Southern Literary Studies
Fred Hobson, Editor

The Narrative Forms
of Southern Community

The Narrative Forms
of Southern Community

SCOTT ROMINE

Louisiana State University Press

Baton Rouge

Copyright © 1999 by Louisiana State University Press
All rights reserved
Manufactured in the United States of America
First printing
08 07 06 05 04 03 02 01 00 99   5 4 3 2 1

Designer: Michele Myatt Quinn
Typeface: A Caslon
Typesetter: Crane Composition, Inc.
Printer and binder: Edwards Brothers, Inc.

Library of Congress Cataloging-in-Publication Data
Romine, Scott.
    The narrative forms of Southern community / Scott Romine.
        p.   cm. — (Southern literary studies)
    Includes bibliographical references and index.
    ISBN 0-8071-2401-X (cl : alk. paper)
    ISBN 0-8071-2527-X (p : alk. paper)
    1. American fiction—Southern States—History and criticism.
    2. Longstreet, Augustus Baldwin, 1790–1870.   Georgia scenes.
    3. Kennedy, John Pendleton, 1795–1870.   Swallow barn.   4. Page,
    Thomas Nelson, 1853–1922.   In ole Virginia.   5. Percy, William
    Alexander, 1885–1942.   Lanterns on the levee.   6. Faulkner, William,
    1897–1962.   Light in August.   7. Southern States—In literature.
    8. Community in literature.   9. Narration (Rhetoric)   10. Literary
    form.   11. Autobiography.   I. Title.   II. Series.
    PS261.R53   1999
    813.009'975—dc21   99-14905
                                                                    CIP

The paper in this book meets the guidelines for permanence and durability of the Committee
on Production Guidelines for Book Longevity of the Council on Library Resources.♾

For my parents, Donna and Jerry Romine

Contents

Acknowledgments

First and warmest thanks to Professors Fred Hobson, Julius Rowan Raper, Lucinda H. MacKethan, Weldon Thornton, Robert L. Phillips Jr., John Shelton Reed, and Kimball King for reading all or part of this manuscript at various stages. Their insights, suggestions, and expertise have been invaluable. A Summer Excellence Research Award from the University of North Carolina at Greensboro was helpful in providing time to complete this project. Thanks also to my colleagues at the University of North Carolina at Greensboro, especially Michael Parker, Russ McDonald, Gail McDonald, Mary Ellis Gibson, and Stephen Yarbrough, for various e-mail correspondence, conversations in the hallway, and offhand insights that have, in one way or another, affected my thinking about the issues raised in this book. An earlier version of chapter 1 was published as "Negotiating Community in Augustus Baldwin Longstreet's *Georgia Scenes*" in *Style* 30, no. 1 (spring 1996): 1–27; and an earlier version of chapter 3 was published as "The Levee and the Garden: Will Percy's Pastoral Aesthetic in *Lanterns on the Levee*" in *Southern Quarterly* 35, no. 1 (fall 1996): 29–42. Thanks to these journals and their editors, James M. Mellard and Stephen Flinn Young, for permission to reprint this material. My wife, Karen Weyler, has been willing to discuss ideas, read drafts of chapters, and mark them with copious amounts of red ink. Lastly, I would like to thank the late Professor Robert Bain, with whom I shared many conversations about southern literature that I value more and more as the years pass.

The Narrative Forms
of Southern Community

Introduction

In his chapter on William Faulkner in *The History of Southern Literature,* Cleanth Brooks writes that a "true community . . . is held together by manners and morals deriving from a commonly held view of reality."[1] It is virtually a cliché that this "true community" is central to southern literature; from the beginning of southern literary studies as an academic discipline, the community has served as a critical touchstone, perhaps most notably in the work of Brooks himself. And yet Brooks makes a mistake so obvious that, like Poe's purloined letter, it threatens to go unnoticed: the commonly held view of reality to which he refers is a fantasy and always has been. I take the very presence of manners—which are, after all, a way of deferring conflict on an everyday basis—to indicate the fantastical nature of a social group that apprehends reality "as one." Manners might be said to produce a commonly held view of reality; they do not derive from it. Writers in the conservative tradition have tended to replicate Brooks's positivist tendencies without replicating his critical acumen, often creating an artificial division between the community's vices and its virtues, a division that allows the recuperation of the one and the repression of the other, as if, say, racial discrimination was an incidental flaw of the southern community circa 1930

1. Cleanth Brooks, "William Faulkner," in *The History of Southern Literature,* ed. Louis Rubin et al. (Baton Rouge: Louisiana State University Press, 1985), 339.

that need not implicate an entire system of cohesive (and presumably otherwise legitimate) social relationships. One pernicious consequence of this view has been the widespread dissolution of the first law of community, which I take to be this: insofar as it is cohesive, a community will tend to be coercive.

A second pernicious consequence has been the representation of community as having primarily positive content, an idea that generally appears couched in a rhetoric of shared values. The difficulty with this logic can be indicated by asking which values produced segregation. Brooks nearly avoids this mistake, placing morals in a subordinate position to a shared perception of reality, which is a necessarily prior assumption. But to the extent that reality is not fully shared, morals cannot be either, except in a negative sense—that is, insofar as they define prohibitions. Communities cohere not by means of values, but norms, which can be comprehensive in a way that values never can. As the French sociologist Emile Durkheim says in elaborating his concept of the common consciousness (or collective mind) in *The Division of Labor in Society* (1893), "we should not say that an act offends the common consciousness because it is criminal, but that it is criminal because it offends that consciousness. We do not condemn it because it is a crime, but it is a crime because we condemn it." Writing of the "sacred taboo" of miscegenation, Will Percy demonstrates the validity of Durkheim's insight in the Mississippi Delta: "It is academic to argue the wisdom or justice of this taboo. Wise or unwise, just or unjust, it is the cornerstone of friendly relations, or interracial peace. In the past it has been not the eleventh but the first commandment. Even to question it means the shattering of race relations into hideous and bloody ruin."[2] Unable to identify the transgressive content of miscegenation, much less the values that define that content, Percy can only verify the norm, and, moreover, the importance of a shared sense of that norm to the continuity of an interracial community. Values might appear as post facto justifications of norms, but the norms are always, already there.

Durkheim established a positive correlation between the common con-

2. Emile Durkheim, *The Division of Labor in Society*, trans. W. D. Halls (New York: Free Press, 1997), 40; William Alexander Percy, *Lanterns on the Levee: Recollections of a Planter's Son* (New York: Alfred A. Knopf, 1941), 307–308.

sciousness and the presence of what he calls mechanical solidarity, an archaic mode of social organization marked by a near absence of specialized divisions of labor, social classes, and individual autonomy. Such solidarity has limited relevance in the context of the southern community except insofar as it points to the simulated consensus—a paradox that intimately informs the works under consideration here—by means of which the South could establish the essentially cohesive nature of its social order. One of the several ironies of southern history is that something approaching mechanical solidarity, in which, as Durkheim says, "the individual consciousness is almost indistinct from the collective consciousness . . . [and] the individual has no sphere of action that is peculiarly his own,"[3] could exist in such a stratified and deeply divided culture.

Allen Tate structures *The Fathers* around a provocative question that assumes the fundamentally negative content of social reality: "is not civilization the agreement, slowly arrived at, to let the abyss alone?"[4] In appropriating Tate's idea of the social negative, I mean to suggest that community is enabled by practices of avoidance, deferral, and evasion; in a certain sense, as Tate implies, community relies not on what is there so much as what is, by tacit agreement, not there. Hence, a new definition of community: a social group that, lacking a commonly held view of reality, coheres by means of norms, codes, and manners that produce a simulated, or at least symbolically constituted, social reality. This study examines how that reality is constructed and maintained in five major narratives of the American South—Augustus Baldwin Longstreet's *Georgia Scenes* (1835), John Pendleton Kennedy's *Swallow Barn* (1832), Thomas Nelson Page's *In Ole Virginia* (1887), William Alexander Percy's *Lanterns on the Levee* (1941), and William Faulkner's *Light in August* (1932).

The works under discussion here are all representative works. By this, I do not mean to imply only that they represent some particular genre, although many of them do. *Georgia Scenes* is generally regarded as the founding text of southwestern or backwoods humor; *Swallow Barn* and *In Ole Virginia* are widely considered the two central narratives in the plantation

3. Durkheim, *Division of Labor,* 140.
4. Allen Tate, *The Fathers* (New York: G. P. Putnam's Sons, 1938), 185–86.

tradition; *Lanterns on the Levee* is an important example of what might be labeled the southern cultural autobiography, a genre in which personal narrative and cultural commentary combine in a complex mediation of self and role; and *Light in August,* perhaps the least representative text generically speaking, epitomizes many of the modernist techniques and themes that characterize the Renascence period. Nor do these works represent the whole of "Uncle Sam's other province": the Tidewater South of Kennedy and Page differs radically from the Longstreet's Piedmont, while Percy's Delta and Faulkner's postage stamp of Mississippi soil are different worlds, despite being separated geographically by just over a hundred miles. Nor, finally, do these works represent the whole of southern culture at any given point and time; the perspectives they offer are unequivocally white, male, and upper class. The specific sense in which I claim that these works are representative lies in the ways they demonstrate how a hegemonic social order in a given place and time attempted to resolve its internal conflicts and legitimate its hegemony. In many ways, these works can be thought of as variations on a paternalistic theme.

In claiming that community is enabled by practices of deferral, I should be careful to avoid the implication that community lacks any content whatsoever. Because deferral itself has a structure, a heuristic model of community is therefore in order. In providing, in a very schematic way, such a model, I want to indicate three conditions or techniques of deferral—drawing boundaries, imagining structures, and creating images—that find expression throughout the works under consideration.

It has been said that in the South a man from the next county is a stranger, and one from the next state is a foreigner. Whatever its truth, this axiom indicates the important role drawing a boundary plays in defining a community's inside and outside, and, more importantly, its conditions of insiderhood and outsiderhood. Although this boundary often has a geographical analog, it does not correspond precisely to a city limit: it resists mapping in a strict sense. Faulkner's Jefferson and Percy's Greenville perhaps come closest to having a geographical boundary, although Mottstown in Faulkner's novel essentially replicates the collective mind of its neighboring city, whereas Percy's boundary is in a constant state of flux, sometimes bordering the South, sometimes Mississippi, sometimes the Delta, sometimes Greenville, and in the end, I argue, bounding only Percy's self, thereby producing something like a community of one. The boundary of Percy's local community is thus, like that of many of the communities I will consider, circumscribed by more distant, concentric boundaries. Kennedy and Page, for example, have boundaries circumscribing the plantation, the local network of plantations, Virginia, and the South. Although Longstreet's community is the most geographically amorphous of them all, his description of one particular town epitomizes the role that boundaries play for all of these writers in defining communities as social units. Espousing the localism of the State Rights' creed, Longstreet writes that Springfield felt "that under the *Social Compact,* she ought to love her own state a little more" than other states, and "admitted frankly, that living as she always had lived, right amidst gullies, vapours, fogs, creeks, and lagoons, she was wholly incapable of comprehending that expansive kind of benevolence, which taught her to love people whom she knew nothing about, as much as her next door neighbors and friends."[5] In thus valorizing localism, Longstreet privileges in absolute terms insiderhood over outsiderhood; to be inside is not equivalent to being more intrinsically worthy of regard, but to be located within a network of social relationships and obligations that does not extend indefinitely.

Longstreet calls attention to another important facet of boundaries: they tend to be drawn in such a way as to divide order from chaos, internal security from external threat. For the citizens of Springfield, the threat consists of hostile natural forces that demand social cohesion; in other cases, the threat is more social or political in origin. Although the threat does not always lie immediately outside the city limits—often, the boundaries of the state or of the South serve that function—the communal boundary does tend to mark a space inside of which social order obtains. The narrative work of *Georgia Scenes* is to establish order in physical locales previously perceived to lack order, and thus to transform locale into community. In contrast to the peripatetic narrators of Longstreet's work, the aristocrats of *Swallow Barn* and *Lanterns on the Levee* are more rigorously bound to their

5. Augustus B. Longstreet, *Georgia Scenes: Characters, Incidents, &c. in the First Half Century of the Republic* (1835; Savannah, Ga.: Beehive Press, 1975), 125.

respective communities and thus tend to defer or project chaos onto the outside world. Mark Littleton, the narrator of *Swallow Barn*, describes the master of the plantation as "quietly observing the tumult of affairs from a position too distant to be reached by sordid passions that sway the multitude," while LeRoy Percy, the hero of *Lanterns on the Levee*, expresses his desire, after his political defeat at the hands of the poor whites, to keep his community, "this small corner of the United States in which I reside, comparatively clean and decent in politics and fit for a man to live in."[6] In each instance the communal boundary marks not merely an already ordered social space, but a space inside of which order can and must be actively maintained. The communal boundary, then, tends to define the limits of social responsibility and social agency.

The order circumscribed by the communal boundary invariably involves an organization of social types along class and race lines. Here localism gives way to a more generically southern symbolic vocabulary. In *Lanterns on the Levee* Will Percy asserts unequivocally that "the basic fiber, the cloth of the Delta population—as of the whole South—is built of three dissimilar threads and only three"—the landed gentry, poor whites, and Negroes.[7] Although Percy's own narrative complicates this tripartite division, a basic division of the community into high white, low white, and African American occurs in each of the works I consider. To be sure, each work places different emphases on these categories: *Georgia Scenes*, for example, does not particularly concern itself with African American characters, nor does *Light in August* place a great deal of emphasis on class distinctions among its white characters. Moreover, several of these works make additional delineations among the three basic groups listed above: *Georgia Scenes*, for example, emphasizes the yeoman (the positive counterpart of the poor white), whereas *In Ole Virginia* distinguishes between slaves who validate the social order

6. J. P. Kennedy, *Swallow Barn; or, A Sojourn in the Old Dominion*, rev. ed. (New York: G. P. Putnam, 1853), 215; Percy, *Lanterns on the Levee*, 152.

7. Percy, *Lanterns on the Levee*, 19. Throughout this study, I use the outmoded term "Negro" to refer to this group as it was symbolically conceived and represented by the white writer in question, all of whom use this term to refer to African Americans. Similarly, the pejorative term "poor white" is used to refer to the category of lower-class whites as mediated by the writer or community in question.

and those who threaten it. But whatever the specific configuration of social types, they remain structural in a strict sense: their categorical integrity is contingent upon the presence of an other. The cultural and narrative logic by means of which these oppositional categories are maintained is a central theme of this study.

Percy's cloth metaphor highlights a central issue concerning social types: for a community to remain a community, the several types must organically cohere in such a manner as to produce a "tight-knit" order (to extend Percy's metaphor). The presence of types presupposes hierarchy, which the French sociologist Pierre Bourdieu usefully defines as the simultaneous presence of unity and division. Division, based on deviation from the norm supplied by the white upper class, requires that deprivileged groups enter the community as limited partners—limited in the sense of having certain social rights and privileges denied to them, partners in the sense that they consensually participate in the social order. To establish itself as an organic order—that is, a natural rather than a constructed or instrumental one—the community and its representatives must therefore establish two things, the natural basis of division and the collective basis of unity. Division, then, is defined from the top down, while unity is asserted from the bottom up. Because deprivileged groups are required to participate consensually in the social order, they acquire a certain power to disrupt community, which can never overtly announce itself as a form of coercion. In Gramscian terms, community can be conceived as a localized form of hegemony dependent upon "spontaneous" consent, and yet, as Gramsci shows, hegemony is never purely consensual. It is precisely the dynamic deferral of coercion into consent that necessitates, as we shall see, the intervention of a narrative apparatus.[8]

The first two conditions of community, a boundary and a structure, are essentially structural (if not perfectly stable); that is to say, they maintain what integrity they have through opposition and difference. The third, an image, is not. In many ways the least tangible element of community, an image permits a mimetic orientation in which the positive attributes of

8. Pierre Bourdieu, *Outline of a Theory of Practice*, trans. Richard Nice (Cambridge, U.K.: Cambridge University Press, 1977), 165; for Gramsci on the "spontaneous" nature of hegemonic consent, see *Selections from the Prison Notebooks of Antonio Gramsci*, ed. and trans. Quintin Hoare and Geoffrey Nowell-Smith (New York: International Publishers, 1971), 5–16.

community (cohesiveness, order, stability, interdependence, and so on) are lent a kind of iconic integrity or, to put the matter another way, are displaced into things. The community's icon permits a way of thinking about community that effaces its status *as* thinking, since the community appears in this configuration as an object there to be perceived rather than as the product of collective or quasi-collective projection. I hardly need add that such icons are highly selective, nor that this selectivity historically has enabled the white South's perennial claim to be judged on the basis of its best icons and not its worst.

Having provided a model of community, I should reiterate that communities do not neatly resolve themselves into models. Even if, as I am suggesting, communities are in no way "objective," people still, for all intents and purposes, live in them. One need only scan any written material on the South, from academic criticism to *Southern Living,* for the phrase "sense of place" to perceive how fully the subjective experience of community historically has been displaced onto objects. And while I shall argue that "sense of place" correlates positively with the less admirable "in their place," it would be grossly misleading to suggest that a sense of place is nothing more than a cynical alibi for exploitation. As Jürgen Habermas says of the lifeworld (*Lebenswelt*), the community's social roles and norms can never be perceived as being instrumental or strategic, as having a *purpose* such as distributing material wealth or social prerogatives in a certain way. To perceive agency in this manner (as if someone so *designed* the community) would be to obliterate instantaneously the perception of community as something always, already there—as part and parcel of what James McBride Dabbs calls the "massive, concrete South."[9]

The rhetoric of the concrete has a long history in the tradition of southern conservatism. But however heavy it sounds, the southern concrete is only a distant relation to Dr. Johnson's rock. As Dabbs argues in *The Southern Heritage,* for all its emphasis on the concrete the South was founded on

9. Jürgen Habermas, *The Theory of Communicative Action,* Vol. 2: *Lifeworld and System: A Critique of Functionalist Reason,* trans. Thomas McCarthy (Boston: Beacon Press, 1987), 113–52; James McBride Dabbs, *The Southern Heritage* (New York: Alfred A. Knopf, 1958), 168.

an abstraction, and a particularly instrumental one. "By a process of violent abstraction," Dabbs writes, "we converted the African Negro into the image of our desire, a slave." When the planter bought the abstract, diagrammatic African, Dabbs continues, "he bought essentially a machine, a stripped-down powerhouse. Into that machine he tried to build certain gadgets. The slave was to be docile, submissive, unreflecting."[10] In transforming this abstraction into a concrete object—for it is unbearable to live with an abstraction—the white South deferred reflection for fear of what it might reveal. The strategies of deferral register intricately in its narratives.

In examining how these narratives establish the concreteness of the community they represent—or, alternatively, how they evade the abstractions implicit in that community—I will emphasize their essentially circular production of an objective social world. As Bourdieu writes in his *Outline of a Theory of Practice,* collective practices (among which I will include narrative) involve "the reconciliation of subjective demand and objective (i.e. collective) necessity which grounds the belief of a whole group in what the group believes, i.e. in the group: a reflexive return to the principles of the operations of objectification, practices or discourses, is prevented by the very reinforcement which these productions continuously draw from a world of objectification produced in accordance with the same subjective principles." Bourdieu is essentially describing a feedback loop that works. By constantly producing objects in accordance with subjective demands, collective practices remove their operations from the realm of reflexive examination, thereby allowing a culture to produce the "naturalization of its own arbitrariness" and establishing "a quasi-perfect correspondence between the objective order and the subjective principles of organization." Bourdieu labels this kind of belief *doxa* "so as to distinguish it from an orthodox or heterodox belief implying awareness and recognition of the possibility of different or antagonistic beliefs." For Bourdieu the unavailability of *doxa* to reflexive or conceptual scrutiny is contingent upon two things: the absence of conflicting world views and the ability to continuously produce an objective world. By "objective," Bourdieu designates something akin to what the conservative tradition labels "concrete," and in both cases the "solidity" of the

---

10. Dabbs, *Southern Heritage,* 170, 172.

object depends largely, if not exclusively, upon the collective nature of the subject involved. To borrow Durkheim's terminology, the concrete presupposes a collective mind. Nevertheless, the ubiquitous presence in the South of conflicting (usually northern) ideologies, combined with the resistance offered by the objects under consideration, has worked to complicate the maintenance of *doxa,* although the South historically has been able, as W. J. Cash points out in his discussion of the savage ideal, to extend its domain to a degree unusual in modern Western civilization.[11]

Since the collective mind must continually "find" objects that fulfill subjective imperatives, the doxic mode involves a constant state of deferral, and thus involves a key component of what philosopher Michael Polanyi calls tacit knowing. In *The Tacit Dimension* Polanyi describes tacit knowing as a process of attending *from* something (the tacit dimension) *to* something else (the focal dimension). In a useful illustration he describes using a stick to feel one's way in the dark. For tacit knowing to occur, our awareness of the stick's impact on our hand must be transformed into a sense of its point touching the objects we are exploring. Polanyi's claim that "[a]ll meaning tends to be displaced *away from ourselves*" holds true for the narratives considered here, all of which tend to externalize and objectify the subjective, tacit construction of social reality that occurs at the level of narrative subjectivity. Polanyi observes that the tacit dimension can be disrupted by making it the object of focal awareness; if we "[s]crutinize closely the particulars of a comprehensive entity," its meaning will be "effaced" and "our conception of the entity is destroyed." In 1926 Donald Davidson proposed a term (and a theory) that essentially replicates Polanyi's insight in a southern context. By "autochthonous ideal," Davidson indicated a condition under which the southern writer was ideally unconscious of his culture as a peculiar environment necessitating either protest or explanation oriented toward some external audience. Faulting Gerald Johnson (among others) for pointing the way to the literature of protest, and DuBose Heyward, who, "encountering a yoke of oxen, is not content to describe them, but is determined to point out that he finds in them 'the unconquerable spirit of these hills' " for com-

11. Bourdieu, *Outline of a Theory of Practice,* 164; W. J. Cash, *The Mind of the South* (New York: Alfred A. Knopf, 1941), 90–91.

mitting the heresy of the travelogue, Davidson advocated that the southern writer *dwell in* (to use Polanyi's phrase) the tacit dimension of his culture rather than focusing on it from a perspective from which it might appear quaint, backward, or ideologically deviant.[12] However reactionary Davidson's development of this idea in his later writings, his insight that focal awareness of tacit knowledge inevitably disrupts that knowledge is a perspicacious one.

The basic structure of Davidson's admonition is prominent throughout the southern conservative tradition, perhaps most notably in its recurring opposition between rhetoric and dialectic. The basic nature of the opposition is stated succinctly by M. E. Bradford, who characterizes the rhetorical mode as "reasoning from axiomatic or 'assumed' principles," whereas the dialectical mode is "defined by an interest in first causes and a disposition to seek the truth through refinements of definition or debate." In "Remarks on the Southern Religion," his contribution to the Agrarian symposium, Allen Tate contrasts John Adams's dialectical reasoning with Thomas Jefferson's rhetorical habits of mind. Where Adams "needs a 'process of moral reasoning,' which forces the individual to think out from abstract principles his role at a critical moment of action," Tate notes that "Jefferson calls his judgment 'taste'—reliance on custom, breeding, ingrained moral decision." In a brilliant essay on John Randolph of Roanoke and American individualism, Richard M. Weaver claims that rhetoric is the more congenial mode for the southerner in general and the aristocrat in particular. The aristocratic mind, Weaver claims, is intuitive, antiscientific, and antianalytical: "It is concerned more with the status of being than with the demonstrable relationship of parts." Although each of these writers subtly inflects the opposition—placing different emphases on historicity, cultural temperament, and ideology, and varying in the degree to which they privilege rhetoric—each finally links dialectic with a process of abstraction antithetical to traditional culture. Rhetoric, which presumes both a stable tacit dimension and an attenuation of individual agency, is said to stand in a causal relation to a concrete world that, in turn, cannot be subjected to focal scrutiny without tradition

12. Michael Polanyi, *The Tacit Dimension* (Garden City, N.Y.: Doubleday, 1966), 12, 13, 18; Donald Davidson, "The Artist as Southerner," *Saturday Review,* 15 May 1926, 782.

being irrevocably—and intolerably—disrupted. As Eugene Genovese remarks in *The Southern Tradition*, a "world self-consciously experienced" as-
saults the "deepest feelings" of southern conservatives and "their belief that
men ought to take that world, natural and social, as a given."[13]

Even to frame the issue this way, as several of these writers were perfectly
aware, involves a level of abstraction antithetical to the way of life being de-
fended. The opposition between rhetoric and dialectic is, after all, dialectical. Nevertheless, the Agrarian project was stated in positive terms as a
defense of a more organic and cohesive way of life than was possible in a
North decimated by industrial capitalism. In "support[ing] a Southern way
of life against what may be called the American or prevailing way," the
Agrarians produced one of America's most powerful critiques of industrialism. Even if, as many commentators have suggested, *I'll Take My Stand* defines its antagonist much more clearly than it does the society it wishes to
defend, the community it does represent conforms fairly closely to our
model, possessing as it does a boundary (roughly the Mason-Dixon line), an
icon oriented around subsistence farmers and Cousin Luciuses, and a social
structure. For the Agrarians a natural hierarchy—a legitimate unity in division—in no way undermines the "right relations of man-to-man" upon
which are founded "the social exchanges which reveal and develop sensibil-
ity in human affairs." One clear implication of the Agrarians' logic is that
hierarchy and community stand in a causal, rather than incidental, relationship; a cohesive social unit does not simply coincide with, but depends upon
the presence of hierarchy. To be sure, there is nothing especially new in all
this. A distrust of abstract egalitarianism and emphasis on the positive role
of social inequality have been cornerstones of southern conservatism dating
back to antebellum defenses of slavery. George Fitzhugh, to take but one

13. M. E. Bradford, "Where We Were Born and Raised," in *The Reactionary Imperative:
Essays Literary and Political* (Peru, Ill.: Sherwood Sugden, 1990), 115; Allen Tate, "Remarks
on the Southern Religion," in *I'll Take My Stand: The South and the Agrarian Tradition*, by
Twelve Southerners (1930; reprint, Baton Rouge: Louisiana State University Press, 1977),
170; Richard M. Weaver, "Two Types of American Individualism," in *The Southern Essays of
Richard M. Weaver*, ed. George M. Custis, III and James J. Thompson, Jr. (Indianapolis: Liberty Press, 1987), 91; Eugene D. Genovese, *The Southern Tradition: The Achievement and Limitations of an American Conservatism* (Cambridge: Harvard University Press, 1994), 20.

example, "plants" his defense of slavery in *Cannibals All!* (1857) on the following passage from Thomas Carlyle:

> To rectify the relation that exists between two men, is there no method, then, but that of ending it? The old relation has become unsuitable, obsolete, perhaps unjust; and the remedy is, abolish it; let there henceforth be no relation at all. . . . Cut every human relation that has any where grown uneasy sheer asunder; reduce whatsoever was compulsory to voluntary, whatsoever was permanent among us to the condition of the nomadic; in other words, LOOSEN BY ASSIDUOUS WEDGES, in every joint, the whole fabric of social existence.

Fitzhugh seamlessly integrates Carlyle's scathing irony into his critique of the abstract "Isms of the North"—abolitionism, socialism, industrialism— that beget revolutions. "When, in time of revolution," Fitzhugh writes, "society is partially disbanded, disintegrated, and dissolved, the doctrine of Human Equality may have a hearing, and may be useful in stimulating rebellion; but it is practically impossible, and directly conflicts with all government, all separate property, and all social existence." For Fitzhugh social cohesion is the necessary, positive consequence of human inequality. Writing of the slave order in an essay on "Faulkner, *Sanctuary*, and the Southern Myth," Allen Tate restates this thesis, writing that "[t]he old order had a great deal of good, one of the 'goods' being the result of the evil; for slavery itself entailed a certain responsibility which the capitalist employer in free societies did not need to exercise if it was not his will to do so."[14]

The connection between egalitarianism, industrialism, and the absence of social cohesion is at work in the rhetoric of the Agrarians, although it is clear that they attacked egalitarianism in more muted tones than they did industrialism. As Weaver himself points out, *I'll Take My Stand* had "something to say about social structure, even though most of this had to be said indirectly, so as not to be too rude to democratic equalitarianism. It freely recognizes differences in people and insists that these differences ought to

---

14. "Statement of Principles," in *I'll Take My Stand*, xxxvii, xliii; George Fitzhugh, *Cannibals All! or, Slaves without Masters*, ed. C. Vann Woodward (Cambridge: Belknap Press, 1960), 8; Thomas Carlyle qtd. in Fitzhugh, *Cannibals All!* 10–11; Allen Tate, "Faulkner, *Sanctuary*, and the Southern Myth," in *Memoirs and Opinions, 1926–1974* (Chicago: Swallow Press, 1975), 144.

be built upon or utilized creatively—this in place of the futile plans for eras-
ing them. The essays on education and on the Negro meet this issue
squarely."[15] In fact, Robert Penn Warren's essay on the Negro, "The Briar
Patch," is a classically evasive defense of segregation, a position he later re-
nounced to the chagrin of Weaver and Davidson. The Agrarians largely deferred potentially troublesome issues of race and class, at least in the context
of their own time; certainly their validation of hierarchy (in the abstract)
does anything but meet squarely the glaring injustices that several of them,
to their credit, later recognized. The key point to be made, however, is that
insofar as hierarchy is based on hereditary categories of race and class, racial
and class discrimination now appear not as incidental flaws counterbalanced
by communal cohesiveness, but as constitutive components of a cohesive social order.

Historically, the conservative tradition has not been especially troubled
by this line of reasoning, since race and class lines generally have been
viewed as natural boundaries marking inferior and superior social groups.
Nevertheless, the ability to state this proposition in positive terms has
clearly declined over time—what is explicit in Fitzhugh is implicit in *I'll
Take My Stand*—and one of the most provocative contemporary statements
of conservative principles, Eugene Genovese's *The Southern Tradition* (1994),
attempts to eliminate it altogether. Genovese attempts to recuperate the traditionalist view of social hierarchy by eliminating altogether the issue of
race. Advocating a "society of orders based on a hierarchy that recognizes
human inequality—that is, inequality as individuals, not as members of a
race," Genovese asserts that this "viewpoint has often accompanied racism,
but it has no necessary connection to it." Revising a Jeffersonian concept of
natural aristocracy that has proven stubbornly resistant to historical articulation, Genovese himself resists the historical fact that discrimination, a
term he is eager to rehabilitate via Burke, inevitably recurs to aggregate
groups. This is not to accuse Genovese of bad faith, but to indicate the abstraction underlying his argument, since whatever the form of the argument

15. Richard M. Weaver, "The Southern Phoenix," in *The Southern Essays of Richard M.
Weaver,* 24.

for hierarchy, its content in the tradition of southern conservatism has invariably gravitated toward race and class. Precisely insofar as these categories threaten to reveal their arbitrary or symbolic constitution, they pose a threat to the autochthonous ideal, which is predicated on the presence of a self-evident world. Yet for Davidson and his fellow conservatives, the cause of the South's "painful self consciousness" is always the external progressive leaders who export abstract isms and require "a repudiation not only of the Southern past but of the elements of the Southern character that are most firmly ingrained."[16] The rhetoric of community thus tends to defer the threat to a position beyond the communal boundary. The narrative of community, however, demonstrates that this deferral is not absolute, that the autochthonous ideal was disrupted internally as well.

"Out of the quarrel with others we make rhetoric; out of the quarrel with ourselves, we make poetry." Yeats's aphorism (a favorite of Allen Tate) bears deeply on the topic of this study, for when we turn from the community produced by rhetoric to the one produced by narrative, the stability of the social order becomes a more problematic issue. In one sense it is difficult to comprehend why this is so. Unbound by any "real world," the writer of narrative might seem free simply to emplot his theories, to create a fictional world such that it offers little resistance to the ideal order he envisions. I take the axiom that "if you ask a southerner anything, he'll tell you a story" to indicate that such parables are especially possible in the South. Yet as Fredric Jameson argues in *The Political Unconscious,* wish-fulfillment in narrative is no simple matter precisely because history does intrude, often in subtle and unexpected ways. If we think of narrative in Jamesonian terms as machinery for ideological investment, we may well find that Willie Stark, who points out in *All the King's Men* that all machines lose energy, proves our axiomatic southerner to be an exception to the rule. Our axiomatic southerner tells a story that makes its point with no loss of energy; he is one of those southerners Allen Tate describes who contemplate history for "the

16. Genovese, *Southern Tradition,* 27; Donald Davidson, "The Southern Poet and His Tradition," *Poetry* 40 (1932): 102.

sake of contemplating it and seeing in it an image of themselves" and thus tend "to like stories, very simple stories with a moral."[17] The narratives under discussion here are not of this type.

A certain loss of energy occurs first in the shift from type to character. Historically, it has never been especially difficult for the southern rhetorician to speak of "the Negro," but for the southern writer to incorporate convincingly an African American character into his narrative has proven to be a different matter altogether. It is probably a fair generalization to say that tension inevitably emerges when a literary character stands in a representative relationship to his or her social group, and from *Georgia Scenes* to *Light in August* variations on this relationship obtain: characters are never just themselves. To be sure, a continuum exists; it is self-evident that Sam in Page's "Marse Chan" is more obviously a type than is Joe Christmas in *Light in August*. And yet, as I shall argue, there is a part of Sam that resists being "Negro," just as Christmas never completely avoids being "Negro." In *Studies in European Realism* Georg Lukács articulates the specific sense in which these characters can be considered types:

The central category and criterion of realist literature is the type, a peculiar synthesis which organically binds together the general and the particular both in characters and situations. What makes a type a type is not its average quality, not its mere individual being, however profoundly conceived; what makes it a type is that in it all the humanly and socially essential determinants are present on their highest level of development. . . . True great realism thus depicts man and society as complete entities, instead of showing merely one or the other of their aspects.

For Lukács, the type allows the "true great realist" to avoid the dead ends of naturalism, which reduces characters to political pawns, and symbolism, which retreats from the world in a sterile valorization of subjectivity.[18] It is doubtful whether all of the writers considered here can be considered "true great realists," but their representation of character nevertheless tends toward the middle ground Lukács privileges.

17. Fredric Jameson, *The Political Unconscious: Narrative as a Socially Symbolic Act* (Ithaca, N.Y.: Cornell University Press, 1981), 182; Tate, "Remarks on the Southern Religion," 173.

18. Georg Lukács, *Studies in European Realism* (New York: Grosset and Dunlap, 1964), 6, 5–6.

The realism of these narratives extends beyond types to the manners that structure social interaction. Returning to Bourdieu's notion that hierarchy presupposes both difference and unity, we should note that the representation of types gravitates toward assertions of difference. Conversely, assertions of unity tend to orient themselves around representations of relationships and of manners conceived in a broad sense. As Dabbs says of racial etiquette, manners bind people together on one level and separate them on another. Indeed, each of these narratives fulfills James W. Tuttleton's definition of the novel of manners as a work in which "the manners, social customs, folkways, conventions, traditions, and mores of a given social group at a given time and place play a dominant role in the lives of fictional characters, exert control over their thought and behavior, and constitute a determinant upon the actions in which they are engaged, and in which these manners and customs are detailed realistically—with, in fact, a premium upon the exactness of their representation."[19] Expanding on Tuttleton's definition, we should add that manners constitute not simply a determinant upon characters, but upon collective characters—that is to say, manners permit the structural configuration of social types.

The confluence of types and manners in these works tends to stabilize the communal icon and create what might be conceived as a pastoral inertia. And yet typically this inertia cannot be sustained in any absolute sense. The interaction between collective characters tends, as well, to produce something like a collective plot that resolves or at least engages those social tensions and contradictions that challenge the integrity of the pastoral icon. This confrontation tends to orient itself in either a progressive or regressive direction. *Georgia Scenes* provides an example of the former, as its narrative work produces a pastoral order; *In Ole Virginia* is an example of the latter, as it charts the declension of the same. *Swallow Barn* exiles narrative altogether from its pastoral community, whereas for Will Percy, the pastoral

19. James McBride Dabbs, *Who Speaks for the South?* (New York: Funk and Wagnalls, 1964), 110; James W. Tuttleton, *The Novel of Manners in America* (Chapel Hill: University of North Carolina Press, 1972), 10. For a brilliant examination of how racial etiquette in a specific community worked to conceal dissent and produce the appearance of cohesion, see William H. Chafe, *Civilities and Civil Rights: Greensboro, North Carolina, and the Black Struggle for Freedom* (Oxford, U.K.: Oxford University Press, 1981), esp. 6–9.

mode permits the aesthetic recuperation of an order threatened by a narrative of degeneration and alienation. The community of *Light in August,* certainly the most complex work considered here, tells stories that construct and preserve order, only to find that these stories spiral out of control, threatening the very order they had originally maintained. Yet however resistant to categorization this confrontation between narrative and pastoral modes, the very fact of its existence indicates the tenuous nature of the social order being represented. If we define narrative as a squaring of circles in the dimension of time, it would be superfluous in a perfectly pastoral world.

In very different ways, then, each of these works involves a community whose ostensibly self-evident organization into class or racial types threatens to be exposed as a matter of coercion rather than consent. Let me clarify that I am not attempting to expose the contradictions and mistakes inherent in these writers' attempts to legitimize the existing order. These mistakes are usually too obvious to need belaboring. Rather, I am dealing with the more specific issue of how these narratives register resistance to their own symbolic operations. As Polanyi notes, meaning tends to be displaced outward, yet as these representative narrators attend to the outside world, they often encounter disorder and discord where they expected stability and consent. They are, in some cases, better realists than they may have intended to be.

In the first sketch of *Georgia Scenes*, Longstreet's upper-class narrator, Lyman Hall, invokes his moral obligation and class privilege in chastising a lower-class farm boy, who, in turn, colorfully rejects his censure. It is a significant moment, for with this breakdown of manners, the tacit ground assumed by Longstreet's narrator is momentarily but effectively obliterated. We might say that the farm boy *textualizes* Hall's tacit norms—that is to say, he indicates in no uncertain terms that what was axiomatic and apodictic is subject to a radically different interpretation. Whereas Hall sees moral obligation, the farm boy sees illegitimate coercion. Whether it be Kennedy and Page confronting a resistant slave, Percy confronting a Negro servant class that rejects aristocratic benevolence, or the community of Jefferson confronting its arbitrary construction of a Negro rapist, each of the narratives under discussion contains a similar moment in which the feedback loop maintaining the coherence of community—that is, the production of social objects in accordance with subjective principles of organization—is disrupted. I will call this the reflexive moment, since what this moment threatens to reveal is the arbitrary, symbolic nature of the tacit norms by which social roles are assigned and the objective world of the text is produced. By objective I mean something similar to Bourdieu's notion of the collectively perceived and to the traditionalist conception of the concrete. In fact, the collective, concrete nature of these social positions or roles is precisely what is called into question at this moment, when hegemony fails, the familiar becomes strange, and cohesion begins to look suspiciously like the product of coercion.

The reflexive moment represents as well a formal crisis—that is to say, the relationship between narrative form and ideology is frequently made problematic at this crucial juncture. In *Problems in General Linguistics* Emile Benveniste contrasts narrative with discourse in terms of the relative objectivity of each. Whereas discourse, according to Benveniste, implicitly or explicitly produces a subject that "maintains the discourse," "the objectivity of narrative is defined by the absence of all reference to the narrator." As the narrator disappears, "[t]he events are chronologically recorded as they appear on the horizon of the story. No one speaks. The events seem to tell themselves." To be sure, Benveniste is defining narrative in a strict sense that I do not wish to retain, but his definition of narrative describes a situation in which the narrator so completely attends to the world that all traces of the tacit dimension are effaced. As Bourdieu puts it, when there is "objective consensus on the sense of the world, what is essential *goes without saying because it comes without saying.*"[20] When "events seem to tell themselves," rhetoric vanishes. It is only when the tacit dimension becomes reflexively available that "telling a story" acquires the connotation of illegitimacy underlying an entire postmodernist discourse of mere textuality (which places and emphasizes the "just" in "just a text") and an entire western discourse of mere rhetoric (which establishes the negative connotation associated with sophistry).

It is here that we find the southern conservative tradition kicking against

20. Emile Benveniste, *Problems in General Linguistics,* trans. Mary Elizabeth (Coral Gables, Fla.: University of Miami Press, 1971), 208; Bourdieu, *Outline of a Theory of Practice,* 167.

the pricks of western foundationalism dating back to Plato, whose opposition between rhetoric and philosophy closely prefigures the Agrarian and neo-Agrarian opposition between rhetoric and dialectic. Where the Platonic tradition has held that reality is available exclusive to philosophy, the conservative tradition has tended to maintain that social reality, at any rate, remains the province of rhetoric. In an essay titled "The Cultural Role of Rhetoric," Richard Weaver finds Socrates, the consummate dialectician, guilty of the very charges for which he was convicted and executed. According to Weaver, Socrates' "exposure of the contradiction" is, by the standards of pure logic, "undeniably convincing." Yet the "very rationality of it," Weaver continues, "suggests some lack of organic feeling." Weaver concludes that

a society cannot live without rhetoric. There are some things in which the group needs to believe which cannot be demonstrated to everyone rationally. Their acceptance is pressed upon us by a kind of moral imperative *arising from the group as a whole*. To put them to the test of dialectic alone is to destroy the basis of belief in them and to weaken the cohesiveness of society. Such beliefs always come couched to us in rhetorical terms, which tell us what attitudes to take. [emphasis added][21]

Weaver's questionable premise—that rhetorical-moral imperatives are collectively derived—indicates, I think, the condition under which dialectic contradiction insinuates itself within the collective mind, making contradiction perceptible as such and thereby introducing the notion of the arbitrary. It is precisely when a society's *givens* appear, as it were, to have been *taken* from some of its members that problems arise. A collective contradiction troubles no one, but a contradiction that calls into question the very ground of collectivity establishes, as a kind of irresistible force, the illegitimacy of rhetoric conceived now as mere sophistry. In this sense morality and collectivity are, as Durkheim's model suggests, consubstantial. To put the matter another way, the threat of dialectic is not that it rationally undermines moral imperatives, but that it undermines their collective basis.

In some ways this appears to be a problem more intrinsic to narrative

---

21. Richard Weaver, "The Cultural Role of Rhetoric," in *Language Is Sermonic: Richard M. Weaver on the Nature of Rhetoric*, ed. Richard L. Johannesen et. al. (Baton Rouge: Louisiana State University Press, 1970), 169, 174–75.

than to rhetoric proper. Southerners have always excelled at quarrels with others, but quarrels among ourselves have tended to be more fitful: we have, for example, no antebellum novel that defends slavery as effectively as any number of proslavery theorists. The narratives under consideration in this study register a level of dissonance that contemporaneous rhetoric tends to exclude, and as a consequence must achieve, however tenuously, what rhetoric assumes as a given: in effect, we might say that narrative ends where rhetoric begins. The dominant narrative work of these texts, then, can be described in broad terms as an attempt to defer reflexivity, to recuperate the autochthonous ideal, and to reclaim the tacit ground that enables the production of an objective social world.

However, this is only the dominant work of these narratives. There is also a less prominent movement in the opposite direction in which social groups or collective characters that reject the communal consensus are declared enemies and exiled beyond the communal boundary. This exclusive movement explains, for example, Longstreet's division of the lower-class white into the "poor white" and "yeoman," the latter of which is integrated within the community while the former is declared beyond the pale. The curious position of African Americans under segregation can also be described in terms of this dual movement. On the one hand claimed as a devoted retainer and virtual member of the family (hence the master code, "we alone know the Negro") and on the other as an alien race and a threat to southern purity (hence their equation with contamination), African Americans existed on the margins of community. To put the matter another way, the Negro was rhetorically integrated into the community even as the African American was physically and symbolically separated from it.

A few words about what *The Narrative Forms of Southern Community* is not. It is neither a history of southern community nor an exhaustive study of southern communities in narrative. I have selected a particular kind of community, which might be labeled the paternalistic or hegemonic community, and provided close readings of what I take to be five major instances of its representation in narrative. Although I would content that this is perhaps the dominant form of community in southern history and southern literature, it is clearly not the only form. This study has little relevance for Appalachian communities, for example, nor does it account for the multitude of alternative communities opposed to, excluded from, or otherwise outside the hegemonic order. That each of the works I consider demonstrates a deep need to establish the collective basis of unity may answer one potential objection to my title: namely, that I use "southern community" where "white community" or "white upper class community" would be more accurate. This objection is perfectly valid except insofar as the narratives themselves attempt to establish the inclusiveness of the communities they represent. In fact, I would contend that most of the narrative subjectivities under consideration are more concerned to establish the collective basis of unity than the natural basis of difference. Moreover, to refer to the "white upper class community" is to ignore, on some level, that reality was not controlled equally. To paraphrase W. J. Cash, if it can be said that for any given place there are many communities, the fact remains that there is also one community.

My concern with the hegemonic community explains the exclusion of works written by female and black southerners, neither of whom had, for obvious reasons, as great a stake in defending the cultural status quo. All of the narratives I have chosen, *Light in August* not excepted, align themselves with the community rather than representing it satirically or otherwise maintaining distance from it. I have therefore excluded from consideration works in which community figures prominently by such diverse figures as George Washington Cable, Mark Twain, T. S. Stribling, Carson McCullers, and Eudora Welty. Several of the works I discuss have counterpart texts that provide a kind of photographic negative of the positive images produced by these conservative narratives. Frederick Douglass's 1845 *Narrative of the Life* systematically inverts the tropes of *Swallow Barn;* Charles W. Chesnutt's *The Conjure Woman* is a direct signification on the dialect tales of Page; and Richard Wright's *Black Boy* obliterates the patrician logic of *Lanterns on the Levee.* Although I do not directly discuss any of these texts, I hope that their latent presence is evident.

I should also, at the beginning of a work concerned with issues of race and, to a lesser extent, class, explain the lack of discussion concerning the third term in that postmodern sequence, race-class-gender. The exclusion of gender issues from this study parallels a general subordination of gender issues in the works I treat, with the significant exception of *Light in August.*

To be sure, female characters appear in the other works, but in none of them is the category of "woman" or "lady" in any way contested. Indeed, there are relatively few works in the tradition of southern literature that undertake to demonstrate the organic nature of gender roles in the South, whereas those that attempt to demonstrate the organic nature of class and race roles are too numerous to count. The relative absence of such works—especially given the plenitude of works representing the constraining, pernicious nature of gender roles—poses an interesting problem, and one that is certainly beyond the scope of this study. Nevertheless, let me offer a few speculations on the matter. First, while the South has had distinctive gender roles, its treatment of women has not differed as substantially from mainstream American culture as its treatment of the white lower class and of blacks, the latter of whom, especially, were for more than a century largely defined as "a southern problem"—with disastrous consequences. As a result, it may be that the South tended to feel less of a rhetorical imperative to explain and defend itself on the issue of gender than on the issues of class and especially race. Second, the regulation of gender roles has historically tended to be defined as a private, familiar matter, whereas race and class have been regulated at a more public, communal level. To the extent that hegemonic narrative represents a public form—and that is a large extent, especially up until the Renascence period—issues of gender tend to manifest themselves less overtly.

A few words about methodology. My general practice is to focus on three key aspects of each narrative: (1) how social roles or character slots are perceived as givens in the narrative community, (2) how the characters inhabiting these roles offer resistance to the hegemonic order, and (3) how the narrative recuperates the hegemonic order, if indeed it does. Individual chapters respond to a plenitude of formal structures—framing techniques, narrative stylistics, master codes, modes of representing individual and collective consciousness, collective plots, embedded storytelling, and so on—through which this master sequence is enabled. As this book concerns itself with the relationship between formal structures and ideology, I should like to reiterate the axiom that a separation of form and content is nearly always an artificial one.

1

Augustus Baldwin Longstreet's *Georgia Scenes*

In 1835 the printing office of the *State Rights' Sentinel* in Augusta, Georgia, issued the first edition of *Georgia Scenes: Characters, Incidents &c. in the First Half Century of the Republic,* authored by a "native Georgian." Consisting of nineteen sketches that had been appearing for the past two years in the *Sentinel* and before that in the Milledgeville *Recorder,* the book was a resounding success. Reviewing the work a few months later in the *Southern Literary Messenger,* a young Edgar Allan Poe affirmed that the anonymous author was endowed "with an exquisitely discriminative and penetrating understanding of *character* in general, and of Southern character in particular," before going on to praise the work as "a sure omen of better days for the literature of the South." Five years later, Harper and Brothers published a second edition of the work that would sell over 8,000 copies before being reprinted seven times before the Civil War. Although its author, Augustus Baldwin Longstreet, could not, of course, have envisioned such a development, *Georgia Scenes* would also inaugurate an important genre of southern literature known retrospectively as "southwestern humor." Although often given its due as the beginning of a tradition that leads to later writers such as Mark Twain, William Faulkner, Erskine Caldwell, and Flannery O'Connor, southwestern humor has long been exiled to the margins of antebellum southern literature. In his 1993 *Yeoman versus Cavalier,* Richie Devon Watson banishes the genre to a subliterary "generic cordon sanitaire" isolated from the more central plantation tradition. Besides being misleading on its own terms, Watson's assertion that in their own time "southwest humorists were simply not considered legitimate writers" has tended, as a general critical view, to legitimate the dismissal of Longstreet and his fellow humorists as literary dabblers whose ideological work is crudely simplistic and easily understood.[1]

Much of this neglect can be traced to the reductive critical lens through which *Georgia Scenes* (and indeed the genre as a whole) has been viewed: Kenneth Lynn's paradigm of the *cordon sanitaire*, which pits gentleman narrators against bumbling and sometimes sinister yokels in a relentlessly repetitive and monological justification of class privilege. But a reconsideration of Longstreet's symbolic organization of collective experience, paying particular attention to a network of tropes of economy, nature, representation, and language games, implicates Longstreet in a complex negotiation of class roles. In tracing the evolution of what I will call the socionarrative style (by which I mean a social style reflected in narrative stylistics) of Longstreet's primary narrator, Lyman Hall, I show that Longstreet's ideal community can be achieved only after the gentleman narrator responds to the dialogic imperative of the lower class.

To speak of Longstreet's community is, however, somewhat misleading in that *Georgia Scenes* represents a complex network of communities ranging from quasi-aristocratic smarts sets of "The Ball" and "The Fox-Hunt" to the backwoods locales of "The Dance" and "The Shooting Match." It is in the context of the latter that the cultural work of *Georgia Scenes* is most complex and, for the modern reader, most compelling. At the heart of Longstreet's narrative lies, essentially, a discourse of colonization through which those previously external, alien, and chaotic backwoods communities are subsumed within the hegemonic order. This extension of hegemony has important historical parallels. The antebellum South was anything but a

---

1. [Edgar Allan Poe], "Georgia Scenes," *Southern Literary Messenger* 2 (1836): 287, 292; Richie Devon Watson, *Yeoman versus Cavalier: The Old Southwest's Fictional Road to Rebellion* (Baton Rouge: Louisiana State University Press, 1993), 57–58, 57. For a discussion that shows how highly Longstreet was regarded by both critics and the reading public, see John Donald Wade, *Augustus Baldwin Longstreet: A Study in the Development of Culture in the South* (New York: Macmillan, 1924), 151–60.

monolithic culture, and one important source of interclass conflict was the clash between the market economics and hierarchical order of a slave society and the subsistence economics and rugged individualism prevalent in backwoods communities. As the historian Stephen Hahn has shown, these backwoods communities were deeply skeptical of the commodity market, which tended to erode the localized autonomy they valued highly and preserved through what Hahn calls "habits of mutuality." According to Hahn, while the antebellum social structure "did not array southern whites, as distinct social classes, in directly exploitative relations," neither did it eliminate class antagonisms, which continued to erupt in political and economic arenas.[2] Writing just as the South was beginning to acquire an acute regional self-consciousness, Longstreet attempts to mediate these antagonisms through a discourse that preserves both cultural unity and class difference.

This is not to say, however, that Longstreet affirms the popularized and mostly misleading division of the antebellum white South into aristocrats and poor whites. *Georgia Scenes* is, on its own terms, as complex a representation of white social classes as Daniel R. Hundley's *Social Relations in Our Southern States* (1860), a work long regarded as a masterpiece of social taxonomy. Yet the acute cultural self-consciousness of Hundley's work, largely occasioned by the national debate over slavery, is nowhere to be found in Longstreet's narrative. Repeatedly disabusing northerners of their egregious misperceptions of the South, Hundley orients his rhetoric externally; Longstreet, in contrast, elides his text's rhetorical dimension. Where Hundley's description of the "Southern Yankee" is largely an excuse for attacking authentic Yankees for their abolitionist tendencies, Longstreet's treatment of social class lacks an overt political context. Given the dates of the two works—one published on the eve of the Civil War, the other just a few years after William Lloyd Garrison was dragged through the streets of Boston for preaching abolition—these differences perhaps should not surprise us. Nevertheless, the centrality of slavery to southern class relations, along with Longstreet's subsequent defense of the institution later in his career, includ-

2. Steven Hahn, "The Yeomanry of the Nonplantation South: Upper Piedmont Georgia, 1850–1860," in *Class, Conflict, and Consensus: Antebellum Southern Community Studies,* ed. Orville Vernon Burton and Robert C. McGrath Jr. (Westport, Conn.: Greenwood Press, 1982), 45–46.

ing the bitter antiabolitionist pamphlet *Letters from the South* (1849), raises the issue of whether slavery acts as an absent cause for Longstreet's negotiation of class roles. Is it specifically the preservation of slavery that necessitates interclass consensus? One of the interesting features of *Georgia Scenes* is how our ability to answer this question is strictly circumscribed. Although slavery is present in *Georgia Scenes* as part of Longstreet's ideal community, it is clearly relegated to the background. Yet the ambiguous role of slavery in *Georgia Scenes*—its absence *as* a cause, if indeed it *is* one—represents but one instance of a paradox present throughout Longstreet's work: as the social order is stabilized, there is a corresponding deemphasis on the *rationale* of that order, on justifying why *this particular order* is necessary or desirable. As the community becomes more concrete, its justification becomes less tangible. In examining how the attenuation of overt rhetoric parallels a gain in tacit norms, I hope to illustrate an essential precondition for community that the later texts I consider frequently cannot sustain: namely, that the cultural logic through which a community coheres cannot be subjected to conscious scrutiny.

Since his stated explanation of his narrative project focused exclusively on issues of preservation and realism, Longstreet himself would have been skeptical of such a project. He wrote of *Georgia Scenes* that "the aim of the author was to supply a chasm in history which has always been overlooked—the manners, customs, amusements, wit, dialect, as they appear in all grades of society to an ear and eye witness of them." In his preface to *Georgia Scenes* he claimed to have used "some little art" only to "recommend [the sketches] to the readers of my own times" in the hope that their initial popularity would increase "the chance of their surviving the author" until a day "when time would give them an interest."[3] Critics such as Kimball King have justly praised Longstreet for his work as a social historian, and James

3. Longstreet qtd. in O. P. Fitzgerald, *Judge Longstreet: A Life Sketch* (Nashville: Publishing House of the Methodist Episcopal Church, 1891), 164; Longstreet, *Georgia Scenes*, 1. This work will hereinafter be cited parenthetically by page number in the text. I have used the Beehive Press edition because it is the only modern edition based on the 1835 first edition, which it corrects in numerous ways. The 1840 Harper edition used as the copy text for most other modern editions employed the Harper's house style, which eliminated much of Longstreet's idiosyncratic grammar, spelling, and punctuation.

E. Kibler has argued for *Georgia Scenes* as a seminal work in the development of American realism. Ranking *Georgia Scenes* alongside *Adventures of Huckleberry Finn* as one of the two works that "are the beginning of modern Southern literature," Allen Tate praised Longstreet for his precise observation of "complete, serious human beings" that evade categorization as stereotypes. Nevertheless, few critics have questioned Robert L. Phillips Jr.'s position that Longstreet's "realism" is at least complicated by the sometimes obtrusive presence of a highly subjective narrator. The view of realistic narrative being somehow objective or value-neutral has, of course, been largely dismissed at least since Wayne Booth's *Rhetoric of Fiction,* and even had it not, such a concept has little relevance for *Georgia Scenes,* a work in which narrative prejudices are in evidence on almost every page. On a formal level, however, *Georgia Scenes* fulfills Roman Jakobson's criterion that metonymy provide the symbolic substructure of realist narrative. Longstreet's description of his sketches as "fanciful *combinations* of *real* incidents and characters" points to a deep structure in which contiguity is privileged over similarity as the dominant organizing principle of his narrative, which often, following Jakobson's formulation, "metonymically digresses from the plot to the atmosphere and from the characters to the setting in space and time." More significantly, this formal metonymic structure is replicated on the level of social interaction. As Jakobson reminds us, a "competition" between metaphor and metonymy "is manifest in any symbolic process, be it intrapersonal or social."[4] In *Georgia Scenes* this competition manifests itself most conspicuously in the way Hall perceives the lower class; as the narrative progresses, his metaphorical equation of poor white and animal gives way to a metonymic knowledge through which he negotiates and establishes a consensual relationship with the white lower class. It is in this context of symbolic competition that the archival nature of *Georgia Scenes*—its status as a

4. Kimball King, *Augustus Baldwin Longstreet* (Boston: Twayne, 1984), 137–40; James E. Kibler Jr., introduction to *Georgia Scenes* (1835; reprint, Nashville: J. S. Sanders, 1992), viii–xiii; Tate, "Faulkner, *Sanctuary,* and the Southern Myth," 147; Robert L. Phillips Jr., "The Novel and the Romance in Middle Georgia Humor and Local Color" (Ph.D. diss., University of North Carolina at Chapel Hill, 1971), 23–53, 137–50; Roman Jakobson, "Two Aspects of Language and Two Types of Aphasic Disturbances," in *Selected Writings* (The Hague: Mouton, 1971), 2:255, 2:258.

repository of a historically located discursive paradigm—can be most fully appreciated.

In his 1959 *Mark Twain and Southwestern Humor*, Kenneth Lynn provides an alternative, but fundamentally flawed, paradigm. Lynn's contribution was his historicization of a framed narrative said to represent the reaction of the Whig gentleman to the uncouth backwoodsman associated with Jacksonian democracy. According to Lynn, "Longstreet and his successors found that the frame was a convenient way of keeping their first person narrators outside and above the comic action, thereby drawing a *cordon sanitaire*, so to speak, between the morally irreproachable Gentleman and the tainted life he describes." This *cordon sanitaire*, Lynn claims, exists on both a moral and a linguistic plane, since the vernacular formally marks the moral inferiority of the "tainted" poor white "Clown." Conversely, the "Self-Controlled Gentleman" employs a literate style that provides a normative ground enabling the didactic evaluation and ultimately control of the lower class. Thus, the narrator's language and the vernacular are rigidly separated, and never the twain shall meet—that is, until Mark Twain. Although he modifies his argument slightly in later claiming that "[i]n his best work, however, Longstreet buries his meanings deep within the concrete action of the comedy," this concrete action merely replicates the antagonistic relationship between the Clown and Self-Controlled Gentleman: the latter simply perceives the Clown's depravity rather than having to comment upon it.[5] In short, Lynn argues that whether primarily mimetic or diegetic in orientation, the narrative frame provides an absolute perspective from which the Clown is measured, evaluated, and found deviant. The *cordon sanitaire* thus presumes a social model in which class relationships are unequivocally antagonistic. Although Lynn is clearly correct in recognizing a class distinc-

---

5. Kenneth Lynn, *Mark Twain and Southwestern Humor* (1959; reprint, Westport, Conn.: Greenwood Press, 1972), 64, 64–65, 68–69, 66. For examples of Lynn's influence on the critical reception of *Georgia Scenes*, see King, *Longstreet*, esp. 58–59; Keith Newlin, "*Georgia Scenes:* The Satiric Artistry of Augustus Baldwin Longstreet," *Mississippi Quarterly* 41 (1987–88): 21–37; William B. Lenz, "Augustus Baldwin Longstreet," in *Fifty Southern Writers before 1900,* ed. Robert Bain and Joseph M. Flora (Westport, Conn.: Greenwood Press, 1987), esp. 315; C. Hugh Holman, *The Roots of Southern Writing* (Athens: University of Georgia Press, 1972), 71–72.

tion, his scheme represents a radical reduction of the complexities inherent in the encounter between gentleman narrators and lower-class whites. As we begin to examine *Georgia Scenes,* we find that, far from asserting his moral superiority to these "tainted" characters, Longstreet's narrator is more likely to elide the social distance between himself and his subject in an effort to engender consensual participation in a common social field.

"Georgia Theatrics," which Lynn takes as an epitome of the *cordon sanitaire,* will serve as a useful point of entry into our examination of Longstreet's narrative dynamics. In this short opening sketch Lyman Hall recounts an 1809 visit he made to Lincoln County, Georgia. Walking in the countryside "[r]apt with the enchantment of the season" (4), Hall overhears what is apparently a vicious fight between two ruffians. Horror-struck upon hearing that one of the combatants has lost an eye, he runs to the spot, where he encounters the "victor":

He looked excessively embarrassed, and was moving off, when I called to him, in a tone emboldened by the sacredness of my office, and the iniquity of his crime, "Come back, you brute! and assist me in relieving your fellow mortal, whom you have ruined for ever!"

My rudeness subdued his embarrassment in an instant; and with a taunting curl of the nose, he replied, "You needn't kick before you're spurr'd. There a'nt nobody there, nor ha'nt been nother. I was jist seein' how I could 'a' *fout.*" (6)

Indeed, as Hall informs his "gentle reader," "his report was true," and the young farmer returns to his plow having performed "nothing more nor less than a Lincoln rehearsal" (6). Lynn presents the sketch as a paradigmatic instance of the Self-Controlled Gentleman confronting the "youthful Clown" from the moral distance provided by the *cordon sanitaire.* Locating the narrative discourse at a strictly normative level, Lynn claims that the boy's use of the vernacular and his "iniquitous crime"—read here as psychological neurosis—mark him as wholly deviant (66–69). This rigid hierarchy hardly holds up under scrutiny; as Keith Newlin notes, Hall shows himself to be "morally righteous, easily duped, and prone to act on insufficient information; in short, Hall is himself a rube in the backwoods, a stranger to what he observes."[6]

---

6. Newlin, "Satiric Artistry," 27.

Having kicked, as the boy memorably puts it, before he is spurred, Hall reveals a tendency to align morality and social class. This tendency is evident from the opening lines of the sketch, where he gives the locale as "The Dark Corner" of Lincoln, explaining, "I believe it took its name from the moral darkness, which reigned over that portion of the county, at the time of which I am speaking. If in this point of view, it was but a shade darker than the rest of the county, it was inconceivably dark" (3). Claiming that in the meantime (the sketch is ostensibly written in the early 1830s) the area had "become a living proof that 'light shineth in darkness' " (3), Hall becomes absorbed in his pastoral reveries until startled by the "loud, profane, and boisterous voices": "In Mercy's name! thought I, what band of ruffians has selected this holy season, and this heavenly retreat, for such Pandëmonian riots!" (4–5). As he approaches, he notes that the "accomplices in the hellish deed" had fled (5). Hall's diction ("[m]oral darkness," "profane" voices, "Pandëmonian riots," "hellish deed") indicates a rigid moral binarism that sanctions his social authority; as righteous stroller in his "heavenly retreat," he appropriates the moral right to intervene in the fracas. Because his narrative style projects moral values onto the narrative landscape, it predicts his social style, which likewise "finds" moral values (or their sinister inversion) in the situation he encounters. When he does intervene, he invokes his hierarchical privilege by calling the boy a "brute" who (illogically) is "morally" bound to return and aid his "fellow-mortal." Thus, in relation to Hall, the boy is characterized as "bestial," an identification reinforced when Hall says that the ground looked "as if two Stags had been engaged upon it" (6), while in relation to his imaginary antagonist, he becomes "human," and thus subject to Hall's moral code. If "fellow-mortal" is the term of unity, "brute" is the term of difference.

Hall's unresolved contradiction is contingent upon two unmediated versions of the "natural." A trope with important implications throughout *Georgia Scenes*, the "natural" invokes, on the one hand, the bucolic nature of pastoral reverie (equated here with heaven and the gentleman), and on the other, the brutish nature of animalistic violence (equated with hell and the poor white). While the former nature is regulated by implicit moral rules—natural law, so to speak—the latter is marked, from Hall's perspective, by a sinister inversion of normative morality; the boy's animalistic excesses thus invert the bucolic splendor of the "sportive streams," "vocal birds," and "blushing flowers" Hall observes during his heavenly retreat. Indeed, Hall begins his description of the countryside with the claim that "[w]hatever may be said of the moral condition of the Dark Corner, at the time just mentioned, its natural condition was any thing but dark" (4). Moreover, the boy's metaphoric status as "animal" symbolically contaminates the contexts in which he appears; as a metonymic stand-in for place (the "Dark Corner") and a synecdochic representative of class (poor whites), the boy, Hall implies, cannot be expected to act morally, despite being "obligated" to do so. One might say that from Hall's perspective, the boy is acting according to *his* "nature" instead of Hall's. In symbolically organizing the situation, then, Hall simultaneously creates and legitimates his social authority. Yet this act of authority fails in two ways. First, Hall's "opponent" is revealed to be exclusively the result of symbolic actions occurring at the level of his subjective consciousness. What purports to be "found" is shown to be "constructed," and in this sense, his opponent is quite as imaginary as the boy's. As James M. Cox says, Longstreet "reveals the refined narrator's impulse to disapprove of the violence. . . . He realizes at once that the refined moralist and violent youth are intricately related to each other."[7] Second, the boy utterly rejects the social authority Hall appropriates, an act of subversion that notably involves another animal metaphor (a spurred horse).

The failure of Hall's socionarrative style in "Georgia Theatrics" results from the absence of dialogic class negotiation; both Hall and the farm boy fail to recognize their common involvement in the same social domain or community. To put the matter this way, however, raises two questionable issues. First, one could argue that the narrative itself does not recognize this common involvement, that it segregates gentleman narrator and poor white for the reader's amusement at the expense of the latter or as a justification of the cultural status quo (this, as we have seen, is Lynn's argument). Second, one could argue that such common involvement is merely an illusion engendered by a narrative designed to serve the interests of an upper class.

---

7. James M. Cox, "Humor of the Old Southwest," in *The Comic Imagination in American Literature,* ed. Louis D. Rubin Jr. (Washington, D.C.: Voice of America Forum Series, 1974), 109.

Such an argument presumes that community is an epiphenomenon of class structure that functions to conceal authentic class antagonisms. The first criticism is much easier to answer than the second, since all that must be shown is a style that dialogically incorporates the voice of the Clown rather than monologically consigning that voice to communal exile. The second is much harder to answer; in some respects, it cannot be answered. Longstreet's negotiation of community is demonstrably dialogic in nature; to use Bakhtin's language, Longstreet's "world is full of other people's words [that he] introduce[s] . . . into the plane of his own discourse, but in such a way that this plane is not destroyed." Yet at the same time, it is impossible to counter the kind of objection raised by Lennard J. Davis, who claims that, while actual conversation is dialogic in Bakhtin's sense of the word, "dialogue in novels lacks this crucial and democratic strand—everything that comes from the author is autocratically determined."[8] In many instances Longstreet's dialogism is autocratic in precisely the way Davis uses the term; the issue then becomes whether Longstreet legitimately integrates the Clown's voice into the plane of his own discourse.

Leaving aside the ethical question of *whether* this particular class hierarchy can be considered legitimate, there are two ways to consider the legitimacy of Longstreet's textual negotiation. My primary aim, after bracketing Longstreet's rhetoric and considering it in the social field produced by the text, is to concentrate on his narrative legitimation rather than its legitimacy per se. Secondly and more provisionally, I want to suggest that Longstreet's textual negotiation has important parallels in the context of antebellum class relations. In attempting to relate textual and historical fields, I will rely generally on the negotiation-based model of social relations proposed by Theodore B. Leinwand, who conceives of social power as a continual discourse of "[c]ompromise, negotiation, exchange, [and] give and take." Leinwand rejects conflict as an inherent "operator" in the field of "sociopolitical and cultural practices," arguing instead that the win-lose/subversion-containment terminology of Foucauldian discourse fails to account for the

8. Mikhail Bakhtin, *Problems of Dostoevsky's Poetics,* ed. and trans. Caryl Emerson (Minneapolis: University of Minnesota Press, 1984), 201; Lennard J. Davis, *Resisting Novels: Ideology and Fiction* (New York: Methuen, 1987), 177–78.

complexity of social relations as they actually exist and are modified over time.[9] Leinwand's model is especially relevant to *Georgia Scenes,* a work in which exchange constitutes an important trope. Throughout the work we find horses, money, promises, oaths, curses, blows, insults, and so on being exchanged, often after a period of literal negotiation. An examination of individual sketches will show that such exchanges provide the opportunity for the negotiation of communal norms, and further, that the final horizon of this negotiation is the relationship between the gentleman narrator and the lower-class whites he encounters.

Briefly, I will define negotiation as intratextually legitimate when it performatively establishes consensus regarding social roles. This definition, of course, relies on consensus as it is represented by the gentleman narrator and thus can be called into question as an ideologically motivated resolution in the same sense that community itself can be considered an epiphenomenon. At the strictly textual level, however, we should briefly note that Longstreet's rhetoric of realism can be construed as an attempt to answer such objections, as can his attempt, which I discuss later, to legitimate his authority to "represent" the lower-class whites in both the political and narrative senses of the word. On a sociohistorical level, however, I want to suggest that the textual dynamics of *Georgia Scenes* parallel in important ways the dynamics of antebellum southern culture. Although it is beyond the scope of this project to historicize in any depth the parallels between Longstreet's rhetoric of consensus and interclass relationships in the antebellum South, much less to claim Longstreet as a precise representative of patrician attitudes, I nevertheless contend that *Georgia Scenes* does indicate the broad contours and essential preconditions for the establishment of such political and cultural cohesion as did develop across class lines, a phenomenon, it should be added, for which Lynn's model cannot account. Longstreet negotiated the middle ground between oligarchy and populism that defined public life in the antebellum South.

Turning to the symbolic preconditions or givens implicit in Longstreet's world, we should reiterate that the narrative negotiation of *Georgia Scenes*

9. Theodore B. Leinwand, "Negotiation and the New Historicism," *PMLA* 105 (1990): 479, 478.

rests largely upon a rhetoric of nature, which finds exaggerated form in both its pastoral and bestial incarnations. As in "Georgia Theatrics," Hall's effete, highly stylized characterization of nature opposes the bestial "nature" of the backwoods poor white. As the narrative progresses, Hall increasingly comes to find a style of narration that will negotiate these two extremes and appear normal (natural) in contrast to their excesses, which find verbal form in the raw vernacular of the backwoodsman and the effete moral rhetoric of the dandy. Thus, "natural" acquires a positive connotation over the course of the work such that its inversion, "unnatural," assumes the rhetorical weight of both "artificial" (in relation to the dandy) and "animalistic" (in relation to the poor white). Contrapuntal to the opposition between natural and unnatural is a second opposition between cultured and uncultured, categories oriented along class lines. Schematized in a Greimas rectangle, the structuring oppositions of *Georgia Scenes* look like this:

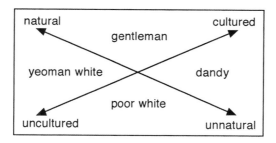

The organizing structure of *Georgia Scenes* thus produces four character types: the yeoman white, the poor white, the gentleman, and the dandy. Whereas the gentleman represents the ideal synthesis between nature and culture, the dandy represents a parody of the gentleman—a man who is cultured, but unnatural and artificial. This character slot is ultimately filled by Abram Baldwin, Hall's narrative counterpart. Similarly, the yeoman, whose presence is pervasive, has a negative counterpart in the poor white, whose lack of culture is not counterbalanced by natural virtue. To briefly schematize the two axes, we might note that the natural-unnatural axis orients itself according to issues of norms and normalcy, of morality, and of behavior; this axis is essentially egalitarian, applying equally to all members of the community, defining what are "right" and "wrong" actions. Conversely, the cultured-uncultured axis orients itself according to issues of propriety, status, and manners; this axis is primarily hierarchical, defining what are "proper" and "improper" actions. As the narrative logic of *Georgia Scenes* unfolds, we find the initially dominant term (cultured) apparently being superseded by the term that allows wider communal participation (natural), the latter having more to do with social behavior than birthright. At the same time, Longstreet's attempt to preserve hierarchy through the mechanism of representation is far from disinterested, and the utopian vision of community portrayed in "The Shooting Match," the final episode of the book, should be interpreted as an ideologically motivated resolution to pressing social tensions.

Before turning to Hall's role in this ideological closure, however, I want first to consider the role of Hall's fellow narrator, Abram Baldwin. As the narrator of only six sketches (out of nineteen), Baldwin has frequently been given short shrift by critics, who have tended to view him either as another mouthpiece for Longstreet or, as James B. Meriwether says, as "a foil to the ultimately much more masculine and successful Lyman Hall." Expanding on Meriwether's argument, James E. Kibler writes that Baldwin looks forward to a common trait of twentieth-century southern protagonists, the "disembodied intellectualism" of a Quentin Compson or an Isaac McCaslin.[10] While there is no question that Baldwin occasionally reflects Longstreet's views, his narrative trajectory firmly establishes his exile from the Georgia community, a situation particularly curious since he, unlike Hall, proclaims from the beginning his devotion to the pastoral ideal embodied in the yeoman farmer. Yet as a chronic offender of Davidson's autochthonous ideal, Baldwin's participation in the community is prevented by the pastoral frame of reference through which he apprehends it.

In Baldwin's first sketch, "The Dance," we find a world-weary gentleman "called by business to one of the frontier counties, then but recently settled" (7). Induced to stay for a dance, Baldwin immediately—and vehemently—insists to his reader that the simple ways of the country folk are far superior

---

10. James B. Meriwether, "Augustus Baldwin Longstreet: Realist and Artist," *Mississippi Quarterly* 35 (1982): 359; Kibler, Introduction, xix.

to those of the city sophisticate. Vigorously defending the early hour of the dance, Baldwin lauds the simplicity of country ways, asserting, "The refinements of the present day in female dress has not even reached our republican *cities* at this time; and of course, the *country girls* were wholly ignorant of them" (9). He goes on, "They had no boards laced to their breasts, nor any corsets laced to their sides; consequently, they looked, for all the world, like human beings, and could be distinctly recognized as such, at the distance of two hundred paces. Their movements were as free and active as nature would permit them to be" (9). Although his reader would surely expect the women to greet with a kiss—"Oh, no; but with something much less equivocal: a hearty shake of the hand and smiling countenances, which had some meaning" (10). The Francophobe Baldwin concludes by adding parenthetically, for his reader's edification, the following: "*Note.*—The custom of kissing, as practised in these days by the *amiables,* is borrowed from the French; and by them from Judas" (10).

Baldwin's pastoralism betrays its own artifice, and the resulting perspective on the "good country people" can only be described as distant and patronizing. Baldwin is himself highly conscious of his status as an outsider and an exile. Upon encountering his self-described "old sweetheart," Polly Gibson, Baldwin thinks back on his youth and subsequent life:

Then, I was light hearted, gay, contented and happy. I aspired to nothing but a good name, a good wife, and an easy competency. The first and last were mine already; and Polly had given me too many little tokens of her favor to leave a doubt now [then], that the second was at my command. But I was foolishly told, that my talents were of too high an order to be employed in the drudgeries of a farm, and I more foolishly believed it. I forsook the pleasures which I had tried and proved, and went in pursuit of those imaginary joys, which seemed to encircle the seat of Fame. From that moment to the present, my life had been little else than one unbroken scene of disaster, disappointment, vexation and toil. And now, when I was too old to enjoy the pleasures which I had discarded, I found that my aim was absolutely hopeless; and that my pursuits had only served to unfit me for the humbler walks of life, and to exclude me from the higher. (14)

Possibly the first character in southern literature who can't go home again, Baldwin is a more profound exile than he realizes, for despite his attempts to use the frontier folk as a didactic stick to beat snobs with, they doggedly resist his efforts to emplot them and reveal the essential snobbery of his attitudes. Baldwin's attempted authorial control thus acquires social content as we find him attempting to orchestrate the scene and failing miserably.

His main failure in the regard centers around his inability to get Polly Gibson to dance with him, or indeed even to recognize him. He first learns that she will be at the dance from Polly's husband, who, after jokingly exacting from Baldwin a promise not to steal her away, offers to introduce him immediately. Baldwin demurs, preferring instead to play the scene to the hilt: "I'll promise not to run away with her, but you must not let her know who I am. I wish to make myself known to her; and for fear of the worst, you shall witness the introduction. But don't get jealous, Squire, if she seems a little too glad to see me; for I assure you, we had a strong notion of each other, when we were young" (11). When the moment comes, Polly refuses to dance with him before Baldwin dramatically reiterates his offer:

> "Well," continued I, (raising my voice to a pretty high pitch, on purpose to be heard, while my countenance kindled with exultation at the astonishment and delight which I was about to produce,) "you surely will dance with an old friend and sweet-heart, who used to dance with you when a girl."
>
> At this disclosure, her features assumed a vast variety of expressions; but none of them responded precisely to my expectation: indeed, some of them were of such an equivocal and alarming character, that I deemed it advisable not to prolong her suspense. (15–16)

Baldwin is here very much the plot maker, having initiated a rising action and eagerly looking forward to the comic denouement. Unfortunately, even after he gives his name, Polly does not remember him, going so far as to claim that she doesn't "think I ever heard the name before," despite remembering very well the other names he provides to jog her memory (16). Before he can make himself known, he is whisked away to the dance floor, where he plans to recall himself to her by his trademark dance step: " 'She'll remember Abram Baldwin,' thought I, 'as soon as she sees the *double cross-hop*' " (16). Alas, this too proves a flat failure, as Polly is called away, while Baldwin learns, to his chagrin, that he is no longer the dancer that he was. Exhausted, he leaves the dance floor, his "moral energies [brought] to a perfect level with [his] physical" (18).

Baldwin's failure to integrate himself within the agrarian community is replicated at a stylistic level. From the opening pages of the story we are made aware that Baldwin *puts* things differently than his hosts. Early on, for example, he is told that he will "be expected at the frolick"—a phrase he carefully sets off in quotation marks—and he consents, "being desirous of seeing all that passed upon the occasion" (17). Baldwin's studied diction, which dominates both his narration and his speech, sets him apart from his fellow characters, but in a manner diametrically opposed to Lynn's *cordon sanitaire*. Even as he values agrarian pastoralism over city sophistication, he reaffirms—in a highly artificial manner—the stylistic boundaries between himself and the country folk; in a typical instance, he describes himself, as he retires from the dance floor, as "to speak in my native dialect . . . '*mortal tired*'" (18). This stylistic dissociation has broader cultural implications; rather than mediating the multiplicity of styles within the community, Baldwin exaggerates them. However much he may praise the simple ways of the frontier folk, he can never engage them directly; his access is mediated through the official language of the pastoral mode. Although he stops short of distributing oaten pipes and shepherd's crooks, it is clear that Baldwin approves of the agrarian icon because it is the sort of thing he has read about in books, perhaps those written by Robert Burns, a poet he approvingly mentions in a later sketch. Ultimately, Baldwin's radical abstraction of—and alienation from—the frontier folk makes it impossible for him to negotiate community.

Although Baldwin is the author of five later sketches, these merely elucidate the narrative alienation of "The Dance." Things are no better for Baldwin when he returns to town, for there his pastoral orientation makes any trace of sophistication literally unbearable. In "The Song" Baldwin recoils so vehemently from a continental song he hears at a social gathering that he returns home "in convulsions," takes sixty drops of laudanum, falls asleep, and has a nightmare in which Hecate (with the face of the singer, Miss Augusta Crump) attacks him amidst an army of French birds and Italian beasts. Although Baldwin admires the music of Ireland and Scotland, which may still "be safely admitted into a land of liberty and sense" (71), the continental fare of Miss Crump proves his undoing. He describes her piano playing as a pitched battle between her hands and the keys, while her voice seems at one point "compounded of a dry cough, a grunt, a hiccup and a whisper," and at another resembles "the squall of a pinched cat" (77, 78). But however bad the music, Baldwin has missed an important element in the episode: Miss Crump is, as her mother claims in an aside, frightened to death, and she plays only out of filial duty and the desire not to disappoint her eager audience. When, after her first song, a bystander pleads for a second, she "looked pitifully at her mama; and her mama looked 'sing' at Miss Augusta: accordingly she squared herself for a song" (77). Baldwin himself applauds Mrs. Crump, who was "kind enough . . . to interpose, and to relieve the company from further anxiety" by commanding her daughter to play (75). Baldwin is thus caught in the double bind of applauding Miss Crump's act of playing—a social imperative—while denouncing the playing itself. That his critical temper overcomes his sense of social propriety makes it impossible for Baldwin to function socially; although he excels as a satirist, his satirical perspective exiles him from the genteel gathering of "The Song" no less effectively than his pastoral perspective exiles him from the frontier community of "The Dance."

Baldwin is unwilling to submit himself to what hermeneutical theorists call objectivation, the process whereby a subject externalizes himself through labor or language and thus becomes an object whose environment may subsequently react back on him.[11] Because he claims sole interpretive authority, Baldwin must reject the essential reciprocity of social life. He thus gradually assumes the role of a distant spectator, a role in which he need not forfeit his prerogatives of cultural authority. When he externalizes himself, as when he takes to the floor in "The Dance," he finds that self-dramatization is at best an unwieldy process subject to the chaos always lurking in the external world of *Georgia Scenes*. Baldwin's third and by far his longest sketch, "The 'Charming Creature' as Wife," is the first in which he does not appear as a character. This withdrawal into pure voice, repeated in his two later sketches, suggests his inability to impose coherence on the world while living it at the same time.

Essentially, "The 'Charming Creature' as Wife," is an object lesson on the dangers of the "charming creature," the spoiled, overly sophisticated female type antithetical to domestic stability. The sketch centers around the

---

11. Joseph Bleicher, *Contemporary Hermeneutics: Hermeneutics as Method, Philosophy, and Critique* (London: Routledge, 1980), 270.

marriage between Baldwin's nephew, George Baldwin, and Miss Evelina Caroline Smith, the charming creature whose ability to dramatize virtues she does not possess leads to a disastrous marriage. Shortly after the two are wed, George and Evelina return to his childhood home, where her true character begins to show through. She refuses to allow George to talk with old friends, and is particularly ill-at-ease around the lower classes, despite the "lessons" he provides for her:

> George had endeavored to prepare her for the plain, blunt, but honest familiarities, of his early friends. He had assured her that however rude they might seem, they were perfectly innocent; nay, that they were tokens of guileless friendship; for the natural disposition of plain, unlettered farmers, was to keep aloof from "the quality," as they called the people of the town, and that by as much as they overcame this disposition, by so much did they mean to be understood as evincing favor. (111)

Throughout *Georgia Scenes,* conversations are a way of negotiating and affirming social relationships and of bridging class divisions. But when these visitors appear, Evelina is hostile toward their blunt, familiar comments: "Having no tact for turning off these things playfully, and as little disposition to do so, she repelled them with a town dignity, which soon relieved her of these intrusions; and in less than a week, stopt the visits of George's first and warmest friends, to his father's house" (114). By invoking class status, Evelina severs the lines of communication between her husband and the lower classes, thereby exiling him from his native community. Although Baldwin's views on women in many ways reflect Longstreet's own, it is equally clear that Baldwin and Evelina share certain key traits. As we know from "The Dance," Baldwin is himself prone to act in such a way as to elicit public esteem, the very characteristic for which he denounces Evelina. And like her, he cannot act naturally; he performs with a clear sense of how his actions will be received—or rather, how he would *like* for them to be received. Even as he damns Evelina for maintaining social distance, Baldwin becomes, not an integrated member of the community, but an exile from it, until he fades from the scene, as Meriwether says, "on a note of futility and passivity."[12]

---

12. Meriwether, "Realist and Artist," 359.

Baldwin begins his last sketch, "A Sage Conversation," by proclaiming his love for the "aged matrons of our land" (216). After an effusive, overblown recital of their many virtues, Baldwin concludes by remarking, "I cannot, therefore, ridicule them myself, nor bear to hear them ridiculed in my presence. And yet, I am often amused at their conversations; and have amused *them* with a rehearsal of their own conversations, taken down by me when they little dreamed that I was listening to them" (216). As in "The Dance," Baldwin's professed admiration for the simple country folk goes hand-in-hand with an assumed superiority that precludes any meaningful contact with them. The plot of "A Sage Conversation" centers around a night Baldwin spends with three elderly women who have put him and his companion, the ever-protean Ned Brace, up for the night. When Ned innocently mentions two men who were married and raised "a lovely parcel of children," the women are incredulous. When Ned and Baldwin retire, the latter "could not resist the temptation of casting an eye through the cracks of the partition to see the effects of Ned's wonderful story upon the kind ladies" (219). What ensues is a conversation that moves from shocked amazement to possible explanations (one of the women suggests that one of the "men" must have actually been a woman) to a rehearsal of stories dealing with love, marriage, death, medical cures, livestock, and family histories. Although Baldwin's intention is merely to amuse his reader by showing the women's gullibility, their conversation serves as a ritualistic forum for sharing communal knowledge and affirming communal relationships. The figure of Baldwin peering through the cracks and covertly recording the conversation is a suggestive one, as is his presentation of the dialogue, which follows dramatic convention in assigning each speech to *"Mrs. S.," "Mrs. R.,"* or *"Mrs. B."* Both features suggest Baldwin's *distance* from the women's dialogue; he provides no narrative medium in which their speech sounds. As he leaves the women's house the next morning, he simultaneously makes his exit from *Georgia Scenes* having utterly failed to integrate himself within the community.

In contrast to Baldwin, Hall becomes, as *Georgia Scenes* progresses, more deeply integrated within his community, his narrative style finally comprising a kind of discursive medium in which class tensions are resolved, even if such a resolution is far from the natural process implied in his narrative closure. Indeed, Hall's narrative style tends to efface the very idea of class, of which he rarely demonstrates a conceptual awareness. In this respect he is quite unlike Baldwin, whose overdetermination of types makes it impossible for him to function socially. Hall's effacement of class, however, must be heavily qualified since Hall finally effaces the content of class rather than the social forms associated with it; to use Polanyi's terminology, class remains an integral part of his tacit knowledge even though it rarely serves as a point of focal awareness. This distinction, in turn, is a lesson he learns in due course; his mistake in "Georgia Theatrics" is precisely a matter of form (taken as the structure of a social hierarchy) and content (the moral characteristics distributed within that structure). Hall assumes that the poor white living in the "Dark Corner" of Lincoln will act out his depraved moral nature, and thereby prevents any interclass relationship from developing. Yet if Hall stumbles in "Georgia Theatrics," he nevertheless avoids the kind of withdrawal that defines the socionarrative style of his fellow narrator, Baldwin. In Hall's defense, moreover, it can be said that at least he vocalizes his class prejudices and thereby allows the possibility of correction and modification.

Consciousness that he too provides a figure to be interpreted by others becomes for Hall an important point of departure in his evolution toward a more egalitarian socionarrative style. His second sketch, "The Horse Swap," begins with a man "cavorting" on horseback in front of an impassive crowd. As Hall approaches, he relates that the man "eyed me closely" before "he fetched a whoop, and swore that 'he could out-swap any live man, woman or child, that ever walked these hills, or that ever straddled horse flesh since the days of old daddy Adam.' 'Stranger,' said he to me, 'did you ever see the *Yellow* Blossom from Jasper?' " (20–21). After being assured by the man that he is, in fact, the celebrated personage in question, Hall relates, "I began to feel my situation a little awkward" until an older gentleman named Peter Ketch "relieves" him by drawing the attention of the Yellow Blossom and engaging him in a horse swap. After a ritualistic series of offers, counter-offers, rhetorical feints, and insults, Ketch and the Blossom finally agree to swap horses. When Bullet, the horse Ketch has obtained, is discovered to have a huge sore on his back, it appears that Ketch has been fooled until his young son reveals that Blossom's new beast, Kit, is both blind and deaf.

In an important essay on the role of games in southwestern humor, Michael Oriard notes that what Ketch actually gains in the exchange is "stature in the eyes of the townspeople." "An audience," Oriard says, "whether simply readers like ourselves or bystanders at the scene, is essential to such contests . . . because it provides the context in which the stake of the game is meaningful."[13] Ketch's rhetorical strategy makes particularly shrewd use of the crowd, relying as it does on the audience's ability to unpack his layered and sometimes subtle ironies. Unlike Blossom, whose hyperbolic self-proclamations are designed to separate himself from those around him, Ketch has a rhetorical style that implicates and involves his audience. When, for example, Blossom comments on the "curious look" in Kit's eyes, Ketch responds, "Oh yes, sir, . . . just as blind as a bat. Blind horses always have clear eyes. Make a motion at his eyes, if you please, sir." When Kit jerks back, Ketch continues, "Stone blind, you see, gentlemen . . . but he's just as good to travel of a dark night as if he had eyes" (26). Finally, when Blossom grumbles, "Blame my buttons . . . if I like them eyes," Ketch responds gracefully, "No . . . nor I neither. I'd rather have 'em made of diamonds; but they'll do, if they don't show as much white as Bullet's." In each instance, Ketch employs what Wayne Booth calls stable irony—that is, irony that re-lies on shared assumptions and contexts to communicate its message.[14] Ketch does not bargain with Blossom so much as he bargains with the spec-tators, winning them to his side through a shrewd series of rhetorical moves. Thus, when Blossom threatens to end the negotiation, Ketch refers to the figure he attempts to project to the townsfolk: "I didn't care about trading; but you cut such high shines, that I thought I'd like to back you out; and I've done it. Gentlemen, you see I've brought him to a hack" (27). And later, when negotiations stall for a second time, Hall reports that "it was pretty unanimously decided that the old man had backed Blossom out" (28) until

13. Michael Oriard, "Shifty in a New Country: Games in Southwestern Humor," *Southern Literary Journal* 12, no. 1 (1980): 14.

14. Wayne C. Booth, *A Rhetoric of Irony* (Chicago: University of Chicago Press, 1974), 5–6.

the young trader backs down and agrees to Ketch's terms. In both instances Ketch's strategy pays concrete dividends. Because he is able to create consensus by manipulating audience reactions, he can bring communal sentiment to bear upon Blossom, whose image as "a *leetle* of the best man, at a horse swap, that ever trod shoe-leather" (21) requires that the community recognize his prowess with each trade.

In the end, however, the joke is on Blossom, who has utterly failed to read the situation correctly. This episode mirrors countless incidents in southwestern humor; indeed, the very nature of the horse swap and its equivalents (games of chance, confidence games, swindles) throughout the genre revolves around the ability both to interpret competently and to objectify oneself so as to deny this ability to others. While in many cases this process works to undermine communal stability—one thinks of Simon Suggs and Sut Lovingood—Longstreet tends, in *Georgia Scenes* at least, to posit some congruity between communal health and the kind of uncertainty created when a character like Ketch misrepresents himself and his immediate situation. If Longstreet's ideal community assumes structured social roles, it also assumes that a measure of uncertainty and instability—in short, a measure of play—is no less necessary for the maintenance of communal norms. Indeed, when we note the numerous cases of false impersonation or misrepresentation in the pages of *Georgia Scenes*—a list that would include, besides Peter Ketch, the character of Ned Brace in both "The Character of a Native Georgian" and "A Sage Conversation," the young gentlemen of "The Wax Works," the debaters in "The Debating Society," and Hall himself in "The Shooting Match"—we come to realize that the motif is an important one in Longstreet's (and particularly Hall's) narrative world. A composite picture of Longstreet's quasi-trickster figure would reveal a gentleman who has mastered the language games of his native community such that he can predict how others will interpret him. Peter Ketch, for example, is marked by his dialect as being of a higher social class than Blossom; although clearly not an aristocrat, his speech and general manner establish him firmly as a middle-class yeoman and, from Blossom's perspective, a dupe. As we have seen, his rhetorical appeal to the community places him in an advantageous position vis-à-vis the exchange he negotiates, an exchange that acquires social significance since his increased stature works to reaffirm existing hierarchies. As the town's representative, in effect, Ketch provides the backwoods youth with something of an education. In "The Character of a Native Georgian" Hall describes a similar kind of misrepresentation directed toward the dandy. Introducing Ned Brace as a man who "seemed to live only to amuse himself with his fellow beings," Hall comments that "[t]he beau in the presence of his mistress, the fop, the pedant, the purse-proud, the over-fastidious and sensitive, were Ned's favorite game. These never passed him uninjured; and against such, he directed his severest shafts. . . . He was admirably fitted to his vocation. He could assume any character which his humor required him to personate, and he could sustain it to perfection" (31).[15]

The ability to gauge one's audience and rhetorically mislead it works performatively to establish social hierarchy; indeed, several of Longstreet's sketches establish a rough correlation between the ability to lead and the facility to mislead. Because such verbal facility represents a special kind of social power, it must be used responsibly. As Jürgen Habermas remarks,

> Thanks to the creativity of natural language the native speaker gains a unique power over the practical consciousness of the members of a community. The career of sophistry reminds us that it can be used for mind-fogging agitation as well as for enlightening people.
>
> There is, however, another side to this power: the specific lack of power of the speaking subject vis-à-vis habitualized language-games; they cannot be modified unless one participates in them. This in turn can be successful only to the extent that the rules which determine a language-game have been internalized. To enter into a linguistic tradition necessitates, at least latently, the efforts of a process of socialization: the "grammar" of language-games has to become part of the personality structure.[16]

15. Although Hall asserts this social value, the sketch itself consists of sometimes mean-spirited practical jokes at the expense of the gullible. In his final prank Brace constitutes a social threat as he interrupts a line of water buckets being carried to a fire so that he can get a drink. For a persuasive explanation of the schizophrenic nature of the sketch, see Wade, *Longstreet*, 171–72.

16. Jürgen Habermas, *Communication and the Evolution of Society*, trans. Thomas McCarthy (Boston: Beacon Press, 1979), 184.

Habermas's equation of language games and socialization processes provides a useful way of approaching the process by which Hall's dialogic encounters during the course of the book necessitate an internalization of language-game "grammar" before he can actively perform and negotiate his social authority, a position from which, in turn, consensus can be established. In early sketches like "The Horse Swap" Hall plays a more or less passive role, allowing someone like Ketch, who functions almost as a surrogate, to enter into the language game with all the social implications that attend it. As his monological narrative perspective begins to absorb the dialogic accents of the lower class, Hall demonstrates a willingness to narrate, understand, and finally engage in the exchanges and language games that define and maintain social order.

As he engages his community through its language games, Hall retains as a rhetorical subtext the trope of nature we have already noted. Most of Hall's sketches, including "The Horse Swap," "The Fight," "The Turn-Out," "The Gander Pulling," "The Turf," "The Fox Hunt," and "The Shooting Match," focus upon gatherings in which characters establish social hierarchies through a game or contest of some sort. As they are represented diachronically, these contests mediate the nature-culture opposition that permeates *Georgia Scenes* and, in doing so, work to naturalize the cultural positions they produce. In "The Fight" hierarchy emerges through physical combat; although the two combatants are described as "admirable specimens of human nature in its finest form" (56), Hall is quick to denounce the fight as a "scen[e] of barbarism and cruelty . . . now of rare occurrence" (70). Social hierarchy performatively established through physical combat thereby partakes of the rhetoric of bestial nature we noted in "Georgia Theatrics," a "nature" here consigned to the past by cultural institutions such as "the Christian religion," "schools, colleges, and benevolent associations" (35). Hall makes a similar temporal contrast in "Georgia Theatrics," for between the erstwhile "moral darkness" of Lincoln and its present respectability, he claims, "I could adduce from this county instances of the most numerous and wonderful transitions, from vice and folly, to virtue and holiness, which have ever perhaps been witnessed since the days of the apostolic ministry" (3).

Nevertheless, this preference for the present over the past is offset by several passages in which Hall makes the opposite comparison. In "The Turn Out," for example, Hall interrupts his tale to describe the lush countryside he and his host, Captain Griffin, see as they walk to the school house. Apologizing to his reader for the "minuteness of the foregoing description," Hall justifies himself by relating the Captain's remark that the surrounding lands "will never wear out" (83). Hall then recounts how, forty-two years later, he visited the same site, which in the meantime had become "barren, dreary and cheerless" (84). This passage subtly emphasizes the loss of the "natural" that Hall laments on several occasions: he begins the tale, for example, by describing the "Georgia Welcome of 1790" that he fears "Georgia will know . . . no more," a clear comparison between present decadence and sophistication and the natural hospitality of what he calls, without a trace of self-consciousness, the "good old days" (80). A similar passage occurs later in the tale, when "the *ruffle-shirted* little darlings of the present day" compare unfavorably with the "hardy sons of the forest" he encounters as he visits Captain Griffin (90). Unlike his fellow narrator Baldwin, for whom the present is always a sorry substitute for the irredeemable past, Hall demonstrates a divided temporal preference: On the one hand, he characterizes the past as simple and natural and the present as precious and decadent; on the other, he characterizes the past as bestial and uncouth and the present as civilized.

Implicit in this contradiction are the two basic narratives of human culture; in the one, culture represents an evolution from a bestial state, while in the other, it represents a devolution from some ideal natural state. While Longstreet's mediation of this contradiction may appear to be simply inconsistent,[17] I would contend instead that it helps delineate the abstract categories necessitating narrative resolution. Referring back to the categories defined earlier, we find that within the opposing pairs of terms cultured-uncultured and natural-unnatural, the historical progression unfolding within Hall's narrative is positive in the former case and negative in the latter; as the community of *Georgia Scenes* evolves, it becomes at once less "bestial" and less "pastoral." A closer examination of these passages, moreover, reveals

---

17. As it does to Richard Gray; see *Writing the South: Ideas of an American Region* (Cambridge, U.K.: Cambridge University Press, 1986), 70–71.

a class context at work; generally speaking, Hall prefers the less bestial lower class of the present, but the more natural upper class of the past. Thus, as the community of *Georgia Scenes* develops over time, the frontier excesses of the poor white tend to disappear as part of the same cultural shift that produces a more decadent and sophisticated upper class. As the poor white is, broadly speaking, transformed into the yeoman, and thus becomes better suited to a respectable position in the community, the gentleman threatens to be transformed into the dandy, who unlike his predecessor can stake no legitimate claim to a position of leadership. The narrative work of *Georgia Scenes*, then, is to produce a gentleman (Hall) able both to reaffirm class hierarchy and to negotiate interclass consensus by internalizing the grammar of the communal contests and language games through which hierarchy is established.

Among the more complex of Hall's later tales in this regard is "The Gander Pulling," which shows his socionarrative style evolving from the rigid moralism of "Georgia Theatrics." The story revolves around a game in which a heavily greased gander is hung upside-down from a loose rope under which competitors pass mounted on horseback; the horseman who pulls the greased fowl's head from his body is declared the winner. As he describes the greasing of the gander, Hall shifts from an objective point of view to a morally interested one:

Abhorrent as it may be, to all who respect the tenderer relations of life, *Mrs.* Prator had actually prepared a gourd of *goose*-grease for this very purpose. For myself, when I saw Ned dip his hands into the grease, and commence stroking down the feathers, from breast to head, my thoughts took a melancholy turn—They dwelt in sadness upon the many conjugal felicities which had probably been shared between the *greaseess* and the *greasee*. . . . And now alas! an extract from the smoking sacrifice of his bosom friend, was desecrated to the unholy purpose of making his neck "a fit object" for Cruelty to reach "her quick, unerring fingers at." Ye friends of the sacred tie! judge what were my feelings, when in the midst of these reflections, the voice of James Prator thundered on mine ear, "Durn his old dodging soul; brother Ned! grease his neck till a fly can't light on it!" (128–29)

In raising the issue of cruelty to animals, Hall exaggerates the linguistic barriers that separate him from the lower class, yet in a manner markedly different from the previous sketches in which this issue is raised. In "The

Horse-Swap," cruelty to animals allows Hall to assert the moral distance between himself and the poor white; after the sore on Bullet's back is exposed, Hall "felt that the brute who had been riding him in that situation, deserved the halter" (28). In "The Gander Pulling," however, Hall presents the same conflation of human and animal attributes ironically; we have little difficulty in perceiving that Hall's overblown rhetoric of moral concern is just as exaggerated as Prator's blunt outburst. The ironic opacity of Hall's rhetoric indicates a language that is no longer a transparent vehicle of absolute social authority. Likewise, his exaggerated sentimentality serves to subvert his characterization of both the birds and their tormentors, the latter of whom, unlike Blossom and the farm boy of "Georgia Theatrics," escape being consigned to the category of brute beast. As Carolyn S. Brown observes, "The Gander Pulling" reveals that "the rewards of contact with the frontier come not from piously condemning but from accepting and appreciating the frontier and frontier tales on their own terms."[18] Less concerned with judging the behavior of the lower class, Hall becomes more engaged in the negotiation of social relationships implicit in the game.

Yet while Hall is less eager to condemn the morals of the lower class, he is equally unwilling to dispense entirely with class distinctions. Early in the sketch, he notes that the "few females" in attendance "were from the lowest walks of life" (128), and later, as the gander pulling commences with the cry "Now blaze away!" he parenthetically glosses the command as the one used "for an onset of every kind, with people of this order" (131). More significantly, the issue of class qualifies Hall's attitude toward the fighting and drinking that follow the gander pulling, neither of which elicits, as we might expect, his moral condemnation. Instead, we find Hall sympathetically portraying the man who brings about these potential transgressions, one Fat John Fulger, the winner of the gander pulling colorfully described by one spectator as "that *gourd* o' hog's *lard*" (133). Although he is among the less skilled contestants, Fulger caps his victory with a speech Hall initially characterizes as being "little calculated to reconcile [the losers and those who had staked bets on them] to their disappointment" (133). "*Boys,*" Fulger be-

18. Carolyn S. Brown, *The Tall Tale in American Folklore and Literature* (Knoxville: University of Tennessee Press, 1987), 47.

gins, "don't pull with *men* any more. I've jist got my hand in; I wish I had a pond full o' ganders here now, jist to show how I could make their heads fly—Bet all I've won, you may hang three upon that rope, and I'll set Slouch at full speed, and take off the heads of all three, with the first grab; two with my hands, and one with my teeth" (134). This mock self-aggrandizement, Hall explains, "was all fun, for John knew, and all were convinced that he knew, that his success, was entirely the result of accident. John was really a 'good natured fellow,' and his *cavorting* had an effect directly opposite to that which the reader would suppose it had—it reconciled all to their disappointment, save one" (134). Fulger knows what people think of him, and thus is able to resolve the tensions accompanying his victory; in a sense, his skill at language games makes up for his ineptitude at gander pulling. In employing stable irony, as Hall carefully explains, Fulger reestablishes harmony in an audience seething with potential violence, the result of an accident disrupting a social ritual in which consensus (here, concerning the probable winners) had already been achieved. From Hall's point of view, Fulger's ability to reestablish the consensus he had disrupted qualifies the morally dubious actions that follow when he spends his winnings treating the company to drinks, "and thereby produced four Georgia rotations [fights]; after which all parted good friends" (134).

Conspicuously absent is any narrative moralizing, especially notable given Longstreet's own commitment to the temperance movement and Hall's frequent condemnation of fighting and drinking on other occasions. Indeed, a later sketch titled "An Interesting Interview" is devoted entirely to portraying the ill effects of "the all-destroying vice" of drunkenness. At the beginning of this tale, which relates a drunken conversation of two "industrious, honest, sensible farmers, when sober" (185), Hall looks forward to the day ten years hence when he hopes to "see [drunkenness] driven entirely, from the higher walks of life at least, if not from all grades of society" (184). This divided sense of class expectation similarly informs the ending of "The Gander Pulling," where instead of judging them for their drunken, brawling ways, Hall presents the lower-class folk sympathetically. Drinking and fighting are not threats to communal relationships, but a means of establishing them—among people of a certain sort. If, as one of his drunkards claims, "circumstances alter cases" (186), Hall's style proves flexible enough to recognize and even sanction the positive consequences of drinking and fighting within the lower class ritual of the gander pulling. If the participants in the gander pulling do not live up to his gentlemanly ideals, they nevertheless affirm their mutual bonds in a way that Hall is reluctant to condemn outright. At the same time, Hall's provisional ethics with respect to drinking and fighting legitimate his tacit sense of social hierarchy. In not holding the yeoman to a strict or absolute morality, Hall neither requires nor expects him to behave according to the moral code that legitimates class distinctions between gentleman and yeoman. This sense of inclusion, then, while broadening the parameters of communal participation, nevertheless fails to eliminate class distinctions.

The maintenance of community requires a socionarrative style flexible enough to sustain engagement with the lower class while simultaneously perpetuating the social gradations that inform *Georgia Scenes* from the beginning. As I have said, this tension between common ground and class distinction constitutes the dominant problem to be resolved through Hall's narrative negotiation. Given Longstreet's lifelong devotion to the ideals of Jeffersonian democracy, the problem of social class orients itself around the perennial problem of how, in a society where all men are created equal, some are more equal than others. In an 1834 editorial in the *State Rights' Sentinel,* the Augusta newspaper he owned and edited, Longstreet confronted the issue of class in the context of American violence. Longstreet wondered how Americans could be as violent as Europeans, or perhaps even more so, given that Americans had "no extremes of grandeur or poverty, of aristocracy and peasantry—no feudal barbarian distinctions of vassal, as in Europe; and that the great mass and bulk of the population are, it may be said, of the middling class, and placed upon an equality of condition certainly as respects their political rights, and in the aggregate they are so also in respect to their morals, their education, and their rank in society."[19] Although Longstreet's language subtly subverts his homage to a (nearly) classless society—equality of rank in society "in the aggregate" clearly collapses into nonsense—it is interesting to note how, following Longstreet's logic, social

19. [Augustus Baldwin Longstreet], "The causes of the frequency of Murders, Suicides, and Insanity in the United States," *State Rights' Sentinel,* 17 April 1834, 1.

hierarchy might (as in Europe) legitimately fuel violence. Longstreet resolves this issue by presenting political rights—suffrage—as the mechanism through which all Americans are "placed upon an equality of condition." This equality of condition does not, however, preclude a hierarchical distinction between representative and represented.

In a post–*Georgia Scenes* sketch titled "Darby, The Politician," Longstreet describes the social chaos that results when an unfit yeoman is elected to political office. The title character is designated in the first sentence of the tale as "the first man who, without any qualifications for the place, was elected to the Legislature of Georgia." Well suited to his role as small merchant, Darby's entry into politics is presented in sinister terms; he repeatedly demonstrates "shrewdness," "low cunning," and knowledge of "the prejudices and weaknesses of the common people of the country, [of which he] had no little tact in turning . . . to his own advantage." After cagily arranging for his friends to urge him to enter the race, Darby eventually debates his gentleman rivals, Smith and Jones. Playing to the hilt the role of the populist demagogue, Darby leads his rivals into a rhetorical trap by forcing them to agree that the poor are just as free as the rich, and then forcing them to defend freehold suffrage, which dictated that only land owners could vote. Although Smith and Jones eloquently (though feebly) attempt to argue their way out, Darby has clearly and effectively—in the minds of the gathered farmers, at any rate—appropriated the ideal of equality for his own selfish ends. Republican ideology, then, serves as a kind of master code through which social discourse must be channeled, and the rhetorical effort expended by Darby and his rivals serves to gain primary access to it. Because Darby's rhetoric forces his opponents into a double bind, the essential contradiction of republican ideology—that equality and hierarchy can coexist—cannot be resolved conceptually, but only, according to Fredric Jameson's formulation, through intervention of a narrative apparatus—in this case, the story of Darby's sordid political career, which demonstrates the yeoman's illegitimacy as a political representative.[20]

The issue of representation permeates *Georgia Scenes* as well. In "The Fight," for example, we find surprisingly little scorn directed at the combat-

20. Augustus Baldwin Longstreet, "Darby, The Politician," in *Stories with a Moral*, ed. Fitz R. Longstreet (Philadelphia: John C. Winston, 1912), 50, 53; Jameson, *Political Unconscious*, 82–83.

ants themselves; instead, Hall censures the combatants' wives (who initiate the fight with their own quarrel) and the conniving Ransy Sniffle, a diminutive poor white who feeds "copiously upon red clay and blackberries," eggs the combatants on by relaying inflammatory information, and finally serves as an object lesson "for the purpose of showing what a great matter a little fire sometimes kindleth" (57, 58). In his moralistic coda to the tale, Hall explicitly condemns the peace officers who "countenance" such "disgrace[s] to the community," asserting that they "deserve a place in the Penitentiary" (70). Hall thus reserves his harshest comments for what we might call inverted representatives (the morally inferior wives and Ransy Sniffle standing in for the parties concerned) and delinquent representatives (the peace officers who fail to represent community interests). If the violence of "The Fight" takes place in a context of egalitarianism run amok—that is, in the absence of properly hierarchical representation—Hall's next sketch, "The Turn-Out," shows a healthier form of transgression sanctioned by a higher level of cultural authority—here, Hall's host Captain Griffin. Immediately after greeting his guest, Captain Griffin explains that the local boys are planning to revolt against the school-master:

The boys . . . are going to turn out the school-master to-morrow, and you can perceive they think of nothing else. We must go over to the school-house, and witness the contest, in order to prevent injury to preceptor or pupils; for though the master is always upon such occasions, glad to be turned out, and only struggles long enough to present his patrons a fair apology for giving the children a holiday, which he desires as much as they do, the boys always conceive a holiday gained by a "turn out," as a sole achievement of their valor, and in their zeal to distinguish themselves, upon such memorable occasions, they sometimes become too rough, provoke the master to wrath, and a very serious conflict ensues. To prevent these consequences, to bear witness that the master was forced to yield, before he would withhold a day of his promised labor from his employers, and to act as a mediator between him and the boys, in settling the articles of peace, I always attend; and you must accompany me to-morrow. (82)

The Captain's account of what will transpire is notable in that he, unlike the participants in the affair, is fully aware of the intersection between the boys' heroic intentions and the schoolmaster's contractual obligations. As both a proxy for the townsfolk and an authority figure for the boys, the Captain countenances the form of the contest while at the same time ensuring that its violent content is kept under control—ensuring, in short, that it remains a game. This level of authority is precisely what is absent in "The Fight," where social hierarchy is determined by physical combat rather than, as with Captain Griffin, preceding and containing it. Indeed, Captain Griffin's representative authority contains, on an almost authorial level, the action he narrates before the fact; whatever chaos ensues, he assures Hall, will be limited by his authority to preserve order.

Although "The Fight" demonstrates the need for the kind of legitimate representation we find in "The Turn-Out," it is not until "The Shooting Match," the concluding sketch of *Georgia Scenes,* that Longstreet engages the issue of representation in the context of social class. Here, Hall's moral fitness to represent the yeoman whites resolves class tension by producing consensual, tacit agreement about class roles. But while such a resolution will necessarily be ideologically interested, it is nonetheless achieved through dialogic negotiation rather than unilateral imposition. From the opening lines of "The Shooting Match" we find Hall actively responding to the dialogic imperative of the lower class using language, as Longstreet says in his preface, "*accommodated to the capacity of the person to whom he represents himself as speaking*" (2).[21] Traveling in a frontier county, Hall comes upon a "swarthy, bright-eyed smerky little fellow," whom he asks if he is "going driving" (229):

"Not exactly," replied he, surveying my horse with a quizzical smile, "I have n't been driving *by myself* for a year or two, and my nose has got so bad lately I can't carry a cold trail *without hounds to help me.*"

21. Longstreet felt compelled to justify himself to those who "have taken exceptions to the coarse, inelegant, and sometimes ungrammatical language, which *the writer* represents *himself* as occasionally using" by reminding his reader that "*it is language accommodated to the capacity of the person to whom he represents himself as speaking*" (2). Although critics have usually interpreted this statement as a justification, on realistic grounds, for the coarse dialect found throughout the book, Longstreet is speaking only of the coarseness of "the writer's" language *as speech*—that is, the language of either Baldwin or Hall as they "accommodate" their language to the "capacity" of their intratextual audience (not the reader of *Georgia Scenes*).

Alone, and without hounds, as he was, the question was rather a silly one; but it answered the purpose for which it was put, which was only to draw him into conversation, and I proceeded to make as decent a retreat as I could.

"I did n't know," said I, "but that you were going to meet the huntsmen, or going to your stand."

"Ah, sure enough," rejoined he, "that *mout* be a bee, as the old woman said when she killed a wasp. It seems to me I ought to know you."

"Well, if you *ought,* why *don't* you?"

"What *mout* your name be?"

"It *might* be any thing," said I, with borrowed wit; for I knew my man, and knew what kind of conversation would please him most.

"Well, what is it then?"

"It *is,* Hall," said I; "but you know it might as well have been any thing else."

"Pretty digging!" said he. "I find you're not the fool I took you to be; so here's to a better acquaintance with you." (229–30)

Although the language game played by Hall and Billy Curlew ends in mutual respect, its unstated rules suggest an initial unwillingness of each to engage the other as an equal; for Billy, this unwillingness is clearly represented as class resentment. According to the unstated rules of the game, hierarchy is established by attributing literal significance to a word or phrase where none is intended; by thus improperly attributing literality to the other's language, Billy and Hall are able, in turn, to make the other look the fool. Hall resolves this antagonism when he demonstrates that he understands the game, after which Billy renews the banter as a way of affirming mutual respect. When Hall asks Billy to "give me your name," the latter replies, "To be sure I will, my old coon—take it—take it, and welcome. Any thing else about me you'd like to have?" (230). In the end, the dialogic instability of language works not to affirm difference, but to define mutual participation within a community.

Throughout "The Shooting Match," Hall's asides to the reader indicate his consciousness of how he relates to the yeomen he encounters: He notes that his initial "silly" question "answered the purpose for which it was put, which was only to draw him into conversation"; he comments that "I knew my man, and knew what kind of conversation would please him most"; and shortly thereafter, upon meeting Squire Sims, he explains, "I am always free and easy with those who are so with me, and in this course I rarely fail to please" (233). Having thus internalized the "grammar" of the language games governing communal interaction, Hall orients his language toward his specific audience so as to make negotiated exchange possible, which in turn is predicated on acknowledging that he is likewise available to their evaluation. As Bakhtin explains, the speaker's "orientation toward the listener is an orientation toward a specific conceptual horizon, toward the specific world of the listener; it introduces totally new elements into his discourse; it is in this way, after all, that various different points of view, conceptual horizons, systems for providing expressive accents, various social 'languages' come to interact with one another. . . . The speaker breaks through the alien conceptual horizon of the listener, constructs his own utterance on alien territory, against his, the listener's, apperceptive background."[22] That Billy represents an alien conceptual horizon is made clear at several points in the story; for example, even after he and Hall establish mutual respect, Billy guesses that "you hardly ever was at a shooting match, stranger, from the cut of your coat" (230). Thus marked as an alien, Hall is nevertheless able to engage Billy's "apperceptive background"—that is, the tacit assumptions that permit him to judge Hall on the basis of his clothing. Hall's coat acts here as a metonymic indicator of class; Billy's prejudice is that Hall's coat is, so to speak, empty. When Hall relates that he has not only been to shooting matches, but also "won beef" at one as a child, Billy is incredulous until he realizes that Hall is the very man of whom his father, who had once won a bet on Hall's shooting, has spoken "many a time" (231–32). Knowing that he can count on the other fellows to make, as he has done, a metonymic association between clothing and character, Billy hopes to "tear the lint off the boys" by betting on Hall at the shooting match. As he tells Hall, "They'll never 'spect such a looking man as you are of knowing any thing about a rifle" (232), a class prejudice he reaffirms

22. M. M. Bakhtin, *The Dialogic Imagination: Four Essays,* ed. and trans. Michael Holquist and Caryl Emerson (Austin: University of Texas Press, 1981), 282.

shortly thereafter when he introduces Hall to Squire Sims, telling him, "for all you see him in these fine clothes, he's a *swinge*-cat—a darned sight cleverer fellow than he looks to be" (233).

Hall's emphasis on reciprocal valuation indicates how substantially the framing dynamics of his earlier tales have become elaborated within the intratextual sphere of action. We have seen in "Georgia Theatrics" how Hall's initial moralistic socionarrative style, when enforced as a "sacred office," leads to a subversion of social authority. If "The Gander Pulling" shows Hall's narrative perspective becoming flexible enough to recognize the social value of the lower class's "uncouth" ways, he still remains a spectator. It is not until "The Shooting Match" that Hall puts into practice as a citizen what he has learned as a narrator. No longer a spectator, he actively participates in the communal ritual, gladly accompanying Billy to the shooting match when invited to do so. This physical act is significant, for here we see a negotiation of class boundaries being effected, literally, on common ground.

Not that any consensus appears imminent upon Hall's arrival at the shooting match; indeed, the very opposite is true, as he finds himself, after Billy enters him in the competition and brags of his shooting prowess, to be the object of intense and generally skeptical scrutiny. As Hall relates, "Every inch of me was examined with the nicest scrutiny; and some plainly expressed by their looks, that they never would have taken me for such a bite" (235). Unwilling to wound Billy's feelings by either shooting by proxy (Hall explains that "by all rules of breeding I was bound to shoot in person") or refusing to shoot at all, Hall reluctantly enters the contest and holds out for the last shot. During the intervening rounds of shooters, he describes in minute detail the rules of the shooting match, its history in the state of Georgia, the types of weapons used, and especially the verbal gamesmanship of the various participants. As in several earlier sketches, insults and word play replace the actual contest as the primary site of competition: Mealy Whitecotton's frail physique, Hiram Baugh's weak boasts, and Simon Stow's ineffectual deliberateness all receive sarcastic commentary from the crowd. When Hall's turn comes, he too becomes the butt of his fellow shooters' comments, for despite Billy's assurances that he is a shooter of great renown, Hall finds that he can hardly raise the yeoman's heavy rifle.

Haplessly attempting to raise the piece amid the men's clever sarcasm—one man explains that Hall "used to shoot well . . . but can't now nor never could," while another warns those standing near the target to be careful, "for I'll be dod durned if Broadcloth don't give some of you the dry gripes if you stand too close thare"(244–45)—Hall fires blindly and immediately begins saving face through self-deprecation. Having learned a lesson from Fat John Fulger, Hall explains that "I have always found that the most credible way of relieving myself of derision, was to heighten it myself as much as possible. It is a good plan in all circles, but by far the best which can be adopted among the plain rough farmers of the country" (245). Fully cognizant of his audience's language games and the potential resentment they harbor, Hall facetiously swears never to shoot for beef again if the cross is not knocked out, then provides a ludicrous explanation of the single and double wabble—shooting techniques, he explains, well known to all the best marksmen. As the men tending the target approach, the irony of Hall's discourse has become apparent to his fellow shooters, who are no longer interested in the accuracy of his shot, since Hall's "airs and harangue" have "put the thought to flight" (246). Astonishingly, however, the men tending the target arrive with the news that Hall's shot is, as one puts it, "only second best after all the fuss" (246), to which Hall exclaims "with uncontrollable transports," "Second best!" From their distant perspective, Hall relates, the combination of Billy's boasting, the courtesy extended to him, and his struggles with the rifle ("taken as the flourishes of an expert who wished to 'astonish the natives' ") have conspired to create in them the expectation of a skilled shot. Although these men are disappointed with Hall's marksmanship, those who have witnessed firsthand his shooting and his facetious rhetoric are incredulous, and their astonishment, Hall explains, "blinded [them] to the real feelings with which the exclamation ["Second best!"] was uttered, and allowed me sufficient time to prepare myself for making the best use of what I had said before, with a very different object" (247).

Because its meaning is open to dual interpretations, Hall's exclamation allows him the opportunity to lament "with an air of despondency" that he is "getting too old and dim sighted to shoot a rifle" (247). Although he later asserts that, in fact, the shot had been the result of pure luck, Hall again demonstrates his facility at language games; marked as different by his clothing and fancy speech, he adapts his speech to demonstrate that he is "one of them." James Kibler thus acts as Longstreet's ideal reader in claiming that despite "superficial" differences, Hall and the shooters "find common ground." As Kibler continues, "There is absolutely no class 'struggle' or resentment because these 'simple' men have the dignity of possessing values in common with the 'high and mighty of land,' the same values that matter more than the trappings of wealth, power, and fame. It is thus finally these shared values that bond them and bind the community into an organic whole. From this common ground, the one 'class' can regard the other with genuine respect across their superficial 'barriers.'"[23] In subordinating class division to the organic unity, Kibler affirms the utopian resolution provided through Hall's narrative negotiation, as does Billy Curlew, who invites Hall home to "swap lies," an offer, he asserts, that "won't cost [Hall] a cent" (248).

This utopian resolution nevertheless restricts the yeoman to a positional entrance into the community. As he is preparing to leave, Hall is stopped by a member of the crowd and asked what he is "offering for." When Hall assures him that he is not a candidate for office, the man replies, "Oh . . . if you're up for any thing you need'nt be mealy-mouthed about it, 'fore us boys; for we'll all go in for you here up to the handle," a sentiment endorsed by Billy, who affirms that if Hall ever should, the "boys of Upper Hogthief" will "go for you, to the hilt, against creation, tit or no tit, that's the *tatur*" (249). Coupled with a severe juxtaposition of high and low dialects, this reference to political patronage suggests the integral role political representation plays in bridging social boundaries; essentially, Hall has achieved a social style capable of creating consensus, a style that encompasses the yeoman farmers of Upper Hogthief as citizens rather than frontier curiosities but recently evolved from the half-horse, half-alligator. But while "The Shooting Match" performs the essential cultural work of reclaiming the poor white of the Dark Corner as the yeoman white of Upper Hogthief, it does so with the understanding that the political role of the latter is defined

---

23. Kibler, Introduction, xviii.

in relation to that of the gentleman. This tacit agreement is a key example of what Jameson calls the ideologeme, that rhetorical construct "susceptible to both a conceptual description and a narrative manifestation all at once." Displayed here in its narrative manifestation, which Jameson describes as "a kind of ultimate class fantasy about the 'collective characters' which are the classes in opposition,"[24] the ideologeme of representation tacitly delimits cultural roles; there is no question of either Hall's fitness to represent or the yeoman's lack thereof. Nor is this resolution presented conceptually, since we have no explanation justifying the men's respective roles. We must therefore view Hall's narrative resolution as more a matter of form than of content since unity is established and mutually affirmed without, and almost at the expense of, an explanation regarding the content of the form. Put another way, as soon as consent is granted and the form of unity established, the content of division—those characteristics that make the yeoman unfit to lead—disappears. Immediately following the yeomen's commitment to "go in for you up to the handle," Hall precisely inverts the metonymic relationship between morality and place he had established as the moralistic narrator of "Georgia Theatrics." Where he had assumed that the "Dark Corner of Lincoln," accurately depicted the morality of its inhabitants, he says of "Upper Hogthief," "The reader will not suppose that the district took its name from the character of its inhabitants. In almost every county in the State, there is some spot, or district, which bears a contemptuous appellation, usually derived from local rivalships, or from a single accidental circumstance" (249). So ends *Georgia Scenes* on a note of class reconciliation.

The tacit resolution provided by "The Shooting Match" legitimates Hall's ability to represent, both politically and narratively, the yeomen of Upper Hogthief; his knowledge of them "as they are" validates, as they recognize, his ability to represent them in a political context. As Kenneth Burke reminded us many years ago, it is "no mere accident of language that we use the same word for sensory, artistic, and political representation" since each realm constitutes a mode of symbolic action.[25] Yet, as in most Jeffer-

24. Jameson, *Political Unconscious,* 87.
25. Kenneth Burke, *The Philosophy of Literary Form: Studies in Symbolic Action* (Berkeley and Los Angeles: University of California Press, 1973), 26.

sonian rhetoric, the representative relationship here is not strictly synecdochic in the sense that the "whole" Hall represents is monolithic, although
the yeomen's perception that Hall is one of them tends to elide class distinctions, as does Hall's narrative style itself. Nevertheless, the relative disappearance of Hall as a moralistic narrator does not occasion a total collapse
of the narrative frame. Hall's narrative style, having been dialogically modified over the course of the book, has become a social style and thus can be
put into play as speech that has social value as a unit of exchange. The verbal give-and-take between Hall and his fellow shooters nevertheless takes
place within a narrative medium in which Hall on several occasions metonymically digresses to provide information or interpretation not explicitly
germane to the action being described. As Hall becomes more of a narrator
and less of a character—that as, as he reestablishes the frame—he tacitly asserts his social authority. In many instances, such digressions show Hall, in
his role as a social historian, providing historical contexts unavailable to his
reader or presumably to the folk of Upper Hogthief. Hall also invokes his
wider frame of reference when, on three occasions, he introduces a particular character and then describes the class or type the man represents. He introduces Squire Sims, for example, as having been "a Justice of the Peace in
his day; (and where is the man of his age in Georgia who has not?)" (232), a
formulation that quickly fixes the Squire in the reader's mind as a minor official and a good fellow. He describes Moses Firmby, one of the better
shooters, as "a tall, slim man of rather sallow complexion; and it is a singular fact, that . . . the mountaineers have not generally robust frames or fine
complexions: they are, however, almost inexhaustible by toil" (240). This
shift from individual to type occurs again with Mealy Whitecotton, introduced as "another Ransy Sniffle" (233). In the sphere of what we might call
social synecdoche, Hall moves with confidence; there is no question, as in
"Georgia Theatrics," of his categorical expectations, his social taxonomy,
being subverted.

Hall's ability to categorize these minor characters quickly and efficiently
represents a kind of social authority resulting from the fact that they are, in
a deep sense, *familiar* to him. As he attains a style that socializes previously
alien and disruptive members of the community, Hall tacitly legitimates his

authority to organize his culture symbolically. His interpretive authority encodes a kind of social power: being an authority on this culture is equivalent to having power within it. For example, Hall's three-word categorization of Mealy Whitecotton is also a way of controlling him; unlike our previous Ransy Sniffle, whose ability to fuel violence as an "inverted" representative constitutes a real threat to community stability, Mealy is dealt with easily: despite his status as the "self-constituted commander-in-chief" of the shooting match (233), he loses authority to Hall. On a more complex level, Hall's social authority is elaborated in his relationship with Billy Curlew, who fully represents Jameson's collective character. Hall's narrative relationship with Billy is, on two occasions, literally that of an interpreter—one who decodes the dialect message of the yeoman. In the first instance Hall glosses in detail Billy's invitation to the shooting match, a "short sentence . . . replete with information for me," thereby demonstrating his intimate knowledge of the offer's social meaning. In the second, which occurs just after the shooting match, Hall relates how Billy "begged me to go home with him for the night, or as he expressed it, 'to go home with him and swap lies that night, and it should'nt cost me a cent,' the true reading of which, is, that if I would go home with him, and give him the pleasure of an evening's chat about old times, his house should be as free to me as my own" (248). This dialogic encounter demonstrates how completely Hall's gentlemanly style has absorbed the yeoman's raw vernacular. In interpreting Billy's coarse economic metaphors, Hall restores the social meaning of the proffered exchange.

Although somewhat redundant, Hall's translation of economic language into the language of community epitomizes the narrative work of *Georgia Scenes*. Unlike Baldwin, whose business trip to the frontier only exacerbates the distance between himself and his hosts, Hall is able to negotiate and establish a social bond with the yeoman. The tenuous nature of that bond, combining as it does both social unity and class difference, can perhaps best be gauged by its eventual demise in the postbellum era, when Bourbons and Populists produced a political culture more bifurcated along class line. Yet there is a more important sense in which the community produced by *Georgia Scenes* survives well into the twentieth century and which indeed may be intrinsic to the experience of community generally. In conceptually repressing how he legitimates the social order, Hall engenders a consensus that rests largely on tacit and unspoken agreement, suggesting that, in the final analysis, we must defer the symbolic procedures through which we resolve social contradiction and experience community.

2

THE PLANTATION COMMUNITY

John Pendleton Kennedy's *Swallow Barn* and
Thomas Nelson Page's *In Ole Virginia*

In contrast to the class tensions that are resolved through negotiation at the conclusion of *Georgia Scenes,* the issue of race proved more intractable during the antebellum era. The primary reason is not difficult to locate: dialogue with one's property posed certain problems. As intellectual historians such as Lewis P. Simpson and Eugene Genovese have shown, the antebellum South had evolved in large measure into a community based on chattel slavery, an ideal social order "built securely, permanently, unqualifiedly on the right of men to hold property in other men." Conceived by southern social theorists as an agrarian bulwark against those insidious "Isms of the North"—industrialism, abolitionism, socialism, equalitarianism—against which George Fitzhugh and other apologists vociferated, the slave community was represented as a utopian icon to be emulated by the western world as the means of preserving a maximum distribution of property and individual liberty. At once reactionary and revolutionary, men such as Fitzhugh, Albert Taylor Bledsoe, Thomas Roderick Dew, Beverley Tucker, James Henley Thornwell, and James Hammond theorized nothing less than a Dixie version of the City on the Hill. And for all its Cavalier trappings, the slave community was not dissimilar from its Puritan counterpart in one fundamental way: both were predicated on a rigid social hierarchy perceived to be both necessary and beneficial. Indeed, John Winthrop's assertion that "in all times some must be rich some poore, some highe and eminent in power and dignitie; others meane and in subjection" so that "every man might have need of others, and from hence they might be all knitt more nearly together in the Bond of brotherly affeccion"—this from the same sermon in which he first used his famous metaphor—might very well have come, minus the archaic orthography, from the pen of any number of proslavery theorists.[1]

Another similarity between the Puritan and Cavalier versions of the City on the Hill is that they both failed to materialize, and for similar reasons, especially their respective failures to recognize the ideological power of bourgeois individualism. The story of the South's revolutionary engine that couldn't is well known. Yet, as Genovese says, the antebellum South was unique among modern slave societies in that it saw itself as the "last genuine hei[r] of Christian civilization and a properly stratified and humane social order" and produced from this vision a broad critique of capitalism and a call for the reinstitution of slavery in industrialized countries. Moreover, southern social theorists presented this vision in a tough-minded, sophisticated, coherent, and intellectually rigorous manner. And yet contrary to Genovese's assertion, and with the odd exception of a work like Henry Timrod's "Ethnogenesis," the southern literary mind could not sustain this vision.[2] Put simply, there is no narrative equivalent of *Cannibals All!* or Bledsoe's *Essay on Human Liberty*. For all its revolutionary rhetoric, the South demonstrated a curious inability to generate stories that were not essentially defensive; it is, in fact, a fair generalization to say the southern literary mind could not—or at any rate, did not—produce the narrative equivalent of the positive good school of proslavery rhetoric.

Antebellum narrative offers a useful arena in which to examine how the achievements of narrative coincide with the givens of rhetoric. It is my contention that the antebellum literary mind devoted its principle energy toward preserving a pastoral vision of chattel slavery that resisted insertion in

1. Lewis P. Simpson, *The Brazen Face of History: Studies in the Literary Consciousness of America* (Baton Rouge: Louisiana State University Press, 1980), 71; John Winthrop, "A Modell of Christian Charity," in *The English Literatures of America, 1500–1800,* ed. Myra Jehlen and Michael Warner (London: Routledge, 1997), 152.

2. Eugene D. Genovese, "The South in the History of the Transatlantic World," in *What Made the South Different?* ed. Kees Gispen (Jackson: University Press of Mississippi, 1990), 12, 10.

a historical sequence or plot. More specifically, the plantation itself did not translate effortlessly into narrative; the literary plantation was in every way a less stable institution than its rhetorical counterpart. Curiously, the two narratives most successful in constructing the plantation myth both fail to produce a stable icon. Since the publication of William Taylor's *Cavalier and Yankee* in 1957, critics have not neglected how John Pendleton Kennedy subtly subverts the plantation myth in *Swallow Barn; or, A Sojourn in the Old Dominion* (1832, 1851). Likewise, a critique of slavery lurks in the pages of Thomas Nelson Page's *In Ole Virginia; or, Marse Chan and Other Stories* (1887), usually cited as the central text of the elegiac school of moonlight and magnolias. The main problem both Kennedy and Page confront, in very different historical contexts and for very different reasons, is how to represent the organic bond between master and slave, that relationship upon which rests the organic social order of the plantation community. In representing "the ties that bind"—a phrase whose literal meaning suggests the essence of the problem—both Kennedy and Page confront a figure of resistance virtually absent from proslavery rhetoric: the slave himself, who exerted a tenacious pressure against the narratives that presumed to contain him.

The problematic status of the literary slave is evident throughout the antebellum period. Beginning with George Tucker's *The Valley of Shenandoah* (1824), the abstract institution of slavery and the actual slave are presented in fundamentally different terms. While Edward Grayson, Tucker's mouthpiece, can provide an eloquent rhetorical defense of slavery as a necessary evil, going so far as to assert that the "error on this subject proceeds from a white man's supposing himself in the situation of a slave" (63), the slave auction presented later in the novel evokes precisely this kind of interracial identification. Even William Gilmore Simms, who by any account must be reckoned the antebellum order's most eloquent literary defender, had difficulty in creating a literary counterpart to the slave he described in an 1837 essay published in the *Southern Literary Messenger.* "There is no propriety," Simms writes, "in the application of the name of the slave to the servile of the south. He is under no despotic power. There are laws which protect him, *in his place,* as inflexible as those which his proprietor is required to obey, *in his place. Providence has placed him in our hand, for his good, and has paid us from his labor for our guardianship.*" In contrast to the hierarchy Simms here attributes to Providence, hierarchy in *Woodcraft*, which Simpson ranks alongside *Swallow Barn* as "probably the most significant fiction written in the antebellum South," is authorized by the slave himself. Coming at the end of Simms's Revolutionary War cycle, *Woodcraft* traces the struggle of Porgy and his band of veterans to reestablish the plantation of Glen-Eberley. At the conclusion of the novel Porgy offers to liberate his faithful slave, Tom. The slave refuses, telling his master that "*You* b'longs to *me* Tom, jes' as much as me Tom b'long to *you;* and you nebber guine git *you* free paper from me long as you lib" (509). The sheerly pragmatic nature of Tom's commitment to Porgy, whose primary virtue for his slave lies in his ability to procure dinner, has evidenced itself earlier when Tom refuses Porgy's request that he kill himself should he come to live under another master. That Tom's instinct for preservation, which disrupts his master's absurd sense of the paternalistic bond, later becomes the basis for that bond suggests the extent to which *Woodcraft* comically obliterates any lofty notions of divinely ordained social hierarchy. Moreover, as Simpson argues in *The Dispossessed Garden*, that the pastoral coherence of the plantation community is validated by the consent of the slave points to a "deep vexation in the Southern writer's attempt to authenticate the South's historical existence as a slave society."[3]

The slave's consent, virtually absent from proslavery rhetoric, thus acquires a potentially disruptive function in Simms's novel and, more generally, in antebellum narrative taken as a whole. In one sense the difference between the narrative slave and the comparatively powerless rhetorical slave is simply a matter of relative abstraction; whereas the latter exists almost exclusively as a concept, a social position, the former comes perilously close to possessing, on an imaginative level at any rate, flesh and blood. That a slave should have a story of his own, as opposed to being a mere appendage to the southern grand narrative, thus represented a kind of crisis, and, as William L.

3. George Tucker, *The Valley of Shenandoah; or, Memoirs of the Graysons* (1824; reprint, Chapel Hill: University of North Carolina Press, 1970), 63; [William Gilmore Simms], "Miss Martineau on Slavery," by A South Carolinian, *Southern Literary Messenger* 3 (November 1837): 657; Lewis P. Simpson, *The Dispossessed Garden: Pastoral and History in Southern Literature* (Athens: University of Georgia Press, 1975), 55–56, 61; William Gilmore Simms, *Woodcraft; or, Hawks about the Dovecote* (1854; reprint, New York: Norton, 1961), 509.

Andrews has shown, the historical introduction of the slave into narrative space was itself occasioned by an overt rupture in the southern image of slavery brought on by the Nat Turner Rebellion. Because the resolution of conflict is a fundamental characteristic of narrative, the general exclusion of the slave from narrative space acted as a kind of formal equivalent to denying the tensions and conflicts inherent in the institution. As a result, instead of situating slavery in history, the southern literary mind tended toward a pastoral ratification of slavery as a static, extrahistorical—and hence, extranarrative—institution, a tendency perhaps most clearly exemplified in William Grayson's "The Hireling and the Slave" (1854), a work in which the narrative impulse is subordinated to an iconic presentation of the slave's contented and carefree lot.

Here we should pause to distinguish between two distinct forms of narrative: first, as a literary mode that mediates an internally contested discursive space and produces a stable social order (essentially the role Bakhtin associates with the monological novel), and second, as a literary mode that presumes a stable social order and produces a culture hero to contend against external enemies on a world historical stage.[4] The absence of the second, epical mode in antebellum letters is, I think, self-evident, but the causes for the South's failure to produce an epic are relatively complex, especially given that this must be considered the genre most theoretically congenial to the kind of society the South imagined itself as being. Although a deep premise of Simpson's study—essentially, that only modern art is possible—might explain the lack of a southern epic, or even a serious attempt at one, an equally likely explanation might be that the monological stability of the social order, the massiveness of cultural givens, was never secured to the degree required to support an epic plot in defense of slavery. What I am suggesting, in short, is that antebellum narrative registers a level of social disso-

4. William L. Andrews, "Inter(racial)textuality in Nineteenth-Century Southern Narrative," in *Influence and Intertextuality in Literary History,* ed. Jay Clayton and Eric Rothstein (Madison: University of Wisconsin Press, 1991), 305–306; for Bakhtin on the monological novel, see *Problems of Dostoevsky's Poetics,* 203–204. Grayson follows Kennedy fairly closely in locating slavery within a narrative. Denouncing the slave trade as cruel and predicting the repatriation of slaves to Africa, he nevertheless, like Kennedy, emphasizes the pastoral condition of the institution as it presently exists. See discussion below.

nance regarding the institution that could largely be elided within, on the one hand, revolutionary rhetoric, and on the (literary) other, the pastoral mode and its deferral or evasion of the conflicts associated with narrativity. If the South could sustain a picture of slavery, it failed to sustain a story of slavery.

This is not to claim that narrativity is absent from literary representations of slavery in any absolute sense. Indeed, what makes *Swallow Barn* such a compelling work, I think, is that it demonstrates in a single text the deep tension between the pastoral and the narrative modes insofar as they are implicated in a defense of chattel slavery. Where the one is committed to an iconic representation of a static, idealized lifeworld, the other offers the possibility of, on the one hand, a dynamic mediation of internal dissent, and on the other, a connection with history, roles we have generically associated with the monological novel and the epic, respectively. (Insofar as the former is concerned, Simpson's contention that the South's alienation from modernity exiled it from the community of letters can be recast in Bakhtinian terms as an exile from the novel form.) As *Swallow Barn* reduces a complex system of social relations to a pastoral image, the resulting icon acquires a kind of fragility. Nothing can happen to it; events conceived as being part of a narrative—that is, a story having a beginning, middle, and end and pointing to, as Jameson says, a utopian resolution to the contradictions confronted therein—threaten the very conception of an event as an endlessly repeatable instance of a stable order. In a fundamental sense the iconic image that dominates the pages of Kennedy's novel cannot be subjected to the concept of sequence. It is my contention that, although *Swallow Barn* incorporates elements of what I am loosely designating as the narrative mode, it ultimately subordinates the two most important such elements—namely, the dialogic accents provided by Mark Littleton and the cultural plot envisioned by the plantation master Frank Meriwether—to a pastoral defense of slavery. In the end, the pastoral stability already secured by history (in that history has happened in order to produce this particular pastoral world) creates a bulwark against which the demands of history and the external world are rendered impotent. In a fundamental sense, the isolation of the plantation acts as a precondition for its existence.

*   *   *

In Kennedy's novel it is the marginal social figure—the slave, the poor white—who most tangibly links the pastoral stability of the plantation to history. As Simpson notes, it is an old freedman who introduces the theme of devolution that later finds more verbose, if less eloquent, expression in the mouth of Frank Meriwether. When Mark Littleton, the northern narrator of *Swallow Barn* who is visiting his southern relations for the first time, arrives in the environs of the plantation, he is met by Old Scipio, who, according to Littleton, "had, from some aristocratic conceit of elegance, indued himself for my service in a ragged regimental coat."[5] Exhibiting "all the unction of an old gentleman," the venerable freedman drives Littleton to Swallow Barn, during which time he "expatiated with a wonderful relish upon the splendors of the old-fashioned style in that part of the country; and told me very pathetically, how the estates were cut up, and what old people had died off, and how much he felt himself alone in the present times,— which particulars he interlarded with sundry sage remarks, imparting an affectionate attachment to the old school, of which he considered himself no unworthy survivor" (22). Scipio is the first in a series of black characters noted by Littleton for their imitativeness. Repeating a "reflection . . . which doubtless he had picked up from some popular orator," Scipio prefigures Jupiter, the "King of the Quarter" described by Meriwether as a "preposterous coxcomb" whose vanity is sated by one of Meriwether's old *chapeaux de bras,* "a relic of my military era," the gentleman explains (452). In both cases the slave's imitation signifies his commitment to the plantation order and enables his sense of personal self-importance.

As Simpson suggests, both characters introduce parodic overtones into Kennedy's representation of the plantation, yet in neither case is the slave conscious of the parody. With respect to Carey, Meriwether's personal retainer, the situation is fundamentally different because his imitation is not, as it were, overtly slavish. Carey arguably *intends* to parody his master. In an amusing vignette that illustrates to Littleton the essential imitativeness of the plantation community, Carey transforms Meriwether's ponderous prediction that "the sovereignty of this Union will be as the rod of Aaron;—it

---

5. Kennedy, *Swallow Barn,* 21. This work will hereinafter be cited parenthetically by page number in the text.

will turn into a serpent, and swallow up all that struggle with it" into the somewhat less grandiose, "Look out, Master Ned! Aaron's rod a black snake in Old Virginny!" (74–75). If imitation is the sincerest form of flattery, then Meriwether should be immensely flattered, yet in reducing Meriwether's ponderous biblical metaphor to a "black snake in Old Virginny," such imitativeness carries with it decidedly parodic overtones. Nevertheless, Meriwether remains flattered. "He does not dislike this trait in the society around him," Littleton notes, after which he relates an incident in which Meriwether overhears a carpenter "expounding . . . some oracular opinion of Frank's touching the political aspect of the country" (75). Such imitation evinces, Meriwether informs his northern guest, "the wholesome tone of feeling in that part of the country" (75). Such evocations of consensus— even (and perhaps especially) those arrived at in a less than tough-minded manner—embody a stable mode of distributing social authority, an aristocratic trickle-down effect, if you will. Yet in the singular case of Carey, this distribution of authority produces a terminal imitator with opaque motives, for Carey clearly performs his scene with an ulterior motive. "Suspect[ing] us of some joke," Carey "asks 'if there is'nt a copper for an old negro,' which if he succeeds in getting, he runs off, telling us 'he is too 'cute to make a fool of himself'" (75).

Crucially, Littleton numbers himself among the men who put Carey up to his parodic performance. But whom is the joke on? Littleton clearly affirms Carey's gullibility in the entire matter; when the men roar with laughter, he relates, "Carey stares with astonishment at our irreverence" (75). According to Littleton, it is only *after* "having been set to acting this scene for us once or twice" does Carey begin to suspect a joke. But surely it is possible to read beneath Littleton's ignorant slave to one who cagily acts the fool perfectly aware of the performative demands being made of him. Read this way, Carey appears as a master actor with (besides a comic gift) a shrewd sense of what his audience wants (a parody of Meriwether's sententiousness) and what it is willing to pay. If we ask of this latent Carey the question Stanley Elkins asks of "Sambo"—"What order of existence, what rank of legitimacy, should be accorded him?"—we are forced to mediate between Littleton's ignorant, reverent slave and one who consciously and cagily accommodates himself to his audience's expectations. As Elkins re-

marks, "the line between 'accommodation' (as conscious hypocrisy) and behavior inextricable from basic personality, though the line certainly exists, is
anything but a clear matter of choice. There is reason to think that the one
grades into the other, and vice versa, with considerable subtlety." If we interpret Carey in light of later examinations of slavery and African American
discourse, works such as Genovese's *Roll, Jordan, Roll* and Henry Louis
Gates's examination of the signifying tradition, a potential trickster figure
emerges almost irresistibly.[6] Is, then, Carey's performance intentionally parodic? Is there a tangible character behind the veil?

Although it is my contention that *Swallow Barn* systematically elides
these possibilities, the means by which Kennedy's narrative ultimately produces the mindless slave are quite complex. Kennedy had ample opportunity to observe slaves at The Bower, the Pendleton plantation that provided
the model for Swallow Barn, and if we cast him in a sheerly mimetic role as
the recorder of actual slave behavior, his portrayal of this imaginary slave
might well register a level of resistance of which he may not and probably
could not have been aware. (In this context we can think of Joel Chandler
Harris's Uncle Remus tales as paradigmatic examples.)[7] Yet as soon as the
slave enters Kennedy's narrative, he becomes subject to an elision of resistance produced by Littleton's framing subjectivity. In this way, the slave's
actions and words—that is, the phenomena by means of which he is objectified—are made to stand for his character not so much through a metonymic equation of outside and inside, but through an outright obliteration
of interiority. This shift toward the construction of a simulacrum, although
implicit in any subjective or narrative act, is essential to the plantation novel
for obvious reasons: it allows the slave to be figured in perfect harmony with
his pastoral setting. Yet I want to suggest that this shift is rarely absolute,

---

6. Stanley Elkins, *Slavery: A Problem in American Institutional and Intellectual Life* (1959;
reprint, New York: Grosset and Dunlap, 1963), 82, 86; Eugene D. Genovese, *Roll, Jordan,
Roll: The World the Slaves Made* (New York: Pantheon Books, 1972); Henry Louis Gates, *The
Signifying Monkey: A Theory of African-American Literary Criticism* (New York: Oxford University Press, 1988).

7. For an insightful discussion of the conflicting messages sent by Harris's tales, see Lucinda H. MacKethan, *The Dream of Arcady: Place and Time in Southern Literature* (Baton
Rouge: Louisiana State University Press, 1980), 61–85.

that the movement from actual slave to narrative slave registers at some level a certain dissatisfaction with its own symbolic operations, leaving what might be called a black hole of intentionality that resists being filled, or rather, like its astronomical counterpart, *keeps* being filled as it exerts something like a gravitation field continually attracting narrative mass.

The trickster figure implied in the character of Carey, potentially anachronistic or extratextual in nature, can be textually grounded in two other episodes that demonstrate the slave's resistance to the role Littleton and especially Meriwether have designated for him. "A Country Gentleman," the chapter that introduces Meriwether, concludes with the reader's introduction to Carey, who, like his master, is a devotee of the "mystery of horse-craft" (36). Littleton describes Carey as "a pragmatical old negro, . . . who, in his reverence for the occupation, is the perfect shadow of his master" (36). The priority assigned by the shadow metaphor is, however, immediately overturned, as Littleton comments that the consultations between master and slave "would puzzle a spectator to tell which was the leading member of the council" (36). Their frequent intercourse, Littleton continues, "has begot a familiarity in the old negro which is almost fatal to Meriwether's supremacy. The old man feels himself authorized to maintain his positions according to the freest parliamentary form, and sometimes with a violence of asseveration that compels his master to abandon his ground, purely out of faintheartedness. Meriwether gets a little nettled by Carey's doggedness, but generally turns it off in a laugh" (37). Clearly, Carey *enjoys* nettling Meriwether. Simpson surely has scenes like this in mind in claiming that Kennedy "plainly wants to suggest that slavery resists embodiment in the hierarchical pattern of society that is in the minds of the masters," and that moreover, Kennedy "insinuates the suggestion, whether deliberately or not, that the slaves dominate the life of the plantation."[8] Horse-craft provides a domain—albeit a trivial one, at least on the surface of things—in which Carey usurps his master's authority, and despite Meriwether's assertion that "it does no harm to humor" his "faithful old cur" (37), the slave's stubbornness refuses Meriwether's attempt at narrative closure.

Just as this episode implies a degree of resistance that cannot entirely be

8. Simpson, *Dispossessed Garden,* 45.

laughed off, a later episode shows Carey demonstrating a perspicuity quite different from the mindlessness he evinces in singing out "Aaron's rod a blacksnake in Old Virginny!" In this episode, Carey wears the mask of a "minstrel of some repute, . . . [who], like the ancient jongeleurs, . . . sings the inspirations of his own muse, weaving into song the past and present annals of the family" (101). As with Old Scipio, this bardic role confers status upon the slave: Carey is "considered a seer amongst the negroes on the estate, and is always heard with reverence. The importance this gives him, renders the old man not a little proud of his minstrelsy" (101). Yet unlike Old Scipio's uncritical nostalgia, Carey's minstrelsy has an edge to it. Although Carey "signified his obedience to our orders [that he play]," the slave demonstrates a kind of authority that discomfits at least one member of his audience. Rehearsing "in a doggerel ballad" the expected arrival of Singleton Swansdown, Ned Hazard's rival for the hand of the beautiful Bel Tracy, Carey predicts "the probable events of his visit, which, he insinuated, would be troublesome to Ned Hazard, and would, as the song went, 'Make him think so hard he couldn't sleep'" (102). When Ned objects to this rough treatment, Carey recounts in song a dream he once had in which a beautiful lady appeared and "told him that he must instruct his young master" in the ways of courtship, the central insight of which is "that women were naturally very contrary, and must be interpreted by opposites" (103). Proclaimed a "true seer" by Harvey Riggs, who later gives Ned identical advice, the old slave retires with a "smile of utmost benignity," having been rewarded with a mint julep. In many ways prefiguring Charles Chesnutt's Uncle Julius, Carey is adept at manipulating the plantation economy, earning its small rewards in return for obligations invoked and services rendered. Like Uncle Julius, Carey is able to do so by recognizing the apperceptive background against which he speaks; in each of the scenes we have considered, Carey demonstrates an uncanny sense of audience: he knows how much he can get away with.

To return to the most important of these episodes, Carey's appropriation of Meriwether's oratory, we find that the slave essentially carries his own accents to Meriwether's discourse, thereby creating a dialogic field where Meriwether had intended a monological, authoritarian one. Meriwether's predilection for monologue is indeed one of his defining character traits. To be more precise, he intones against a quasi-dialogic background, frequently anticipating the resistance his pseudo-audience might offer. In the following passage, Littleton calls attention to this tendency to disguise monologue as dialogue:

[Meriwether] lately began a conversation, or rather a speech, that for a moment quite disconcerted me. "After all," said he, as if he had been talking to me before, although these were the first words he uttered—then making a parenthesis, so as to qualify what he was about to say—"I don't deny that the steamboat is destined to produce—but after all, I much question—(and here he bit his upper lip, and paused an instant)—if we are not better without it. I declare, I think it strikes deeper at the supremacy of the states than most persons are willing to allow. This annihilation of space, sir, is not to be desired." (72)

Concluding his *speech*—and Littleton's correction is a significant one—by quoting "Splatterthwaite Dubbs of Dinwiddie" to the effect that "the home material of Virginia was never so good as when her roads were at their worst," Meriwether is met with silence; his audience fears "dispute" and "seems to understand the advantage of silence when Meriwether is inclined to be expatiatory" (73). The context and content of the speech thus converge, for Meriwether valorizes the boundaries defining the local discursive hierarchy. The subordinate classes, Littleton notes, "have a natural bias to this venting of upper opinion, by reason of certain dependencies in the way of trade and favor" (73). Within the community, then, what we have called the aristocratic trickle-down effect works without a serious loss of energy, and Meriwether's pronouncements remain largely uncontested. As Littleton relates using an interesting organic metaphor, "There is nothing more conclusive than a rich man's logic any where, but in the country, amongst his dependents, it flows with the smooth and unresisted course of a full stream irrigating a meadow, and depositing its mud in fertilizing luxuriance" (35). Carey is the potential fly in the ointment. If his performative rendering of Meriwether's words were intended to be parodic, he would disrupt the community's hierarchical dissemination of rhetoric.

That Littleton refuses this interpretive option is significant, for in supplying a motive—namely, that Carey considers Meriwether's "sentiment as importing something of an awful nature" (75)—and in refusing to admit that Carey might here as elsewhere be manipulating his audience rather than vice versa, Littleton assimilates the slave's voice within the discursive hierarchy of the plantation community. In thus producing a mindless slave, Littleton's interpretive act produces a discursive field in which Carey does not exist as an agent; unlike "horse-craft" and "love," fields in which Littleton recognizes Carey's satiric authority, "politics" is declared off-limits. This is especially salient given that Carey imitates state rights rhetoric directly relevant to his status as chattel property. By thus mindlessly participating in the consensus of the plantation community, Carey demonstrates his fitness as a slave.

Littleton denies Carey access to precisely that which he claims as his prerogative: a satiric, dialogic ground against which the speech of the plantation community resonates. As Meriwether delivers his monologue, Littleton provides sufficient cues to expose the planter as a windbag: how seriously, after all, can one regard a speech that follows a dramatically bitten upper lip? Littleton's satire, however, fails to extend to the bond between master and slave. *Swallow Barn* insists upon slaves who hold Meriwether "in most affectionate reverence, and, therefore, are not only contented, but happy under his dominion" (34). Yet while Littleton is fully complicit in assimilating the slave within the pastoral icon, he also systematically exposes Meriwether's dominion as something of a farce. As William Taylor observes in *Cavalier and Yankee,* he is "an emotional Indian giver, giving a flattering image of 'feudal' Virginia and then withdrawing it silently."[9] Yet in considering Littleton's satiric stance toward the subplots that dominate the middle portion of *Swallow Barn*—especially the courtship plot between Ned and Bel Tracy and the legal battle over the swamp—it becomes evident that narrative (conceived as an integrated sequence of events) is systematically divested of ideological content, and thus engages only a simulated conflict that recuperates rather than tests the stability of the pastoral icon.

9. William R. Taylor, *Cavalier and Yankee: The Old South and American National Character* (1961; reprint, New York: Oxford University Press, 1993), 185. Most critics have agreed with Taylor that Kennedy's satire of the plantation community, which he softened in 1853 from the 1832 first edition, is "gentle, smiling satire" (183). The exception to this view is Jan Bakker; see note 12 below.

In a peculiar sense *Swallow Barn* is a novel hostile to narrative. In his 1832 preface to the novel, Littleton announces his original intention "to portray the impressions which the scenery and the people of that region made upon [the author], in detached pictures brought together with no other connexion than that of time and place." Due, however, to his becoming "engaged in the various adventures of domestic history," *Swallow Barn*, he explains, "has ended in a vein altogether different from that in which it set out. There is a rivulet of story wandering through a broad meadow of episode" (vii). I have suggested that Kennedy's plantation community is unsuited to narrative in a way that it is not unsuited to the pastoral, a mode more theoretically congenial to the stable social relationships presumed to exist within its boundaries. To put the matter another way, the plantation resists representation as a social totality evolving in time, since any narrative momentum presumes a conflict or set of contradictions necessitating resolution in the first place. To constitute an organic social order, Swallow Barn must remain motionless.

The static quality of the plantation encompasses both its natural setting and its social rituals. Noting the slow pace of life on the plantation, a contemporary reviewer in the *New England Magazine* denounced "insipid" gentlemen such as Ned Hazard "who are ignorant of every useful way of passing the time," concluding that "[t]he whole book is a picture of the stillest of still life." Noting a similar quality in Littleton's idyllic description of a river scene, Jan Bakker finds "something wrong" in *Swallow Barn*'s "stultifying" and "lifeless" imagery of nature. I would contend, however, that Kennedy's still-life aesthetic produces a kind of pastoral inertia, aligning nature and social ritual against the ideological pressures of the outside world. As Bakhtin says, "In the presence of the monological principle, ideology—as a deduction, as a semantic summation of representation—inevitably transforms the represented world into a *voiceless object of that deduction*," and it is precisely the voicelessness of the plantation—or rather, its exclusion of contending voices—that enables its imagistic integrity as pastoral icon.[10] To put

10. Anonymous review quoted in William S. Osborne, Introduction to *Swallow Barn* (1851; reprint, New York: Hafner Publishing, 1962), xxvi; Jan Bakker, *Pastoral in Antebellum Southern Romance* (Baton Rouge: Louisiana State University Press, 1989), 47; Bakhtin, *Dostoevsky's Poetics*, 83.

the matter another way, it is only *as* a voiceless object of monological deduction that the plantation community can appear as a series of "detached
pictures brought together with no other connexion than that of time and
place," a formulation that configures time and place as "concrete" (nonideo-
logical, noncontested) entities with no sequence or story associated with
them. Nowhere is the drowsy, languid texture of plantation life so apparent
as in a chapter titled "A Country Gathering," which describes a day-long
dinner party thrown at Swallow Barn. Although this ritual would not meet
the reviewer's criteria of "a useful way of passing the time," Littleton contrasts it favorably with its "premeditated, anxious" counterpart "in town"
(314). Taken as a group, these social rituals receive little of his satiric wit.

The same cannot be said of the two subplots that dominate the middle
portion of *Swallow Barn*. Both the courtship plot between Ned Hazard and
Bel Tracy and the legal battle over the swamp show the plantation community at its most frivolous and indeed, most ridiculous. Nevertheless, these
dual drives toward resolution and closure, while being situated within a
markedly satiric narrative ground, do not undermine the organic stability of
the plantation so much as demonstrate its intransigence to conflict. In indicating the extent to which the plantation resists narrative, these subplots indirectly work to affirm a pastoral mass against which the return to narrative
and the figure of the slave—a figure largely absent from both subplots—
must contend in the concluding section of *Swallow Barn*.

As several critics have shown, Littleton's primary satiric technique centers on the plantation's absurd appropriation of medieval manners and institutions.[11] Nowhere is this satire more evident than in the relationship that
develops between Bel Tracy and Ned Hazard, both of whom suffer griev-
ously from what Mark Twain would label half a century later the "Sir Walter disease." Prior to the events recounted in the novel, the aptly named
Hazard had been "seized with a romantic fervor which manifested itself
chiefly in a conceit to visit South America, and play knight-errant in the
quarrel of the Patriots," a crusade from which "he came home the most dis-
quixotted cavalier that ever hung up his shield at the end of a scurvy cru-

11. See J. V. Ridgely, *John Pendleton Kennedy* (New York: Twayne, 1966), 60–64; Simpson, *Dispossessed Garden*, 44–45; Lucinda H. MacKethan, Introduction to *Swallow Barn*
(1853; reprint, Baton Rouge: Louisiana State University Press, 1986), xxiii.

sade" (52, 53). Unlike his Spanish precursor, who ultimately renounces knight-errantry, Hazard persists in perceiving—or lacking that, creating—a parallel between medieval romance and his life at Swallow Barn. In this respect he would seem to have found an ideal match in Bel Tracy, who, according to Littleton, "is a little given to certain romantic fantasies, such as country ladies who want excitement and read novels are apt to engender" (228). Smitten by the age of chivalry, Bel goes so far as to dress a petty thief in medieval costume and attempt to pass him off as a minstrel. Initially suspicious of Hazard's frivolity, Bel is eventually won over when her suitor rescues her hawk Fairbourne, an affectation of hers attributed to "the picturesque associations of falconry with the stories of an age that Walter Scott has rendered so bewitching to the fancy of meditative maidens" (228).

The ludicrous nature of all this is not lost on Littleton, who satirizes the lovers' pseudo-medievalism to great comic effect. In a chapter titled "Knight Errantry," as he and Hazard are searching for the missing hawk, Littleton facetiously swears "by our lady!—I mean our lady Bel . . . for henceforth I will swear by none but her" that he will refuse sleep until the ungrateful bird is captured (354). When shortly thereafter Hazard thrashes a ruffian who insults Isaac Tracy, Littleton compares the situation with a joust, and the two return "covered with dust and glory; our enemies subdued and our lady's pledge redeemed" (368). Harvey Riggs, who acts as something of Littleton's alter ego, likewise facetiously avers to Bel that Ned's exploits "are in the very best strain of a cavalier devoted to his lady-love" (394). In the end, the marriage comes to pass, "Bel having, at last, surrendered at discretion" (504), as Littleton relates in a postscript. Kennedy's depiction of the marriage plot involves a kind of comedy in reverse: instead of the paradigmatic plot in which the hero wins his beloved by forging a closer relationship with established society, Hazard does exactly the opposite, winning Bel by participating in her medieval fantasies. To be sure, his studied gravity near the end of the courtship has something to do with overcoming Bel's objections, but it is clear that despite assuming the adult role of husband Hazard remains a child at heart. In a letter written to Littleton after his return to New York, Harvey Riggs describes Hazard's reversion to type following the marriage:

Ned relapsed into all his extravagancies. In truth, I believe Bel grew heartily tired of that incompatible formality of manner which he assumed at our instigation. It sat upon him like an ill-fitted garment, and rendered him the dullest of mortals. Bel took the matter into consideration, and at last begged him to be himself again. Never did a schoolboy enjoy a holiday more than he this freedom; the consequence was, that the wight ran immediately into the opposite extreme, and has carried the prize, notwithstanding he had trespassed against all decorum, and had been voted incorrigible. (504)

Hazard's refusal to conform to the social obligations normally implicit in the marriage contract suggests the extent to which the courtship plot involves no social principle. In sum, there is nothing at stake in the farcical romance between Bel and Childe Ned.

The same can be said of the boundary dispute between Swallow Barn and the Brakes, the neighboring plantation owned by Bel's father, Isaac Tracy. The land in question had been purchased from Isaac's father for a mill-pond constructed by Ned Hazard's grandfather. Ill-fated from the beginning, the mill-dam was eventually destroyed by a flood, leaving some question as to whether the land purchased for the mill-pond reverted to the Brakes following the pond's destruction. Although originally involving serious political overtones—the Hazards had been patriots, the Tracys Tories during the revolutionary period—the boundary dispute has, in the meantime, become a joke to everyone except Isaac Tracy, for whom it remains an *idée fixe*. In an effort to have done with the matter, Meriwether conspires with his attorney to have the case won by Tracy. Again, Littleton ironically situates the story within a feudal context, writing of the original disputants that "[n]ever were there, in ancient days of bull-headed chivalry, when contentious monk, bishop or knight appealed to fiery ordeal, cursed morsel, or wager of battle, two antagonists better fitted for contest than the worthies of my present story" (149).

Just as the conflict between the two plantations is, from Meriwether's perspective at least, a quasi-conflict, so the closure brought about via Meriwether's machinations is a markedly trivial one. And yet here as with the romance plot, the basic form of the narrative might well encompass more

serious issues. It is not difficult to imagine a scenario in which conflict between neighboring plantations might entail ideological differences, nor to
imagine a marriage plot in which these divisions might be resolved. (Page
would employ this very formula in "Marse Chan.") Harvey Riggs explicitly
suggests such a plot in relating the words of "Mammy Diana," a "true sybil,"
to the effect that "the landmarks shall never be stable until Swallow Barn
shall wed The Brakes" (91). Yet because this conflict is but a simulation of
conflict, both subplots remain on the same trivial level; they are ideological
in that they refuse ideology. It is in this sense that narrative is exiled from
the plantation, its absence corresponding to an insular pastorality predicated
on the absence of conflict; indeed, it is precisely this absence that leads Ned
and Isaac Tracy virtually to *invent* conflicts—or in Ned's case, to borrow
them from earlier narratives—as a way of passing the time. Only Meriwether is truly at home in this environment. A visit to Washington only re-
inforces his provincialism, as he returns telling "curious anecdotes of certain
secret intrigues which had been discovered in the affairs of the capital" (32).
Rejecting such vile plots and "[r]elaps[ing] into an indolent gentleman of
the opposition" (32), Meriwether speaks, Littleton later relates in a description that uncannily prefigures Will Percy, "like an ancient stoic, removed
from all ambition to figure on the theatre of life, and quietly observing the
tumult of affairs from a position too distant to be reached by the sordid passions that sway the multitude; or, in other words, he discourses like an easy
and cultivated country gentleman" (215). Meriwether's refusal to play an external role, to figure in history, is not necessarily a serious shortcoming. Because of the stable social order over which he presides, Meriwether need not
act the role of the hero, which is reserved (significantly) for the impetuous
Hazard, whose temperament is clearly regarded as being ill-suited for the
master of a plantation. Even in Ned's case, heroism is impossible within the
plantation community—hence his quixotic adventures in South America.
In sum, the border of the plantation marks the boundary outside of which
narrative occurs.

In its novelistic incarnation, narrative resolves social phenomena perceived
as internally contradictory. Insofar as the white community of *Swallow Barn*
is concerned, no such contradictory phenomena are encountered—that is to

say, it excludes contradiction in an effort to preserve something approaching a monological space. In a revealing act, Meriwether, "like a man who was not to be disturbed by doubts," subscribes to only one partisan newspaper, "as it was morally impossible to believe all that was written on both sides" (32). Within this space, dialogic discourse is impossible, and the epic plots inhabited by Ned and Bel, while not theoretically incompatible with the monological nature of the plantation, are rendered laughable by Littleton, whose dialogic accents expose romance as sheer farce. Yet Littleton's multiple ironies do not so much subvert his pastoral representation of *Swallow Barn* as indicate how the plantation community maintains its boundaries in order to preserve its pastoral integrity. That the quotidian aspects of plantation life do not resolve themselves into a narrative pattern does not render the resulting icon repulsive or undesirable. On the contrary, Littleton is drawn to it:

This course of life has a winning quality that already begins to exercise its influence upon my habits. There is a fascination in the quiet, irresponsible, and reckless nature of these country pursuits, that is apt to seize upon the imagination of a man who has felt the perplexities of business. Ever since I have been at Swallow Barn, I have entertained a very philosophical longing for the calm and dignified retirement of the woods. I begin to grow moderate in my desires; that is, I only want a thousand acres of good land, an old manor-house, on a pleasant site, a hundred negroes, a large library, a host of friends, and a reserve of a few thousand a year in the stocks,—in case of bad crops,—and, finally, a house full of pretty, intelligent, and docile children, with some few et ceteras not worth mentioning. (310–11)

To be sure, Littleton's facetiousness prevents taking him seriously, but by the same token his tone hardly suggests an outright hostility toward the plantation community, as one critic has maintained.[12]

Significantly, Littleton includes "a hundred negroes" among his list, thereby reducing the slaves of Swallow Barn to the status of scenery. Indeed, during the middle section of the novel, slaves appear as but another part of

---

12. As part of his argument that *Swallow Barn* is a "subtly vicious criticism of the plantation way of life in the South," Bakker argues that Littleton here is "eager to get away from the idle, petty, ill-fated place and its soporific, self-absorbed landscape. He actually has to laugh at his misdirected pastoral urge" (*Pastoral in Antebellum Southern Romance,* 42).

the pastoral landscape—that is to say, as another voiceless object of mono-logical deduction. This changes dramatically near the end of *Swallow Barn,* when Meriwether escorts Littleton to "the Quarter" shortly before his de-parture. Before their morning visit, however, Meriwether first takes Little-ton to see the horses he and Carey have painstakingly bred. As in the first chapter, Carey, whose professional preeminence requires that he gainsay Meriwether in matters of horse-craft, refuses to submit to his master's au-thority. Carey's obstinacy would be trivialized save the great importance Meriwether attaches to the horse, a subject which he had, only the night be-fore, orated most eloquently, going so far as to assert that "[t]he improve-ment of the stock of horses" is "one of the gravest concerns to which a landed proprietor can devote his attention" (437). Moreover, Meriwether's asseveration of surrender—"This old magnifico will allow no man to have an opinion but himself. Rather than disturb the peace, I must submit to his authority" (448)—is couched in language that could be applied to Meri-wether himself, whose audience, we have seen, typically "fears dispute" and "seems to understand the advantage of silence when Meriwether is inclined to be expatiatory" (73). Once again, Carey's imitation of Meriwether has an edge to it: as the perfect shadow of his master, Carey comes perilously close to overshadowing him. The latent dissonance present in this scene acts as an overture to the more serious threat to authority posed by Abe, the only overtly transgressive slave in the entire work.

In claiming that Carey potentially disrupts the plantation hierarchy, I should be careful to reiterate that his transgression does not register as such with either Meriwether or (more importantly) Littleton, both of whom laugh off the slave's truculence. Despite his status as an outsider, Littleton fully assumes the racial rhetoric of the plantation community; indeed, this is virtually the only subject on which he fails to provide a dialogic counter-point to the authorized speech of Swallow Barn. As he visits the Quarter, Littleton compares his expectations of slavery with his firsthand experience of it:

> The air of contentment and good humor and kind family attachment, which was apparent throughout this little community, and the familiar relations existing be-tween them and the proprietor struck me very pleasantly. I came here a stranger, in

great degree, to the negro character, knowing but little of the domestic history of these people, their duties, habits or temper, and somewhat disposed, indeed, from prepossessions, to look upon them as severely dealt with, and expecting to have my sympathies excited towards them as objects of commiseration. I have had, therefore, rather a special interest in observing them. The contrast between my preconceptions of their condition and the reality which I have witnessed, has brought me a most agreeable surprise. I will not say that, in a high state of cultivation and of such self-dependence as they might possibly attain in a separate national existence, they might not become a more respectable people; but I am quite sure that they never could become a happier people than I find them here. (452–53)

Littleton continues in this vein, describing the Negro as intellectually feeble, "essentially parasitical in his nature," "in his moral constitution, a dependant upon the white race," and "without foresight, without faculty of contrivance, without thrift of any kind" (453)—all of which conspire to create a "helplessness" that is "an insurmountable impediment to that most cruel of all projects—the direct, broad emancipation of these people" (453–54). Assuming the voice of the southern apologist, Littleton apparently forgets that Carey, the slave with whom he has had the most personal contact, exhibits few of these traits except in the field of action we have designated "political," where his mindless imitation of Meriwether's rhetoric allows Littleton to figure the trope of the helpless slave. But even given Carey's limitation, Littleton can assume the apologist's voice only by tacitly dismissing Carey as a type, a representative slave. Littleton thus gains as a rhetorician what he loses as a direct observer, since his argument is enabled by the abstracted, pictorial slave generic to proslavery rhetoric. But while his racial typology of the Negro and his positive comparison of slaves with other lower classes are standard apologist fare, Littleton disrupts his stable picture of slavery by locating the Negro within a narrative of racial progress.

Against a logic that would represent the Negro as perfectly content with his station, Littleton writes that "Interest, necessity and instinct, all work to give progression to the relations of mankind, and finally to elevate each tribe or race to its maximum of refinement and power," a law to which, he continues, "We have no reason to suppose that the Negro will be an exception" (454). Although it is unclear whence this instinct for ascent originates in a people without "foresight" or "faculty of contrivance," it is nevertheless apparent that the Negro asserts a certain narrative pressure against the pastoral stability of the plantation. These contrary logics likewise manifest themselves in Meriwether's discourse, although in a slightly different way. Undertaking a pastoral defense of slavery, Meriwether asserts that slaves work less than voluntary laborers; that they are more comfortable than rural populations of other countries; that they are punished "pretty much as disorderly persons are punished in all societies"; and that public opinion prevents "cruelty in masters" (457). Nonetheless, Meriwether admits that "slavery, as an original question, is wholly without justification or defence" (455). Viewed synchronically, then, slavery is "theoretically and morally wrong" (455). Yet as the consequence of an external and tacitly northern plot, a "premeditated policy which put them [slaves] upon our commonwealth" (455–56), slavery becomes bearable, even defensible.[13] Mediating between the two master discourses of apologist rhetoric—slavery as "a necessary evil" versus "a positive good"—Kennedy refuses the teleology of the latter, which would involve a cultural narrative producing the pastoral icon of the plantation community. Here, the narrative teleology carries sinister overtones, but the ensuing state receives pastoral absolution.

Its beginning blamed on the North and its middle justified as a benign state of things, the master plot of slavery nevertheless requires a utopian resolution. "When the time comes," Meriwether says, "as I apprehend it will come,—and all the sooner, if it not be delayed by these efforts to arouse something like a vindictive feeling between the disputants on both sides—in which the roots of slavery will begin to lose their hold in our soil; and when we shall have the means for providing these people a proper asylum, I shall be glad to see the State devote her thoughts to that enterprise, and if I am alive, will cheerfully and gratefully assist in it" (456). According to Meriwether, it is the abolitionists who prevent his utopian plot, since "the question of emancipation is exclusively our own, and every intermeddling

13. The basic outlines of this argument permeate proslavery rhetoric. In one of its more extreme incarnations, Augustus Baldwin Longstreet claims that the South "delivered [slaves] from the most cruel bondage that man ever groaned under," before going on to ask Massachusetts (his imaginary interlocutor), "Does it become the *Mother* of Slavery to revile the *Heir* of Slavery?" (*A Voice from the South* [Baltimore: Samuel E. Smith, 1848], 10, 18).

with it from abroad will but mar its chance of success" (457–58). The injustices of slavery must and will be removed by the southerner since "all others are misled by the feeling which the natural sentiment against slavery, in the abstract, excites" (458). The operative words here are "in the abstract," which remove slavery from the demands of history and place it firmly on pastoral ground.

The utopian plot of slavery, then, can only be set in motion if its pastoral stability is first secured. What Meriwether asserts, in sum, is that the authorial control of the emancipation plot must remain a southern prerogative. Thus, he counsels the "real friends of humanity . . . to endeavor to encourage the natural contentment of the slave himself, by arguments to reconcile him to a present destiny, which is, in fact, more free from sorrow and want than of almost any other class of men occupying the same field of labor" (458–59). For Meriwether, the slave's assent is thus, paradoxically, a precondition for his ascent. Although it is interesting to note that the (literal) "field of labor" is conspicuously absent in the novel, the more interesting feature of Meriwether's advice is his oxymoronic reference to the slave's "present destiny," a phrase that precisely captures the nuanced interplay of the narrative and pastoral modes. Insofar as concrete action is concerned, Meriwether proposes that slave marriages be recognized, which would render the plantation community more impervious to "intermeddling" and hence (by a peculiar logic, since this plan would appear to stabilize the social order) better able to initiate the utopian plot. Meriwether also describes to Littleton a "scheme" of his to establish older slaves as landholding tenants, but as his guest points out, the two likely candidates, Carey and Jupiter, each would refuse such a plan, believing their station "not to be enhanced by any enlargement of privilege" (460). Again, the symbolic action of Kennedy's text is such that the concrete slave produced by the pastoral order resists insertion into the emancipation plot, which must then remain at the level of abstraction. It should be noted, moreover, that the emancipated slave Meriwether desires to produce has already been encountered in the form of Old Scipio, perhaps the most conservative character in the book in that he longs for the "good old days" most vehemently.

We can roughly describe this circular logic as the absorption of narrative by the pastoral, whose inertia precludes any forward momentum toward the utopian state Meriwether envisions. In more concrete terms the plantation absorbs the abstract slave with his instinctive will to power and transforms him into a concrete bulwark of conservatism and positive commitment to the status quo. This absorption, however, is not complete, as evidenced by the figure of Abe, who exerts more fully than any other character what might be conceived as narrative *pressure* against the pastoral stability of the plantation. The son of two faithful slaves, Abe associates with "the profligate menials" of Swallow Barn and its environs and eventually hardens into the "most irreclaimable of culprits" (467). After joining "a band of out-lying negroes"—here as elsewhere, action is marginalized to the boundaries of the pastoral order—and annoying "the vicinity by nocturnal incursions of the most lawless character," Abe is banished from Swallow Barn and sent to work on a sailing ship in the Chesapeake Bay. Here, he literally doth suffer a sea-change, eventually becoming an intrepid pilot. During a storm Abe attempts to rescue a stranded brig when all white sailors refuse. Sailing into the storm with a crew of Negro sailors, Abe is lost at sea. "Still, it was a gallant thing," Littleton writes, "and worthy of a better chronicler than I, to see this leader and his little band—the children of a despised stock—swayed by a noble emulation to relieve the distressed; and (what the fashion of the world will deem a higher glory) impelled by that love of daring which the romancers call chivalry. . . . I say, it was a gallant sight to see such heroism shining out in a humble slave of the Old Dominion!" (482–83). Several critics have questioned the significance of, as Lucinda MacKethan puts it, "Abe's noble enactment of a code Kennedy lampoons throughout the novel."[14] Lewis Simpson suggests that while Abe's story potentially involves "a slave possessed of the conviction that slavery is an apostasy to freedom," it ends by producing a "slave who is in a perfect relationship with his masters. He gives his life in their service." In an essay on "inter(racial)textuality"

14. Only one other figure in Kennedy's novel legitimately enacts the chivalric code. As he prepares to depart from Swallow Barn, Littleton peruses the story of John Smith, "the founder of Virginia" and "True Knight of the Old Dominion" (500). Despite their respective validations of chivalry, little would seem to link Smith and Abe. But as I suggest below, the connection is real: whereas Smith's chivalry produces the pastoral icon, Abe's recuperates it. The code of chivalry thus appears solely in a causal relationship with the plantation, which, once produced, renders the code superfluous.

in antebellum southern narrative, William L. Andrews argues that Abe's apostasy is "domesticated" when his actions "become explainable according to prevailing white southern norms." The story of Abe, Andrews suggests, thus writes in reverse the Nat Turner phenomenon, taking the "transformed," apostatic slave and (literally) re-forming him so that he reinscribes dominant racial ideologies.[15]

In arguing that the story of Abe bears close similarities to what Fredric Jameson has called the "wish-fulfilling daydream or fantasy text," I want to suggest that the presence of a pastoral community represents what Jameson calls "those conceptual preconditions of possibility or narrative presuppositions which one must believe, those empirical preconditions which must have been secured, in order for the subject successfully to tell itself this particular daydream"—the specific daydream in question being Abe's heroic sacrifice. Although Andrews rejects Simpson's tentative but still overstated argument that Abe is a revolutionary "who yearns, possibly without articulate consciousness, to transform the garden of the chattel into a domain of pastoral freedom, an Eden of freed slaves," he nevertheless retains the idea that "Kennedy's 'positive' variant of the narrative of the transformed Negro" presupposes a political consciousness on the part of the slave. Noting that Abe's antisocial behavior cannot be ascribed to either mistreatment or a desire for emancipation—both of which the narrative explicitly rejects—Andrews suggests that Kennedy "makes possible the conclusion that an able, spirited, and intelligent black man needs no particular motive for resisting his bondage."[16] The ensuing narrative, however, appears to displace bondage as that specific thing that Abe resists. Although Littleton employs a rhetoric of change, this rhetoric depends at least as much on the change of scene as on any change of character. In his life as a sailor, Littleton relates, Abe finds "a vent for inclinations which, when constrained by his former monotonous avocations, had so often broken out into mischievous adventures" (475). The narrative logic here produces a plantation that, when viewed in the retrospective lens of Abe's story, is not so much oppressive as boring. What

15. MacKethan, Introduction, xxvi; Simpson, *Dispossessed Garden,* 51; Andrews, "Inter(racial)textuality," 307, 310, 309.

16. Jameson, *Political Unconscious,* 181, 182; Simpson, *Dispossessed Garden,* 50; Andrews, "Inter(racial)textuality," 309.

Abe appears to reject, then, is not white authority per se, but white authority that circumscribes and limits the expression of his exceptional nature, which remains largely constant. What threatens to be exposed as intrinsic resentfulness against the pastoral order becomes transformed into a more readily explainable need for the romantic adventure unavailable on the plantation, a need all the more fundamentally conservative as it resonates in the white community—at least in the figures of Bel and Ned—as well.

It seems, then, that Andrews's description of Abe's "militant antisocial activism" presumes a political consciousness that Littleton's narrative systematically erases. As the logic of Littleton's story displaces authentic resentment with a simulation of resentment, Abe's truculence begins to appear nothing more than a thirst for adventure such as drove Ned Hazard on his quixotic quest to South America. Chivalry, then, is not simply a code that allows Abe's actions to be domesticated after the fact; it is a code that he has lived by, after his fashion, all along. This is the sense in which the pastoral community is a precondition for Littleton's fantasy text; were the plantation order perceived by Abe to be antithetical to his freedom—that is, if he were reacting *against* white authority—it would be impossible for him to refuse emancipation and, more importantly, to go to his death affirming that he "always obeys orders!" (479). In Hegelian terms Abe's narrative replaces formal freedom—freedom *from* coercive authority—with substantial freedom, which assumes the individual's identification with hegemonic structures. In the end, the entry of the slave into narrative space simply recuperates the organic bond between servant and master, that bond upon which Kennedy's pastoral ratification of slavery rests.

Just as Kennedy's emancipatory plot is contingent upon the pastoral community of masters and slaves, so the story of Abe validates the essential cohesiveness of that community, even if the plantation cannot supply the exceptional slave with the proper context in which to demonstrate his fidelity and obedience—to consent, in other words, to being a slave. In considering the fantasy texts of cultures that do not share our fundamental ideological premises, there is a great danger that they will appear as *mere* fantasy—simply wish fulfillments unhindered by any notion of a reality principle. Yet if the story of Abe threatens to reveal Kennedy as a dreamer, it is worth remarking the words of a contemporary who argued, in terms that closely echo Meriwether's emancipation plot, that slavery is "one of those evils which divine Providence does not leave to be remedied by human contrivances, but which, in its own good time, by some means impossible to be anticipated, but of the simplest and easiest operation, when all its uses shall have been fulfilled, it causes to vanish like a dream." The author is Nathaniel Hawthorne, and his evasive rhetoric here replicates, as Sacvan Bercovitch has persuasively argued, the evasive utopianism at work in his most famous novel. Wish fulfillment is not, as Jameson notes, "a simple operation, available at any time or place for the taking of a thought," a point we should be careful to keep in mind as we turn to Thomas Nelson Page, a writer whose fantasy text strains modern credulity.[17]

The basic outlines of this fantasy text are well-known. Like Longstreet, Page employs a literate frame narrator who confronts and contains dialect-speaking characters (former slaves, in Page's case); like Kennedy, he employs a stranger to the slave-holding region who is shown the organic cohesiveness of the slave order. In the first three tales of *In Ole Virginia* the former slave narrates the epic adventures of the aristocratic gentleman during the halcyon days of moonlight and magnolias, thereby asserting his consensual participation in the antebellum social order and lamenting its passage into the irretrievable past. Yet in producing the strongest—and in many ways the most durable—iconic vision of the plantation as pastoral community, Page provided an implicit critique of that vision as well. Consider the following situations found in *In Ole Virginia:* a former slave who chides a dog—"think 'cuz you's white and I's black, I got to wait on yo' all de time"; a slave whose master orders him into a burning barn to rescue his horses, and who nearly dies as a result; a master who sells his slaves and attempts to prevent a neighboring slave owner from purchasing them in order to keep a slave marriage intact; a slave owner who divides a family and reneges on his promise to re-

---

17. Jameson, *Political Unconscious,* 182; passage from Hawthorne's campaign biography of Franklin Pierce quoted in Sacvan Bercovitch, *The Office of the Scarlet Letter* (Baltimore: Johns Hopkins University Press, 1991), 87. Bercovitch finds this evasive tendency at work in the conclusion of *The Scarlet Letter,* where an authorial skepticism toward radicalism (including abolition) is implied by Hester's renunciation of radical gender politics. For further discussion, see Bercovitch, *Office,* 124–54.

unite them, leaving the slave father alone, helpless, and delirious; a slave owner who decapitates a slave; and a white community that lives in constant fear of a slave uprising. How do we account for the presence of these features in the work of an author who "more than any other . . . created the elegiac image of the 'Old South,' a garden world of noble cavaliers and faithful retainers that has left his mark on the popular imagination to this day"?[18]

The darker side of Page's plantation myth has not gone unnoticed. In *The Mind of the South*, W. J. Cash suggests that "there are even passages in Thomas Nelson Page, the very forefront of propaganda, in which the advocate is all but submerged in the artist." Writing of "Marse Chan," Kimball King notes that "consciously or unconsciously the author included disturbing details that make his story deeper, and more interesting, than he probably intended. . . . Sam does not understand, nor is it likely that his creator realized, the extent to which the slave has been victimized by the old order." Louis Rubin has called attention to the brutal side of slavery depicted in "No Haid Pawn," a story that, as we shall see, poses the greatest threat to Page's pastoral icon. After an extensive inventory of the problematic nature of Page's tales for the modern reader, Lucinda MacKethan concludes that "[t]he situation of the black man in Page's pastoral kingdom is ambiguous at best, though it was clearly the author's intention to depict plantation life as the ideal mode of existence for both master and slave. . . . That Page never consciously explored the flaws of the Old South, that he failed to see the ambiguities of his own re-creations of the plantation as an ideal world, is only too clear a fact." Collectively, these critics tend to account for the presence of these ambiguities as unconscious "slips" on Page's part that he "failed to see" (to use MacKethan's interesting metaphor). In discussing the stories that comprise *In Ole Virginia*, I want to interrogate further this notion of authorial blindness—arguably as much an achievement as a given—in order

18. Thomas Nelson Page, *In Ole Virginia; or, Marse Chan and Other Stories* (1887; reprint, Chapel Hill: University of North Carolina Press, 1969), 3. This work will hereinafter be cited parenthetically by page number in the text. The representative claim regarding Page's place in southern literature appears on back cover of the J. S. Sanders reprint of *In Ole Virginia* (Nashville, 1991).

to account more systematically for Page's latent critique of the pastoral community of masters and slaves.[19]

Before turning to the stories themselves, we should first clarify that Page was not defending slavery per se. Like most southerners of his generation, Page regarded slavery as having been "well-ended," but as MacKethan argues, Page's pastoral defense of the Old South involved a "positive, assertive direction" in the context of race relations in the postbellum South. Page's defense of slavery thus involves a fundamental displacement, since his apologist rhetoric is not in defense of the institution itself, but of the paternal bond between master and slave insofar as something like it might be reestablished in his own time. The deferrals and evasions involved in Page's defense of slavery are clear in his essays as well. As he writes in "The Old-Time Negro," "One need not be an advocate of slavery because he . . . sets forth facts that can be substantiated by the experience of thousands who knew them at first hand," the primary such "fact" being the "relation of warm friendship and tender sympathy" between master and servant. The destruction of this relationship, Page goes on to suggest, explains "not the least part of the [current] bitterness of the South over the Negro question." Insofar as slavery involved an organic and hierarchical interracial bond, Page defends it. Yet, even within his defense, irruptions of black resentment threaten to expose the fundamentally coercive nature of the institution. Thus, as we find Page extolling the virtues of the slave order, asserting that the "relation of masters and servants was one of close personal acquaintance and friendliness" and that ownership was unequivocally reciprocal, certain memories prove troublesome for the apologist to synthesize: a "curious recollection" of his "mammy" arguing against slavery, and the admission that, following emancipation, house-servants, who presumably were more deeply integrated within the plantation "family," were more likely than field hands to "hear the song of the siren" and desert their masters. Both passages run counter to the point Page is making at the time: in the first instance, that the

19. Cash, *Mind of the South*, 143; Kimball King, Introduction to *In Ole Virginia* (Chapel Hill: University of North Carolina Press, 1969), xx; Louis D. Rubin Jr., "The Other Side of Slavery: Thomas Nelson Page's 'No Haid Pawn,' " *Studies in the Literary Imagination* 7 (1974), 95–99; MacKethan, *Dream of Arcady*, 58–59.

mammy was not merely a servant, but "a member of the family in high standing and of unquestioned influence," and in the second, that during the war, "slaves not only remained faithful to their masters . . . the stress of the time . . . appeared to weld the bond between them," thus underscoring that the vast majority of slaves "identified themselves with their masters, and this union was not one of lip-service, but of sentiment, of heart and soul."[20]

As I have suggested, a similar tension between Page's narrative rhetoric and certain disruptive details manifests itself in *In Ole Virginia* as well, a work in which "lip service" and authentic sentiment are contested in the voice of the former slave. In examining how Page's narrative absorbs these disruptions, I want to call attention to a recurrent *sequence* Page employs in which a first term, which I will call the critical term, demands the narrative resolution provided by the second, which I will label the recuperative term. "Marse Chan," the first tale in *In Ole Virginia* and usually considered Page's finest elegy for the lost age of heroic gentleman and contented slaves, offers a paradigmatic example of this sequence. Early in the tale Marse Chan's father sends a slave, Ham Fisher, into a burning barn to rescue his horses. When Ham fails to return from the burning structure, the "old marster" risks his life to save him. Rescuing his slave, Mr. Channing is dreadfully burned and permanently blinded, although the slave escapes virtually unscathed. As MacKethan notes, "Page must have meant for the incident to show a master's willingness to risk his own life for his slaves. For the modern reader, however, this motive hardly disguises the fact that it was the 'blind' master who unthinkingly exposed his slave to the danger in the first place."[21] For

20. MacKethan, *Dream of Arcady*, 40–41; Page, "The Old-Time Negro," in *The Old South: Essays Social and Political* (New York: Scribner's, 1906), 304, 304, 307, 312, 316, 324, 315, 323–24. Regarding Page's attitudes toward slavery, Louis D. Rubin Jr. points out that "[a]fter the surrender in 1865, what is striking is the alacrity with which almost all Southerners not only accepted the demise of slavery but both publicly and privately expressed their relief at its passing," a circumstance Rubin ascribes to the absence of a true "Master Class" during the antebellum era (*The Edge of the Swamp: A Study in the Literature and Society of the Old South* [Baton Rouge: Louisiana State University Press, 1989], 38). Page's recollection that house servants fled before field hands has some historical validation: Joel Williamson notes that this was true in South Carolina as well; see *After Slavery: The Negro in South Carolina during Reconstruction, 1861–1877* (Chapel Hill: University of North Carolina Press, 1965), 34.

21. MacKethan, *Dream of Arcady*, 55.

MacKethan's modern reader, the first (critical) term of the sequence (master unthinkingly commands slave) lingers and therefore negates the second (master rescues slave). Yet we should note that the second term in no way *requires* the first in order to function: Page could have had Ham Fisher volunteer to save the horses (or any of a number of alternative scenarios in which a command was not involved), in which case Mr. Channing's heroism would have been "purer." What I am suggesting is that Page is not blind to the critique of slavery implicit in the first term, but that he includes that term as a surmountable obstacle or test that the second term in the sequence overcomes or abolishes. Moreover, in this specific instance the second (recuperative) term elucidates the obligations inherent in the first: to have Mr. Channing's power to command entails a deep sense of personal responsibility such that his heroism "rescues" the potential illegitimacy of his authority just as he physically rescues his slave.

Page's recuperative strategy extends to more fundamental features of his narrative, especially to the voice of the former slave. It is as if Page continually poses objections to the fantasy text in which the former slave finally authenticates the utopian dimension of the Old South: "Dem wuz good ole times, marster—de bes' Sam ever see! Dey wuz, in fac'! Niggers didn' hed nothin' 't all to do—jes' hed to 'ten' to de feedin' an' cleanin' de hosses, an' doin' what de marster tell 'em to do; an' when dey wuz sick, dey had things sont 'em out de house, an' de same doctor come to see 'em whar 'ten' to de white folks when dey wuz po'ly. Dyar warn' no trouble nor nothin'" (10). Sam's validation of the "good ole times" epitomizes the narrative work of *In Ole Virginia,* yet his voice, like those of Page's other former slaves, does not serve as a perfectly transparent vehicle for southern ideologies of race. Even a critic as conservative as Clyde N. Wilson qualifies the authenticity of the former slave's voice in claiming that "[t]he voices that Page creates in his work, black and white, are authentic Southern voices. Public voices, perhaps, that do not say everything they know and feel, that tactfully treat some troublesome subjects, and that consciously dramatize themselves—all of which are things that Southerners, black and white, are wont to do in real life. But they are real voices, in their own terms." By qualifying their authenticity as a dramatic, performative authenticity—a crucial qualification indeed—Wilson registers a certain uneasiness with the former slave's voice.

From the perspective afforded by W. E. B. DuBois's theory of double consciousness and Charles W. Chesnutt's conjure tales (not to mention more
recent work by critics such as Gates and Houston Baker), it is difficult to
conjoin the notion of authenticity with the performative demands placed on
African Americans during the postbellum era. But even so, it is interesting
to speculate as to how the black dialect Page employs might, as Robert L.
Phillips Jr. has suggested, evade the rhetorical and political intentions of the
white author.[22] But insofar as the performative demands placed upon Sam
are concerned, speculation is unnecessary, for in "Marse Chan" Page positively indicates them. As the anonymous frame narrator comes upon Sam,
the freedman is walking Marse Chan's dog, who is waiting for an obstacle to
be removed from his path. "Entirely oblivious" to the white narrator's proximity, Sam chides the dog: "Jes' like white folks—think 'cuz you's white and
I's black, I got to wait on yo' all de time. Ne'm mine, I ain' gwi' do it!" (3).
When he notices the white narrator, however, he quickly changes his tune:

> "Sarvent, marster," he said, taking his hat off. Then, as if apologetically for hav-
> ing permitted a stranger to witness what was merely a family affair, he added: "He
> know I don' mean nothin' by what I sez. He's Marse Chan's dawg, an' he's so ole he
> kyahn git long no pearter. He know I'se jes' prodjickin' wid im." (3)

Sam's stark assertion of racial resentment acts as the critical term in a sequence requiring both his overt renunciation ("He know I don' mean
nothin' by what I sez") and the narrator's metaphoric representation of the
quarrel as "merely a family affair." The narrator's recourse to family as a recuperative metaphor displaces the racial content of conflict, and in so doing
epitomizes the centrality of interracial "family" to Page's narrative. But insofar as it lingers, Sam's racial resentment qualifies his tale as a performance,
as the strategic construction of a veil behind which lurks a man discontent
with his place in the social order. Page thus *explicitly* (since there is no other

---

22. Clyde N. Wilson, Introduction to *In Ole Virginia* (1887; reprint, Nashville: J. S.
Sanders, 1991), xvi. Phillips suggests that Page's mimetic representation of black dialect—
which he, like Mark Twain, claimed to have rendered authentically—permits the black narrator to "sometimes . . . escap[e] from the obvious intention of the European rhetorical master"
("Multiculturalism and the Scholarly Journal" [Paper delivered at SAMLA Annual Convention, Knoxville, Tenn., November 1992]).

reason to include the comment) raises the possibility that public racial identity is performative—that is to say, motivated by the dialogic pressure exerted by the white interlocutor rather than originating from some core commitment to hegemonic structures. Like Page's mammy (another "family member") arguing against slavery, Sam potentially disrupts the order of things. The narrative work of *In Ole Virginia*, then, is to recuperate the former slave's authentic, rather than performative, commitment to the social order.

Although in no manner of speaking a "short-story novel," even in the limited sense of a work such as *Georgia Scenes, In Ole Virginia* is not without structure. The first three tales in the collection—"Marse Chan: A Tale of Old Virginia," "Unc Edinburg's Drowndin': A Plantation Echo," and "Meh Lady: A Story of the War"—constitute what I call the constructive sequence of *In Ole Virginia*, as they progressively recuperate a vision of the pastoral community that is tested and even subverted by the tales that follow, especially "Ole 'Stracted" and "No Haid Pawn," which define the virtues of the Old South as essentially negative virtues. By negative virtue, I mean virtue predominately perceptible as an absence, as when, in these later stories, the positive qualities of the plantation community and the social relationships found therein become apparent largely when they are no longer present.

Slavery is not depicted as a flawless institution in the early tales, especially insofar as the conflicts driving these tales are concerned. Usually interlinked with a courtship plot, conflict is limited to white characters, although its consequences extend to their black retainers, who, in the first two stories, are involved in a kind of reflected courtship plot. The conflict in "Marse Chan" centers around the political tension between the Whiggish family of the title character and the family of his beloved, Anne Chamberlain, whose father is a rabid Democrat and fire-breathing secessionist. Col. Chamberlain's radical politics are associated with an irresponsible notion of slavery, for after losing a Congressional election to the "ole marster," Col. Chamberlain suffers financial hardships and puts his slaves up for sale, going so far as to prevent his rival from purchasing the wife of one of his own slaves in order to keep a slave marriage intact. With the war looming on the horizon, Col. Chamberlain debates the more moderate Marse Chan over the question of secession, and insults Marse Chan's father as "a wuss ab'litionis' dan his son" (17). Living up to the southern code of honor, Marse Chan challenges him to a duel, during which he gallantly fires into the air and proclaims to the older man, "I mek you a present to yo' fam'ly, seh!" (21). Dishonored, Col. Chamberlain forbids his daughter to see Marse Chan. When the war breaks out, Marse Chan refuses a captaincy, enlisting as a private only after Virginia secedes. Accompanied by Sam, he repeatedly proves his valor on the battlefield. Eventually, Sam arranges a reconciliation between Marse Chan and Anne, but shortly after the soldier receives her letter accepting his offer of marriage, he is killed in battle.

As MacKethan notes, Page's plantation is a "breeding ground for heroes."[23] In this respect he differs from Kennedy, whose plantation conspicuously fails to produce heroes, with the important exception of Abe. Here, however, we find a certain confluence between the two works, for in both cases it is the slave who validates the code of chivalric honor: Abe by living the code, Sam by bearing witness to the heroism of his master. To the extent that Marse Chan acts as his community's epic representative, the community is divested of its ideological baggage: hotheadedness, destructive pride, radical politics, and an autocratic disregard for slaves, all of which are displaced to the character of Col. Chamberlain. In this respect Col. Chamberlain represents something like a critical term, the recuperative term of which is Marse Chan himself. Curiously, however, the action that permits the two families to be reconciled is the younger man's defense of Col. Chamberlain when a poor white—a "half-strainer," as Sam calls him—has the temerity to assert that the Chamberlains "wuz all on 'em a parecel of stuck up 'risticrats, and [Col. Chamberlain] wan' no gent'man anyway . . ." (30). This is a legitimate critique insofar as vicious slander and contempt for the welfare of one's slaves are antithetical to the code of noblesse oblige. Page's logic thus works in different directions. On the one hand, "Marse Chan" suggests that the legitimacy of the social order can only be actualized by the true gentleman. This point is subtly emphasized when Marse Chan offers to free Sam should he die in the duel, the implication being that the benignity of slavery as an institution cannot be trusted in the absence of the morally upstanding slave owner. On the other, Page's narrative implies that the social hierarchy,

23. MacKethan, *Dream of Arcady*, 48.

among whites at any rate, must be maintained in an absolute sense: under no circumstances can the "half-strainer" be permitted to question the authority of the gentleman. Here the complexity of the former slave's voice enters the equation. Sam participates in the aristocratic feud between the Channings and Chamberlains as a member of the family—a "Channing" by association. When the issue of class status arises, however, Sam immediately suspends whatever social critique is involved in his treatment of Col. Chamberlain and asserts the more generically aristocratic privilege conferred upon him by his familial relationship to Marse Chan. Although the subtle shift of Sam's alignment from family to class recuperates the legitimacy of a broadly conceived aristocratic hegemony, the contingent nature of this alignment fails to eliminate, and even implies, the possibility that Sam's devotion is more a matter of status ιthan an "authentic"—and here the problematic nature of authenticity asserts itself—commitment to the plantation order.

The issues of class status and family standing dominate the next tale as well. In every respect a less fitful defense of the Old South than "Marse Chan," "Unc' Edinburg's Drowndin': A Plantation Echo" begins with an interesting vignette that indicates the former slave's ability not only to possess status, but to confer it as well. When Unc' Edinburg meets the narrator to drive him to the plantation, he is suspicious because of the "unfortunate fact" that the narrator's luggage consists solely of a hand-satchel. Unc' Edinburg had been informed, he tells the visitor with an air of disdain, "as how you might bring a trunk" (40). Unc' Edinburg is indeed a formidable figure, informing the narrator "decisively" that a short visit is out of the question and intimidating him to the extent that he keeps to himself his low opinion of coon meat. When Unc' Edinburg begins his tale of the Old South, the issue of status remains in the foreground. Like "Marse Chan," "Unc' Edinburg's Drowndin' " involves a love affair disrupted by a family rivalry, although in this case the courtship comes to fruition. When Marse George (Unc' Edinburg's master) and Miss Caroline first meet, Unc' Edinburg is forced to defend the family honor to Miss Caroline's maid, Judy, when the latter questions the standing of Marse George's family:

Well, dat outdaciousness so aggrivate me, I lite into dat nigger right dyah. I tell her she ain' been nowhar 'tall ef she don' know we all; dat we wuz de bes' of quality, de ve'y top de pot; an' den I tell her 'bout how gret we wuz; how de ker'idges wuz al'ays hitched up night an' day, an' niggers jes thick as weeds; an' how Unc' Torm he wared he swaller-tail ev'y day when he wait on de table; and Marse George he won' wyah a coat mo'n once or twice anyways, to save you life. Oh! I sutney 'stonish dat nigger, 'cause I wuz teckin up for de fambly. (47)

The operative word in this passage is "we," which firmly installs Unc' Edinburg as a member of the family, and extends so far as to implicate him loosely in the ownership of slaves, as he later refers to "we all's Tubal" (48).

Compared with "Marse Chan," the blocking action in "Unc' Edinburg's Drowndin' " is less implicated in potentially problematic social issues, for Miss Caroline's stepfather's vice is limited to having bad politics—in this case, those of the Locofocos, a radical wing of the Democratic party. The true villain of the tale is Judge Darker's son, a plagiarist, coward, and bully who beats Unc' Edinburg when he finds the slave visiting Judy on his plantation. In response, Marse George cowhides Mr. Darker and then, to indicate his scorn for his antagonist, refuses to duel him, informing him that he would "cowhide him agin ef he ever heah any mo' from him, an' he 'ain't" (63). Unlike Col. Chamberlain, Mr. Darker loses his social status, as everyone comes to share the opinion that "he so low down an' wuthless dee kyarn nobody stand him" (70). Thus, the division preventing the love affair between the hero and heroine assumes a less political, more sentimental texture; indeed, it is pride more than anything else that keeps the lovers separated. In the end, the lovers come together when Miss Caroline visits Marse George as he lies near death, the result of his heroic rescue of Unc' Edinburg from a flooded river. (This rescue is itself a reworking of the fire episode in "Marse Chan," with the significant difference that the slave willingly puts his life in danger in "Unc' Edinburg's Drowndin'.")

For all its ideological smoothness, "Unc' Edinburg's Drowndin' " contains a single incident that threatens to disrupt the utopian order Page is concerned to establish. When Unc' Edinburg goes on his ill-fated visit to see Judy, who has light skin and hair "mos' straight as white folks" (46), she calls him a "black nigger." He responds, " 'Who you callin' nigger, you impident, kercumber-faced thing you?' Den we shake hands, an' I tell her Marse George done set me free—dat I done buy myself; dat's de lie I done lay off to tell her" (60). Although Judy is not impressed with this line of persuasion—she taunts him later in the tale as "dat free nigger" (69)—it is interesting to note how Unc' Edinburg privileges status as a "free nigger" over the status he has claimed earlier as a member of Marse George's family. Status, as Unc' Edinburg conceives it, is always associated with whiteness: to be free (like whites) is to trump having white physical characteristics such as light skin and straight hair. This desire to associate with whiteness potentially disrupts Unc' Edinburg's contentment with his station as a slave, just as his assertion of freedom potentially qualifies his family loyalty as a mere matter of status. In any event, he is willing and even eager to claim independence from Marse George when he perceives his status to be threatened.

Teasing out the logical problems with Page's tales ignores, however, the suspension of logic engendered by the authorial and narrative appeals to sentiment, which, if the tears shed over "Marse Chan" by erstwhile abolitionists such as Thomas Wentworth Higginson and Henry Ward Beecher are any indication, were quite powerful to a contemporary audience. In an important sense, sentimental appeal acts as a dominant recuperative term in *In Ole Virginia,* a work whose manipulation of sentimental power, rhetorical facility, and genius for creating powerful racial icons curiously recalls the work of Beecher's sister, the author of *Uncle Tom's Cabin.* Yet in dwelling on the narrative problems I have labeled critical terms, I should reiterate that as the constructive sequence of *In Ole Virginia* progresses, these critical terms become less prevalent and less problematic. However disruptive Unc' Edinburg's desire for freedom might be, it is clear from the narrative frame that his devotion to the family has survived emancipation. Virtually the only critical term in "Meh Lady: A Story of the War," the third tale in *In Ole Virginia,* concerns the treachery and desertion of certain slaves near the end of the war. But even the aptly named Ananias—a "weevly black" "po' white folks nigger" (109), according to the former slave who narrates the tale—refuses to show his face in public, and his "two or th'ee fellow deserters" feel compelled to assert that the Yankees "cyar[ied] 'em off" (110). Moreover, the deserters are shamed into this confession by their fellow slaves, who thus exert the only overt coercion in the entire work. This incident can hardly be labeled a critical term, so completely does the tale recuperate the slave's loyalty to the social order. Indeed, this sequence might well be considered a recuperative term in relation to status as it figures in the earlier tales, for rather than gaining status as a result of claiming their freedom, these slaves lose it instead.

Other than its complete severance of status and freedom, "Meh Lady" is a formulaic allegory of sectional reconciliation. Meh Lady is a young plantation mistress whose brother, Phil, dies heroically in battle. As the Union armies advance, a dashing Union officer saves the plantation from marauding Union soldiers and later, after being wounded in battle, spends a period of convalescence at Meh Lady's estate, where the two fall in love. Unwilling to marry the enemy, Meh Lady spurns his romantic advances and refuses his financial aid, preferring to labor in poverty after the war ends. Eventually, however, through the intermediation of the slave narrator, Old Billy, and his wife, the lovers marry. In the ceremony Billy asserts his prerogative to give away the bride, thus claiming—if, as King notes, somewhat tentatively—his status as a member of the family.[24] This status is emphasized in the closing lines of "Meh Lady" when we learn that the heroine's second child is named for him, the first having been named after her dead brother. After the ceremony, Billy relates that he "sort o' got to studyin'": "hit 'pear like de plantation 'live once mo', an' de ain' no mo' scuffin', and de ole times done come back ag'in" (138). So ends the utopian drive toward sectional reconciliation and the recuperation of the plantation myth of the interracial family.

If the conclusion of "Meh Lady" represents the culmination of Page's fantasy text, the obliteration of the critique of slavery lingering in the pages that precede it, we should be careful to note that it is a utopian moment Page does not sustain, as the two stories that follow—"Ole 'Stracted" and "No Haid Pawn"—present the interracial community in a less favorable light than any that have come before. Interestingly, the increased pressure exerted by slavery coincides with the loss of the black narrator, for unlike the previous tales, both "Ole 'Stracted" and "No Haid Pawn" are narrated by a white voice. But before turning our attention to these stories, let us first reconsider an issue raised earlier: the question of why a writer so concerned to legitimate the social order of the Old South should include what we have called critical terms in the first place. One is struck by how easily Page could have

24. King, Introduction, xxx–xxxi.

eliminated them, from Sam's assertion of resentment to Ananias's desertion to the Yankees, without structurally damaging his stories; indeed, Page's critical terms seem, in most cases, to be almost superfluous. But Page, like any writer dealing with a historical subject, was forced to take his material from history, and if he was an evasive writer, he was not as evasive as many critics and readers have imagined. He confronted a past in which slaves wanted their freedom, deserted their plantations en masse at the conclusion of the war, and actively voiced their discontent; a past in which slaves were harshly punished and forcibly separated from their families; a past in which the slave exerted tangible pressure against the pastoral icon. By including critical terms, Page incorporated and countered this pressure, and in so doing assimilated a critique of slavery within his myth-producing narrative. Writing for a national audience moving toward white supremacy as a cultural norm, this assimilative technique was rhetorically shrewd, especially for a writer who once remarked that he sold more books in Boston than in the entire state of Virginia. But whatever pressure they may exert, Page's critical terms do not disrupt what we might call his meta-logic, which dictates that whatever its flaws, the slave order produced a cohesiveness whose virtues could only be appreciated fully in its absence. In this master sequence slavery acts as something like the critical term, and its absence as the recuperative term.

In "Ole 'Stracted," the negative virtues of slavery are clearly in evidence. The title character is, like Sam and Unc' Edinburg, a personal retainer of a master who, unlike Marse Chan and Marse George, had fallen upon hard times and been forced to sell his slaves. Divided from his wife and child and sold down the river, Ole 'Stracted makes his way back to his old plantation after the war ever hopeful that his master will return and fulfill his promise to reunite the slave family. Ole 'Stracted's dream is a hopeless one, since communal rumor has it that his master had died "of a broked heart torectly after dee tech he niggers an' sell 'em" (145). A parallel plot involves a freedman, Ephraim, whose dream of owning a farm is thwarted by the ruthless "half-strainer" who owns the land and house he and his family rent. At the conclusion of the tale, Ephraim learns that he is Ole 'Stracted's son, and through a *deus ex machina* resolution, the money he needs to purchase his farm appears in the form of $1,200 Ole 'Stracted had saved to purchase his family. MacKethan argues that "Ole 'Stracted" resists, more than any other tale in the collection, the ideological intentions of its author, who refuses to minimize Ole 'Stracted's tragic situation with any "propaganda of white benevolence," and who "lets us feel [that Ephraim] has every right to realize [his dream]" (56–57). As MacKethan notes, Page's typical attitude toward the freedman, or "new issue Negro," was one of scorn and contempt, echoes of which are clear in one of Unc' Edinburg's asides that "'lections wus 'lections dem days; dee warn' no bait-gode 'lections, wid ev'y sort o' worms squirmin' up 'ginst one nurr, wid piece o' paper d' ain' know what on, drappin' in a chink."[25] Certainly it is difficult to reconcile the image of the vote-selling "new issue Negro" with the sturdy yeoman farmer of "Ole 'Stracted" whose agrarian independence aligns him, unlike Page's previous black characters, with neither aristocrat nor poor white.

"Ole 'Stracted" also diverges from Page's conception of the black family. In "The Old-Time Negro," Page asserts that the "family instinct" had never "taken much root" in Negro culture, owing either to its subordination to "a tribal instinct" or, interestingly, to "the very nature of the institution of slavery" (312). Raising this environmental argument only as a possibility, Page emphasizes familial structure as a race characteristic differing dramatically between Negroes and "Anglo-Saxons," a "race whose history is founded upon the family instinct."[26] "Ole 'Stracted," however, places a positive emphasis on black domesticity. Ephraim's wife is a devoted mother and wife, and Ole 'Stracted's heroic efforts to accumulate the $1,200 are directed toward reuniting the family separated by slavery. Yet to indict slavery in this manner is to resist Page's narrative logic. If "Ole 'Stracted" is a partial indictment of slavery, it is, in aligning the pathos of the independent Negro with the decline of aristocratic power, a massive indictment of the absence of slavery. When confronted with the news that they are to be evicted, Ephraim's wife "instinctively" thinks of her old master, Marse Johnny, only to have Ephraim dash her hopes: "He ain' got nuttin, an' ef he is, he hyarn

25. MacKethan, *Dream of Arcady,* 58.

26. Page goes on to defend slavery as an institution that promoted "family ties among the Negroes," noting that "marital fidelity" had declined following emancipation. In a curious argument, Page asserts that "the instances of desertion of husbands, of wives, of parents, or children [following emancipation] would possibly offset any division that took place under that institution [of slavery]" ("Old-Time Negro," 311–12).

get it in a week" (148). Although Ephraim is designated as her "proper support," Page makes it clear that the domestic ideal is unavailable in the absence of white benevolence. The true villain of the tale is the "po' white trash" who has supplanted the aristocrat in the postbellum social hierarchy and who shares none of the aristocrat's paternalistic concern for the Negro.

In a similar vein, the pathos of Ole 'Stracted's situation is directly attributed to the absence of his master. So deep is the former slave's dependence upon his master that Ole 'Stracted is "unable to give any account of himself" except insofar as that relationship is concerned (153). When Ephraim asks for his name, Ole 'Stracted cannot provide it, asserting, however, that "dat ain' nuttin. *He* [Marster] know it—got it set down in de book" (157). Intentionally or not, Page here inverts an enabling premise of the antebellum slave narrative: that the slave's deep sense of identity extends beyond his social position and thus provides a ground antithetical to his status as chattel property. For Page the slave's identity and his social role are identical, or to put the matter another way, his identity is contingent upon his place in the social hierarchy. Like Joel Chandler Harris's Free Joe, without a master, he is no one. Just as the slave narrative provided a powerful form for critiquing slavery, so Page has Ole 'Stracted's story, his fantasy text of white protection, exert power over Ephraim and his wife. Although fully aware that Old 'Stracted's dream is a fantasy, Ephraim is nevertheless deeply affected by "the beauty of the sublime devotion of this poor old creature to his [master's] love and his trust, holding steadfast beyond memory, beyond reason, after the knowledge even of his identity and of his very name was lost" (151). When the couple visits Ole 'Stracted, the old man reaffirms his belief that his master will return:

"He's comin', too—nuver tol' me a lie in he life—comin' dis evenin'. Make 'aste." This in tremulous eagerness to the woman, *who had involuntarily caught the feeling*, and was now with eager and ineffectual haste trying to button his shirt [emphasis added]. (159)

Ephraim and his wife consume Ole 'Stracted's fantasy text, and for good reason: like him, they do not have available the aristocratic benevolence that makes life as a Negro bearable.

Or so, at least, is the interpretation that I contend made the tale bearable for Page. In fact, the fragility of this interpretation—and indeed the very idea of slavery having negative virtues—produces something like a self-consuming text whose author comes perilously close to making the mistake of the man in the joke who beats his head with a hammer because it feels so good when he stops. It is almost as if the tests or objections Page poses for his fantasy text threaten to overwhelm that text and the organic social order it assumes. This trend continues in "No Haid Pawn," a story that marks a notable generic shift within the collection from the sentimental to the gothic. As several critics have noted, "No Haid Pawn" borrows a number of tropes and images from Edgar Allan Poe's "Fall of the House of Usher," among them the burial of live persons and a house that falls into a body of water—in Page's case, the "pawn" of the story's title.[27] Yet to a greater extent than Poe, Page links the gothic atmosphere of "No Haid Pawn" to the social context of the tale.

The action of the "No Haid Pawn" begins about halfway through the tale, the first half of which recounts the plantation's dark history. The plantation had been built by strangers to the community, and as a consequence, "no ties either of blood or friendship were formed with their neighbors, who were certainly open-hearted and open-doored enough to overcome anything but the most persistent unneighborliness" (166). From the beginning, an "evil destiny had seemed to overshadow the place" (167). Various local legends circulate concerning dungeons built for "awful" if "indefinite" purposes, a Negro builder who had been decapitated in "some awful and occult rite connected with the laying of the cornerstone," and slaves who were buried alive and arose to haunt the pond (167–68). Eventually the house had been inherited by a sinister and brutal West Indian who decapitated a slave and flung the body from a window down to where his horrified slaves watched below. Clearly a curious tale to have been written by an apologist for the Old South, "No Haid Pawn" is nevertheless, as MacKethan suggests,

27. "No Haid Pawn" ostensibly refers to the pond's lack of a source, although the motif of decapitation associated with the plantation makes it a particularly apt name. Page exploits the traditional gothic trope of the house as psychological analog for its inhabitants. For a discussion of how "No Haid Pawn" inverts Page's usual association of plantation houses with their owners, see MacKethan, *Dream of Arcady*, 44–46.

consistent with Page's intention elsewhere in demonstrating "what happens to the plantation ideal when unworthy beings attempt to imitate its concepts."[28] Hence the racial difference between the sinister giant and his fellow planters, who brand the West Indian as a pariah: "His brutal temper and habits cut him off from even the small measure of intercourse which had existed between his predecessors and their neighbors, and he lived at No Haid Pawn completely isolated" (169). The white community acquits itself admirably, publicly hanging the West Indian after his final outrage. Indeed, it is they and not the slaves who are outraged, since after their master's hanging, his "negroes all lamented his death, and declared that he was a good master when he was not drunk" (170).

In any event, were the story to end with the sinister giant—who, after all, effectively serves as a scapegoat who absorbs the evils and abuses of slavery—then "No Haid Pawn" would not resist Page's narrative logic in the way that it finally does. This level of resistance comes in the contemporaneous setting of the story, which takes place during the 1850s. Abolitionists are in the neighborhood:

No idea can be given at this date of the excitement occasioned in a quiet neighborhood in old times by the discovery of the mere presence of such characters as Abolitionists. It was as if the foundation of the whole social fabric was undermined. It was the sudden darkening of a shadow that always hung in the horizon. The slaves were in a large majority, and had they risen, though the final issue could not be doubted, the lives of every white on the plantations must have paid the forfeit. Whatever the right and wrong of slavery might have been, its existence demanded that no outside interference with it should be tolerated. So much was certain; self-preservation required this. (174)

The presence of these "secret agents" accounts for a curious inversion: whereas the slaves of a brutal master validate his goodness, the slaves of his upright neighbors—at least "more than a usual number" of them (171)—flee from the benevolence of their masters, a point that surely contradicts Page's representation of the contented slave. One of the runaways, the black

28. Ibid., 45.

leader of the Abolitionists' secret meetings and the only runaway still at large, is a brutal giant whose master, "instead of being commiserated on the loss of his slave, was congratulated that he had not cut his throat" (173). Having thus set the scene, Page's narrator recounts how he had foolhardily transgressed the boundaries of No Haid Pawn during a solitary duck hunt. When a thunderstorm arises, the narrator is forced to seek refuge in the plantation house, where he falls asleep. Awakened by a curious sound, the narrator catches a brief glimpse of a man in a boat approaching the "haunted house." Terrified, the narrator describes how the man makes his way into the house and is illuminated by a flash of lightning: "Directly in front of me, clutching in his upraised hand a long, keen, glittering knife, on whose blade a ball of fire seemed to play, stood a gigantic figure in the very flame of the lightning, and stretched at his feet lay, ghastly and bloody, a black and headless trunk" (185). The narrator "staggered to the door and, tripping, fell prostrate over the sill," returning later only to find that the "haunted house" had been set afire by the lightning and "reclaimed" with "all its secrets" buried by the dark waters of the pond (186).

So Page ends his tale without explaining the connection between the escaped slave and what is apparently the ghost of the former master dragging his decapitated victim. E. L. Burlingame, the editor of *Scribner's Magazine*, suggested to Page that he bring out a bit more clearly the "dimly suggested connection of the runaway negro & his booty with the climax." Louis Rubin, noting that the "pure ghost story" was a genre in decline when Page was writing, suggests that the "ghost" is actually the escaped slave, and the "black and headless trunk" is that of a stolen hog. Although there is some evidence for this scenario—the runaway is a renowned hog thief, and No Haid Pawn would be an ideal hideout—it is curious that Page's narrator refuses to affirm or even offer this explanation, which remains, as Burlingame says, only dimly suggested. Like Henry James's "Turn of the Screw," Page's tale preserves the moment that Tzetvan Todorov labels the "fantastic" in which the reader is obliged "to hesitate between a natural and supernatural explanation of the events described." If anything, the contiguity of the supernatural destruction of the house, which itself is explicitly described as "haunted," pressures the reader away from a natural explanation. (Could the slave have *burned* the house?) A natural explanation would involve several disturbing elements, foremost among them, as Rubin notes, the perception that the slave community is actively aiding the runaway, since the noise that awakens the narrator is apparently a communication of some sort.[29] Furthermore, other details from the story threaten to appear in a new light; for example, the slaves' active dissemination of horrific tales might be interpreted as having the strategic intention of keeping people far from No Haid Pawn. What I am suggesting is that Page offers a rational explanation, only to withdraw it at the very end, where his recourse to the genre of the ghost story allows him to negate as fantasy the disturbing implications of his tale. To admit otherwise would have been too dark altogether.

Nonetheless, the repressive texture of "No Haid Pawn" represents a stark departure from the fantasy of Negro consent that dominates the earlier tales. To return to the issue of Abolitionists and their efficacy in undermining the "foundation of the whole social fabric"—an interestingly mixed metaphor that has both horizontal and vertical dimensions—we should note that while the narrator's comment is true enough for the antebellum culture he describes, it had for Page a certain resonance in the postbellum era as well. In an essay titled "The Negro Question," originally published in *The Old South* (1892) and reprinted with slight revisions in *The Negro: The Southerner's Problem* (1904), Page blasts a Massachusetts senator for predicting "a harvest of horror and blood" should the South continue on its course of disenfranchisement:

Had he understood the true gravity of that problem, his cheek, as he caught the echo of his own words, would have blanched at the thought of the peril he is transmitting to his children and grandchildren; not the peril, perhaps, of fire and massacre, but a peril as deadly, the peril of contamination from the overcrowding of an inferior race. All other evils are but corollaries: the evil of race-conflict, though not so awful as the French Revolution or San Domingo; the evil of growing armies with their menace

29. Burlingame quoted in Jay B. Hubbell, *The South in American Literature, 1607–1900* (Durham: Duke University Press, 1954), 801; Rubin, "Other Side of Slavery," 97, 99; Tzetvan Todorov, *The Fantastic: A Structural Approach to a Literary Genre,* trans. Richard Howard (Cleveland: Press of Case Western Reserve University, 1973), 33.

to liberty; the evil of race-degeneration from enforced and constant association with an inferior race: these are some of the perils which spring from that state of affairs and confront us.[30]

In this context far from the scene of moonlight and magnolias, the narrator's comments in "No Haid Pawn" concerning the requirements of white self-preservation acquire a new, more immediate dimension. The possibility of an uprising of either slaves or freedmen deals a fatal blow to the notion that interracial relationships are more consensual than coercive. To put the matter another way, Page dispenses with his fantasy text of happy darkies and honorable gentlemen when the former become transformed, as if by magic, into the descendants of Nat Turner. At this crucial moment, the interracial contact previously validated as an organic bond becomes a "peril of contamination," an intolerable "association with an inferior race." "No Haid Pawn," then, exposes the sheer contingency of Page's organic social order, representing the final breakdown of family as a functional metaphor for the interracial community.

In Ole Virginia stands at a critical juncture in southern literary history. In *The Strange Career of Jim Crow,* C. Vann Woodward contrasts the "patronizing, sentimentalized, and paternalistic . . . [but never] venomous or bitter" portrayals of black characters in the work of writers like Page with the venomous portrayals of blacks in Thomas Dixon's *The Clansman* and *The Leopard's Spots,* works that were "the perfect literary accompaniment of the white-supremacy and disenfranchisement campaign." Working with the same Page-Dixon axis, Walter Benn Michaels argues that the interracial family metaphor in Page's *Red Rock* produces "blacks [who] present no real racial threat and stand instead as a kind of bulwark against the new whites." In *Red Rock,* according to Michaels, "whiteness doesn't yet have any real meaning."[31]

30. Page, "The Negro Question," in *The Negro: The Southerner's Problem* (New York: Scribner's, 1904), 213–14. Fred Hobson notes that Page replaced "The Negro Question" with the less polemical "The Old-Time Negro" when he reissued *The Old South* in 1912, possibly because widespread disenfranchisement and the institution of Jim Crow made the polemics of the excluded essay less urgent; for further discussion, see *Tell about the South: The Southern Rage to Explain* (Baton Rouge: Louisiana State University Press, 1983), 146.

31. C. Vann Woodward, *The Strange Career of Jim Crow,* rev. ed. (New York: Oxford University Press, 1957), 78; Walter Benn Michaels, *Our America: Nativism, Modernism, and Pluralism* (Durham: Duke University Press, 1995), 18.

Whatever the truth of Michaels's provocative claim in terms of Page's reconstruction novel, it is clear in "The Race Question," published just five years after *In Ole Virginia,* that white supremacy and disenfranchisement were central tenets in Page's racial program. In an indirect manner, *In Ole Virginia* as well provides a perfect literary accompaniment of the white-supremacy and disenfranchisement campaign—one certainly less virulent than Dixon's, but perhaps more effective precisely for that reason. Having spent the bulk of *In Ole Virginia* affirming the slave's consensual participation in the paternalistic order, Page suggests in "No Haid Pawn" that should this consent not be forthcoming, the white community had best be prepared to see to its preservation at all costs.

Page's implicit program of consent when possible, coercion when necessary, suggests the deep interrelationship between paternalism and white supremacy. For Page, black consent enables the family metaphor through which the interracial community becomes possible, but the absence thereof exposes the dark side of blackness, now conceived as a biological and social contaminant. Page thus predicts Dixon, a writer for whom the absence of black consent defines the Negro as a contaminant in an absolute sense, but who himself preached paternalistic doctrines throughout his career. Dixon, in short, looks squarely at the latent vision of "No Haid Pawn." It is not so much that race has no real meaning in Page, as Michaels suggests, but that consent masks and conceals that meaning. And for a writer whose entire narrative works toward producing and affirming black consent, the presence of a contingency plan does much to subvert the authenticity of the consensus thus produced. In defining the contingent logic of the paternalism, Page provides a useful point of departure for the two narratives we will consider next: William Alexander Percy's *Lanterns on the Levee,* which explores the terminal limits of the interracial community, and William Faulkner's *Light in August,* a work in which white supremacy structures the community in ways it can barely perceive.

3

THE AESTHETICS OF COMMUNITY

William Alexander Percy's *Lanterns on the Levee*

By no means did the rhetoric of paternalism end with the fin-de-siècle paeans to the Old South of Thomas Nelson Page and his contemporaries. Even a writer so obsessed with interracial contamination as Thomas Dixon could, without apparent sense of contradiction, evoke "memories of the dear old nurse in whose arms the weary head of my childhood so often found rest, at whose feet I sat and heard the sad story of the life of a slave until I learned to hate slavery as I hate hell" and claim to speak "with the kindest and tenderest feelings for the Negro race." For Dixon, however, and to a lesser extent for Page as well, the paternalistic bond was most tangible as an absence, as an integral part of a vanished society. The racial animosities of reconstruction and, as the century waned, the rise of racial demagoguery and Jim Crow, made paternalism under slavery a distant memory. However, the continued economic and social interaction between white and black southerners, by now reestablished on a firmly—and, from the white perspective, properly—hierarchical ground, necessitated a new paternalism, one certainly less central to southern society given the deep divisions involved in segregation, but one that nevertheless preserved at least a family resemblance to its antebellum ancestor. No less than under slavery, paternalism under Jim Crow required a fully elaborated mythology of black labor and black consent. As Robert Penn Warren once pointed out, it is a very difficult thing for a man simply to admit that he oppresses another. The intolerable nature of exploitation—in some ways, as intolerable for the exploiter as for the exploited—necessitated that brute economic necessity be translated into a rhetoric of interracial dependence and an image of a social order hierarchically divided by innate differences, yet bound together by common manners, codes, and mutual responsibilities. In short, what James McBride Dabbs says of slavery applies to segregation as well: "one either develops the manners suited to it or becomes a barbarian."[1]

William Alexander Percy was no barbarian. The quintessential southern aristocrat—even W. J. Cash, who tended to doubt the breed's existence, admitted as much—Percy was a planter, a minor poet, and the author of a classic autobiography, *Lanterns on the Levee: Recollections of a Planter's Son* (1941). Often read as a paradigmatic elegy for the lost age of southern heroes, *Lanterns on the Levee* is a more fitful narrative than has generally been acknowledged. As James E. Rocks has suggested, "[t]he art of Percy's autobiography is the art of opposition and tension." Rocks rightly suggests that one fundamental tension centers around Percy's experience of private and public selves, an "interaction of 'being' and 'doing' " reflected in the textual "combination of private reminiscences and public memoirs."[2] I hope to elucidate this interaction by showing how *Lanterns on the Levee* confronts two basic narrative problems: the tenuous configuration of the pastoral community and the loss of cultural energy embodied in the relationship between the heroic father and the passive son. Although Percy's primary strategy in dealing with these problems is to locate some culpable antagonistic force outside the boundaries of the community, his pastoral world erodes in excess of what he can ascribe to these external forces. In the end Percy withdraws from the concrete world of social interaction—a withdrawal embodied in his pervasive rhetoric of failure—because he cannot negotiate his community's tacit logic, especially where racial paternalism is involved.

Often dismissed as paternalistic rhetoric, *Lanterns on the Levee* is interesting precisely for that reason; perhaps more than any other single text, Percy's work registers and attempts to resolve the contradictions of southern

1. Thomas Dixon, "The Southern Question," in *Living Problems in Religion and Social Science* (New York: Charles T. Dillingham, 1889), 247; Dabbs, *Southern Heritage,* 139.

2. James E. Rocks, "The Art of *Lanterns on the Levee,*" *Southern Review* 12 (1976), 815, 817.

paternalism. It requires no great insight to locate these contradictions and the premises that authorize them, but the manner in which Percy conceals them—from his reader and from himself—eludes crude attempts to deconstruct what might (erroneously) appear to be sheer rhetorical violence undertaken in the name of class defense. As Hayden White has suggested, the putative content of any narrative works to mask the ideological operations at work on a formal level, and Percy's narrative in particular repays careful attention to the hierarchy of codes through which the elaboration of cultural "content" (class and racial characteristics, historical processes, cultural mores, and so on) is made to appear self-evident.[3] Essentially, Percy employs two such codes—the ethical and the aesthetic—through which social phenomena accrue meaning. Although Percy's critics have dealt implicitly with his ethical code—a code that works to define and legitimate social hierarchy—insufficient attention has been paid to his aesthetic code, which allows him to preserve the coherence of a community that threatens to be exposed as a coercive, sheerly symbolic entity. By directing attention to the aesthetic ground of *Lanterns on the Levee,* the form of the text—especially the loss of narrativity in its final chapters—can itself be seen as a meaningful attempt to preserve an idealized image of the social order Percy held so dear.

Lanterns on the Levee can be divided into four main sections: chapters 1–2, which serve as a kind of overture for the ensuing narrative; chapters 3–12, the *bildung* chapters that provide an account of Percy's various educations; chapters 13–20, which show Percy entering history and assuming a public role; and chapters 21–27, in which Percy withdraws from history and conceptually elaborates his worldview. From the opening pages of the text, nature begins to accrete social meanings. Chapter 1, "The Delta," frames a brief synopsis of Delta history with a description of the land and the Mississippi River. The early inhabitants of the Delta were forced both to battle and cultivate nature in order to domesticate it. Yet, whether construed as enemy or friend, nature remains an alien presence; as Percy says of the river, "Man draws near to it, fights it, uses it, curses it, loves it, but it remains remote, unaffected. . . . As a thing used by men, it has changed: the change is

---

3. Hayden White, *The Content of the Form: Narrative Discourse and Historical Representation* (Baltimore: Johns Hopkins University Press, 1987), 202–204.

not in itself, but in them."[4] Such a view of nature tends to collectivize those perceiving it, and indeed, Percy tends to portray Delta inhabitants as a homogeneous group synecdochically represented by the planter. As a corrective, he begins chapter 2, titled "Delta Folks," by only half-facetiously asserting, "I may seem to have implied that all Delta citizens were aristocrats traveling up and down the river or sitting on the front gallery, a mint julep in one hand and a palm-leaf fan in the other, protected from mosquitoes by the smudge burning in the front yard. If so, I have misinterpreted my country" (16). Percy devotes the remainder of this chapter to an inventory and analysis of the different Delta social groups. After briefly cataloging "river rats," Jews, and foreign immigrants, all of whom inhabit the periphery of Delta culture, he asserts unequivocally that "the basic fiber, the cloth of the Delta population—as of the whole South—is built of three dissimilar threads and only three" (19): the landed gentry, the poor whites, and the Negroes.

Whatever its merits as a sociological claim, this tripartite division is essential to the narrative work of *Lanterns on the Levee*. With virtually no exceptions, social groups possess for Percy absolute characteristics that allow him to rationalize the social order. Although much of his narrative concerns the poor white, the nature of this group provides little resistance to Percy's worldview: They are "not blessed with worldly goods or mental attainments" (19); their "breed is probably the most unprepossessing on the broad face of the ill-populated earth" (20). "I can forgive them," Percy writes, "as the Lord God forgives, but admire them, trust them, love them—never" (20). In contrast to the poor white, the Negro is presented ambiguously: "His manners offset his inefficiency, his vices have the charm of amiable weaknesses, he is a pain and a grief to live with, a solace and a delight" (21). Unlike the poor white, the Negro possesses aesthetic attractions that mitigate his ethical shortcomings; such is the pure language of paternalism. But if Percy's portrayal of the Negro presumes at times to be authoritative, a strong rhetorical countercurrent suggests otherwise. Although he concludes that "darkies" are "the only Southerners worth talking about," he asks rhetor-

4. Percy, *Lanterns on the Levee*, 13–14. This work will hereinafter be cited parenthetically by page number in the text.

ically, "what can a white man, north or south, say of them that will even approximate the truth?" (22). This tension between the deeply familiar and the utterly inscrutable nature of the Negro resonates throughout *Lanterns on the Levee.*

In an inaugurating event for the remainder of his narrative, Percy ends the chapter by shifting his focus from individual social groups to a consideration of how collective experience is made possible. "So the Delta problem," he writes, "is how all these folks—aristocrats gone to seed, poor whites on the make, Negroes convinced mere living is good, aliens of all sorts that blend or curdle—can dwell together in peace if not in brotherhood and live where, first and last, the soil is the only means of livelihood" (23–24). Percy thus assigns a *place* in history—not simply a collection of pertinent historical facts, as we find earlier in the chapter, but a teleological position or *role* in the plot of history—to each group: for the aristocrats, history assumes the form of devolution; for the poor whites, ascendancy. For the Negro, given his "obliterating genius for living in the present," history is a null category; he "is interested neither in the past nor in the future, this side of heaven. He neither remembers nor plans" (23). Thus divided by group traits and history itself, the "Delta problem" would appear to be a terminal case. Yet Percy claims that "we of the Delta have been fortunate in our misfortunes. Time out of mind we have been gifted with common disasters that have united us or at least made us lean together" (24). Nature, in the form of yellow fever epidemics and floods that produce "that cozy one-family feeling of the inmates of the Ark" (24), thus acts as a common antagonist by means of which social divisions are suspended or abolished. Yet within the cohesive order so produced—and this becomes clearer as *Lanterns on the Levee* progresses— the natures of social groups usurp the antagonistic function of nature itself, acting as the quasi-common opponents against which the community must defend itself. Rhetorically, this construction involves a shift in the referent of the first person pronoun, as Percy's quasi-collective first person elides the distinction between the community and the planter, who thereby assumes his proper role as the community's representative. To take but one example of a strategy found throughout *Lanterns on the Levee,* Percy asserts that "moderate poverty" acts as an excellent "cement for a people" ("No class or individual with us has ever known riches"), before going on to report that "[s]ome years the crop and prices are good and we take a trip or sport an automobile or buy another plantation" (24). Although it is superfluous to point out that this "we" would include neither poor white nor Negro, Percy's reference to "common" poverty rhetorically obliterates the role played by capital within the community, which he is eager to portray as an organic social order rather than one based on economic hierarchy. Similarly, Percy's "soil" acquires an agrarian connotation as a site of cultural cohesion rather than a mere means of producing material wealth.

Percy's quasi-collective "we," which comes before us here as a logical scandal, appears again, less egregiously, as he brings his chapter to a lyrical, if conceptually fitful, close: "Behind us a culture lies dying, before us the forces of the unknown industrial world gather for catastrophe. We have fields to plow and the earth smells good; maybe in time someone will pay us more for our cotton than we spend making it. In the meantime the darkies make up new songs about the boll-weevil and the river, and the sun pours over us his great tide of warmth which is also light" (24). Again, Percy implicitly substitutes an aristocratic perspective for a collective one, here within the context of history. Yet if a dying culture represents only the historical vision of the planter class, another alien antagonist, the "unknown industrial world," makes collective history at least a possibility. Within the social order of the Delta community, however, the quasi-collective first person breaks down yet again in terms of logical reference; the "we" who plows and the "us" who gets paid represent two distinct social groups, as a later chapter, "Planters, Share-Croppers, and Such," makes abundantly clear. Nevertheless, Percy's quasi-collective first person tentatively resolves a problem that manifests itself with greater force as his narrative progresses: the fundamentally illusory nature of a cohesive social order revealed either as a polite fiction or as a temporary experience possible only in moments of "all-inclusive tragedy." (There are few such moments in the text: one rather problematic flood and no yellow fever epidemics.) Because of the attenuation of collective identity—and hence, the increasingly tenuous nature of the collective first-person—the more important stylistic feature here is found in the shift from history ("Behind us . . . before us . . .") to aesthetic experience. As the chapter comes to a close, history ends. When Percy says that "the darkies make up new songs" (the creation of beauty in response to the alien antagonist), he speaks not of an actual event but a mythical and even magical one, an event that invokes a fullness of meaning alien to history. The basic style of this passage occurs throughout the coda to chapter 2, finding perhaps its purest form in the statement, "If we become too prosperous . . . the levee breaks" (24). These statements constitute what Kenneth Burke calls magical language; their implied forms are "*let the* darkies make up songs," and "*let the* levee break," respectively.[5] Both images are thus "conjured up" in response to communal threat, whether it be prosperity, which would exacerbate class division and preclude that "cozy one-family feeling," or the nightmare of history from which Percy is here, as always, trying to awake.

If the image of community that closes chapter 2 represents an escape from history, we should investigate more thoroughly what this history is made of, a question particularly pertinent given my assertion that history happens only in the third section of the book. Perhaps the clearest portrayal we have comes as Percy justifies his narrative project in his foreword: "So while the world I know is crashing to bits, and what with the noise and the cryings-out no man could hear a trumpet blast, much less an idle evening reverie, I will indulge a heart beginning to be fretful by repeating to it the stories it knows and loves of my own country and my own people." Again employing the language of magic, Percy will repeat his stories as a charm against the onslaught of history, which appears here in its typical form as an alien, dispossessing force threatening the community. Although this statement ostensibly refers to *Lanterns* as a whole, its elegiac overtones are most clearly evinced in the second section of the book, which recounts Percy's childhood experiences, his education at Sewanee and Harvard Law, his travels abroad, and his return to Greenville. The organizing metaphor of this section is education, the dominant relationship that between pupil and mentor. The scene of Percy's education is roughly equivalent to what Jürgen Habermas calls the "lifeworld" *(Lebenswelt)*, a symbolically constituted conception of everyday life opposed to the domain of history in which action is strategic, instrumental, and—from Percy's perspective—dispossessing.[6] Even in these early chapters, history lurks just outside the lifeworld and continually en-

5. Burke, *Philosophy of Literary Form*, 4–5.
6. See especially Habermas's critique of Charles Parsons's "system theory of society" in *Lifeworld and System*, 204–34.

croaches upon it; eventually it will erode the apodictic ground of Percy's so-cial identity.

Although Percy devotes significant attention to the education he receives from his father, another category of teacher shapes him in such a way as to render his father's heroism unavailable and tacitly undesirable. In the *bildung* of an aesthete recounted in these chapters, the first of what I will call Percy's aesthetic mentors is his black nurse, Nain, who remains in his memory as "more of an emanation or aura than a person" (27). Recalling his first memory as a song sung to him by Nain—a song whose "words and tune have gone, but not what they did to me" (26)—Percy goes on to comment on his memory: "A poor sort of egotistic memory I know, that records nothing of the outside world, but only how certain bits of it pleased or distressed me, yet mine, and no better now than it was then, and no different" (27). In some ways this representation of a self divorced from the outside world can be taken as emblematic of the entire section, in which a highly subjective, elegiac mode replaces the authoritative voice of the first two chapters. Aesthetic experience takes precedence over ethical instruction. Nain's singing, Percy writes, "opened vistas and induced contemplations" of musical forms that, "awakening kindred compassions in the core of my being, have guided me more sure-footedly through life than all ten of the Commandments" (27). Although "allergic" to the biblical lessons of his paternal grandmother Mur, Percy learns from her a more important lesson: "She taught me to see flowers, and of course anyone who sees them loves them. It would have gone hard with me in certain later hours without that training" (32). When not "Bible-minded," Percy recounts, Mur read to him "superb things": "Grimm and Hans Anderson, *Huckleberry Finn* and *Uncle Remus, The Rose and the Ring,* and *A Christmas Carol, Pilgrim's Progress* and *Alice in Wonderland* " (33). Acknowledging its practical uselessness, Percy nonetheless celebrates his education:

Perhaps a diluted course in Lenin and Marx with passages from *Mein Kampf* or a handbook on electricity and aviation would have better prepared a youngster for life as it is. But not, I think, for life as it should be. Old orders change, I know, and Mur knew, having herself lived through the death throes of one with all its wreckage of aspirations and possibilities, with bitterness to master and new hope to create. But new orders change too. Only one thing never changes—the human heart. Revolutions and ideologies may lacerate it, even break it, but they cannot change its essence. After Fascism and Communism and Capitalism and Socialism are over and forgotten as completely as slavery and the old South, that same headstrong human heart will be clamoring for the old things it wept for in Eden—love and a chance to be noble, laughter, and a chance to adore something, someone, somewhere. Mur and her books did not inform me, they formed me. (33–34)

This passage contains a number of features that recur throughout *Lanterns on the Levee:* a renunciation of instrumentalism and "practical" education, an emphasis on "life as it should be" (always antithetical to instrumentality), a perception of history as transitory and cyclical, and a valorization of the eternal verities that somehow mitigate history's dispossessing force. History is redeemed, then, when (and only when) it is viewed as *form* rather than *scene,* a dialectic fundamental to Percy's narrative negotiation. The essentially aesthetic vision of history (as pure form) is predicated on a stoical abstraction of history's cycles. When, however, Percy speaks, as he does in "A Side-Show Gotterdammerung," "not from a peak in eternity but from the ephemeral now," history appears as a monstrous, vulgar assault on tradition. Later in that same chapter, however, he returns to the cyclical form of history, suggesting that "in every age an aristocracy is dying and one is being born" (62), an idea he qualifies as "chilly comfort, however, to the living members of an aristocracy in the act of dying" (63). Percy's dialectic of history, then, mediates between action and abstraction, between role-playing and aesthetic contemplation. Although history in its abstract form is tolerable, it comes at the price of positive public action. Thus, the language of the charm, which wards off history's intolerable dispossession, is also the language of stasis since, in its tendency toward monumentalism (to borrow Richard King's useful label), it precludes goal-oriented behavior, which by definition is subject to instrumental critique.

As Percy's education takes shape, the division between subjective experience and the outside world becomes increasingly pronounced. At the conclusion of chapter 4, devoted to his maternal grandparents Mere and Pere, Percy asserts that "[t]he color of our temperament, our chief concern, is nothing of our making. . . . If we see the world through mauve glasses, there's no sort of sense in wishing they were white" (45). For Percy an aesthetic temperament has its compensations, since viewing the world through "mauve glasses" lends a "certain opalescence . . . denied the truer and cruder white noons of the desert" (45). At the same time, such a temperament lends itself to loneliness, exile, and a sense of futility. In a pattern Percy will later repeat, most of Percy's aesthetic mentors live apart from history and from the community. Pere, with his passion for opera, is a failure in farming and in "one business venture after another," and "his life petered out in a drab little country town" (37). Judge Griffin, Percy's early tutor who introduced him to Dante, Milton, and Shakespeare, "gained knowledge of every world but this one" and, as he grew older, "became poorer and retired farther from community life to his own family and his own thoughts" (81). Father Koestenbrock, Percy's religious mentor and a passionate admirer of Haydn, "stayed drunk in his room, alone, for weeks and weeks," eventually retiring, as "an old man and very tired," to "a home for superannuated priests, leaving his little church and us" (89, 90). The last chapter of this section, "The Return of the Native," is largely devoted to Percy's "favorite friend," Caroline Stern. "Miss Carrie," Percy writes, "had failed in everything—in painting, in poetry, in making money, in winning love, in dying easy. Yet she was one of the few successes I ever knew. I think I learned more from her of what the good life is and of how it may be lived than from almost anyone else" (139). The collective identity of Percy's aesthetic mentors is thus organized around tropes of withdrawal, privacy, beauty, materialistic failure, and "the good life"; Miss Carrie in particular epitomizes the theme of failure-as-success that permeates *Lanterns on the Levee* no less than it does Thoreau's *Walden* or *The Education of Henry Adams.*

Paul John Eakin has suggested that autobiography requires its subject to mediate between the experience of personal autonomy and "models of identity," or "example[s] of selfhood or character that a given culture offers for imitation."[7] Of the culture-specific models available to Percy, the aesthetic mentor represents but one option. The competing model is offered by his father LeRoy, who, although curiously absent from his son's formative years—Percy claims to have no memory at all of his parents during his first four years of life (26)—represents an absolute ideal against which the son

7. Paul John Eakin, *Touching the World: Reference in Autobiography* (Princeton: Princeton University Press, 1992), 72.

measures himself and invariably finds himself wanting. In contrast to the aesthetic mentor, LeRoy Percy is the public man of action; in one of his first appearances, he forbids Percy's Aunt Nana from reading to him *In Silken Chains*—"[t]he most moving book ever written"—substituting instead the more manly fare of *Ivanhoe* (56–57). Scott's novel, Percy relates, "produced unpredictable results . . . I, far from being inspired to knightly heroism, grew infatuated with the monastic life, if it could be pursued in a cave opening on a desert. . . . It was hard having such a dazzling father; no wonder I longed to be a hermit" (57). Percy's reaction to *Ivanhoe* is emblematic of his general reaction to his father; instead of imitating the hero's "knightly heroism," he withdraws to a private space.

In "A Small Boy's Heroes," Percy initiates the narrative tension between himself and his heroic role models that receives full-scale treatment in the third section of the text. Unlike that section, however, "A Small Boy's Heroes" is set in a private space, the front gallery of the Percy home on which LeRoy and his friends frequently met and drank mint juleps. Like Percy's aesthetic mentors, these men are categorically unwilling to engage in instrumental machinations. General Catchings, the local congressman, "could not kiss babies and considered it indecent to rhapsodize over the purity of Southern womanhood"; consequently, "he was always about not to be elected," a situation Percy analogically internalizes in "vaguely" realizing "that he was always about to be crucified by the people for serving them so devoutly" (67). As a group, these men

were leaders of the people, not elected or self-elected, but destined, under the compulsion of leadership because of their superior intellect, training, character, and opportunity. And the people were willing to be led by them because of their desperate need of leadership in those tragic times, because they recognized their fitness to lead, tested and proved in the series of revealing crises that only began with the war, and because they came from the class which traditionally had led in the South. Applause or aggrandizement played no part in their calculations. (69)

This hagiographic passage follows Percy's account of the historical role played by these men, who during Reconstruction had "stole[n] the ballot-boxes which, honestly counted, would have made every county official a Negro, [and] who had shaped the Constitution of 1890, which in effect and legally disenfranchised the Negro" (69). Although sparsely attended with authorial commentary, these actions (at the very least) diverge from an ideal course of ethical action. Discussing in a later chapter his grandfather's actions during that era, Percy describes the "vote-buying, the stuffing of ballot boxes, chicanery, [and] intimidation" as "[h]eart-breaking business and degrading, but in the end successful" (274). In both instances Percy comes perilously close to dismissing ethics altogether by arguing that the end justifies the means, a contradiction he resolves through recourse to the concept of role, which locates authority and destiny at the collective rather than the personal level. Rather than acting for applause or aggrandizement, these men act for the public good, even when—as is most often the case barring cultural emergencies—the public (in the antagonistic form of Demos) fails to authorize their leadership. "When they lost," Percy writes with no hint of irony, "it was a public loss" (70). Ethical action is thus enabled by the community; moreover, the ethical code of noblesse oblige hierarchically structures the community since these men are, by definition, the only ones ethical enough to act for the public good.

Community thus figures as both the cause and effect of aristocratic action; acting as its representative and in its name, the aristocrat secures the community's survival. This reciprocity is not, however, unproblematic, primarily because community is, in Roland Barthes's sense of the term, a myth. The structural Barthes of *Mythologies* defines myth as a second order semiological system in which the literal signified becomes the mythic signifier. To take Barthes's not irrelevant example, a picture of a black soldier saluting a French flag has a literal signified, or "meaning" ("a black soldier is giving the French salute"), that in turn signifies or invokes the mythic content ("that France is a great empire, that all her sons, without any color discrimination, faithfully serve under her flag"). According to Barthes, myth therefore "impoverishes" literal meaning, "distorts" it, although it does not "make it disappear" because the literal meaning supplies its "nourishment." In *Lanterns on the Levee* the literal, concrete community is similarly "emptied out" as it signifies the mythical community in relation to which aristocratic action assumes its final form. When action occurs within the literal community, there remains the opportunity for it to resist mythological signification, to refuse to transform contingency into an eternal and natural "state of things." More significant than the ubiquitous resistance offered by external-ized enemies (industrialism, the poor white) is aristocratic action that threatens to call attention to its status as pure contingency that does not permit itself to stand mythically for collective action. Because such action fails to accomplish what Barthes calls the "principle of myth"—"to trans-form history into Nature"—the organic community, in an almost literal sense, is called into question.[8]

One such action involves General Ferguson, a friend of LeRoy Percy who, despite being a "man of unimpeachable rectitude, of untarnished honor" (70), fled to South America after $20,000 in Levee Board funds had gone missing under his watch. Despite flatly contradicting Percy's represen-tation of aristocratic role, this episode is nevertheless rescued through nar-rative sleight-of-hand. Although he never admits that General Ferguson stole the money (and even goes so far as to suggest otherwise, implying that the missing funds were due to the General's lack of experience in account-ing, and pointing out that he had nothing to show for it), Percy absolves General Ferguson because he goes insane from guilt: "Going mad for honor's sake presupposes honor" (72). In breaking the code of southern honor, General Ferguson affirms the code by imposing upon himself its rig-orous penalty. However tenuous this ethical rationalization, "l'affaire Fergu-son" offers itself as a key episode in what we might call, with full cognizance of its dual meanings, the aristocratic plot. On the one hand, this plot ap-pears as a grand narrative, an enabling destiny that configures aristocratic action as collective action; on the other, it appears as a scheme, a way of achieving material ends by using collective action as an *alibi*. Because Percy's narrative contains numerous gaps between aristocratic action and collective action, the resulting *aporia* subvert the mythic community and the aristocratic role contingent upon it, and in so doing, generate a logical im-passe against which the narrating subject must contend.[9]

Nevertheless, the dominant narrative impetus of *Lanterns on the Levee* is

8. Roland Barthes, *Mythologies*, trans. Annette Lavers (New York: Hill and Wang, 1972), 114, 116, 118, 129.

9. For an informative discussion of the Ferguson affair, see William F. Holmes, "William Alexander Percy and the Bourbon Era in the Yazoo-Mississippi Delta," *Mississippi Quarterly* 26 (1972–73): 71–88. Although Percy configures the opponents of General Ferguson as enemies,

to preserve at least—and I shall argue, at *most*—the memory of the "pattern" that gave LeRoy Percy and his peers "strength and direction, that kept them oriented, that permitted them to be at once Puritans and Cavaliers" (74). It is the decline of this pattern, Percy writes, that has led to a "disintegration of that moral cohesion of the South which had given it its strength and its sons their singleness of purpose and simplicity" (74). The essential quality of this pattern lies in its ability to reconcile contradictions, an ability Percy associates with strength and power. On the one hand, the pattern dictates an absolute commitment to ethical propriety; on the other, it involves the ability to influence events in the public arena. "Anybody who was anybody," Percy writes, "must concern himself with good government, must fight, however feebly or ineffectually or hopelessly, for the public weal" (74). Yet participation in this public domain involves contact with a less-than-ideal world and a consequent muddying of hands—at least, that is, if public action is not undertaken (as is often the case, given Percy's narrative logic) with the tacit understanding that such action *will* be feeble, ineffectual, or hopeless. Percy's rhetoric of failure often invokes precisely this antithetical relationship between action and ethics in suggesting that the public performance of ideals will be, by definition, ineffectual, although (perceived as a form) aesthetically pleasing. As he writes in his Foreword, "It is better to watch the spread and pattern of the game that is past than engage feebly in the present play." At other times, however, and this is particularly true as he contemplates his father's heroic energy, Percy portrays his enervation as a failure to inherit those qualities that gave the South its moral cohesion. For Percy, failure thus comes in bifurcated form; on the one hand, it represents a principled refusal to succumb to the instrumental code of Demos, and on the other, it represents an inability to replicate his father's public heroism. Taking, therefore, ethics and activity as antinomies, we can schematize the social positions available in Percy's community according to the following Greimas rectangle:

Holmes interestingly shows that they differed little in political philosophy or social class. For a discussion of how the epic hero embodies his culture's destiny, see Georg Lukács, *The Theory of the Novel,* trans. Anna Bostock (Cambridge: MIT Press, 1990), 66–67. Barthes uses the analogy of the alibi to describe the distortive nature of mythical signification; see *Mythologies,* 115.

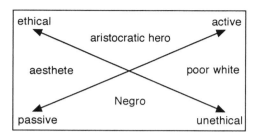

Whereas LeRoy Percy represents the ideal synthesis between ethics and activity—he exists in a cultural space in which, as Michael Kreyling says, "contingency never undermines the purity of action"[10]—the poor white, driven by illegitimate resentment, moves in a world of pure contingency. Forever enacting the alien forces of cultural chaos and ethical degeneration, he is out for what he can get. The Negro's passivity and ethical immaturity make him the white man's burden, although this space, as we shall see, represents both a threat and a solution to Percy's portrayal of an organic community. The space allotted to the aesthete, in whom value and passivity are conjoined, is the space Percy finally inhabits at the price of heroically performing the social role he inherits.

In the third section of *Lanterns on the Levee*, Will Percy leaves the private setting of the preceding chapters and lives in history. For Percy, history obtains meaning in relation to the community. Each of the three main historical events set in Mississippi—LeRoy Percy's defeat in the 1911 senatorial election, the Ku Klux Klan battle of 1922, and the Great Flood of 1927—constitute crises in which social order is disrupted and the ideal relationships between the three primary social groups are altered or at least threatened. Although we have seen that Percy represents history as an external encroachment upon the community, its ramifications are local and intimate.

If the dominant metaphor of the second section is education, then the dominant metaphor of the third is conflict. Yet, as I hope to show, the real

10. Michael Kreyling, *Figures of the Hero in Southern Narrative* (Baton Rouge: Louisiana State University Press, 1987), 155.

threat posed by history is not simply a threat to a way of life, but to the cultural logic that allows that way of life to sustain and justify itself. Nowhere does this anxiety manifest itself more than in Percy's relationship with his father. In his Freudian reading of *Lanterns on the Levee,* Richard King argues that "[f]or all the positive influence of his father, Will Percy was in some fundamental way unmanned by him." According to King, LeRoy acted as a psychological "block" who "overwhelmed" the younger Percy, who "could only obliquely register his protest" through telling silences and "extraordinary reticence." In *Figures of the Hero in Southern Narrative,* Michael Kreyling represents Percy as "the extraneous man, the hero crippled by recollections of an ideal order and an eminent father but impotent in realizing heroic actions and figures in his own life." In contrast, Fred Hobson sees the relationship as a less antagonistic one, suggesting that Percy's "idealization" of his father "was in many respects an idealization of what that [older] South had been." Although Hobson is correct in asserting that Percy celebrated "this ideal gentleman, and the old order over which he presided," the hagiographic style of this celebration conceals important contradictions, deferrals, and outright evasions, since in the end it is LeRoy Percy himself who threatens to unravel the aristocratic plot. When applied to LeRoy Percy and the role he represents, the ethical code through which Percy interprets social conflict fails to resolve the scandalous actions intrinsic to living in history. If, as Hobson suggests, noblesse oblige was no abstraction for Will Percy, as represented by his father it threatened to become one.[11]

Percy's configuration of history presumes that conflict exists because the ethically impoverished are unwilling to accept the leadership of the ethically gifted. This is especially true of the first two historical events Percy describes, the election of 1911 and the Klan battle of 1922, both of which pit LeRoy Percy as a representative aristocrat against the advances of the poor white. The first episode, recounted in a chapter suitably titled "The Bottom Rail on Top," is immediately preceded by a brief episode that subtly contextualizes the action that follows. In this episode Percy describes launching into a moral diatribe aimed at a married friend who had brought on an ex-

11. Richard King, *A Southern Renaissance: The Cultural Awakening of the American South, 1930–1955* (New York: Oxford University Press, 1980), 97, 98, 94; Kreyling, *Figures of the Hero,* 164; Hobson, *Tell about the South,* 284.

tramarital miscarriage, an act which he felt "merited social ostracism" (141).
When LeRoy demurs, it finally "dawned" on Percy that his father "knew all
about it and was not aghast" (141). "He knew," Percy continues, "that a narrow idealism at the start is bracing and formative" (142). The young Percy's
ethical rigor, we infer, is something rather effete in the real world, where a
"narrow idealism" is surely out of place. This ethical gray area, sanctioned
here by his father's "voice of experience," is conspicuously absent in Percy's
treatment of the election, where the absolute purity of his father's motives
stands in stark contrast to the ethical depravity of James K. Vardaman and
his ilk. But as Percy enters history, he demonstrates (if surreptitiously) a certain unease with his father's code that culminates in a more dramatic, if
equally oblique, fashion during the flood of 1927.

In the election episode as elsewhere, history is configured as an intrusion;
originating at a distance, only later do its local ramifications become clear.
Just as, later, reports of the Klan revival in Atlanta seem distant and trivial
(232), news that the sitting senator has died does not at first appear especially
significant. It is, for Percy, "a death that did not stir my pulse or suggest to
me consequences that might have any personal bearing on me or mine. It was
a turning point in my life" (143). According to his son, LeRoy Percy entered
the ensuing election simply to prevent Vardaman from gaining the majority
necessary to assume the vacant seat; only after the other anti-Vardaman candidates withdrew was LeRoy elected to serve out the remaining two years of
the term. Emphasizing his father's altruistic motives, Percy writes that he
"did not want to be senator from Mississippi, but he wanted to keep Vardaman from being" (144). In the next election, however, LeRoy Percy's in-
born sense of noblesse oblige proves to be no match for the Negro-baiting
demagoguery of Vardaman, the Great White Chief whose "qualifications
as a statesman," Percy wryly notes, were that he "stood for the poor white
against the 'nigger' " (144). Amidst false allegations of bribery, LeRoy Percy
encounters "the unanswerable charge . . . that he was a prosperous plantation-
owner, a corporation lawyer, and unmistakably a gentleman" (147).[12]

---

12. For an interesting discussion of the election, see Bertram Wyatt-Brown, *The House of
Percy: Honor, Melancholy, and Imagination in a Southern Family* (New York: Oxford University
Press, 1994), 178–91.

Such was the noisome situation in which Father found himself mired and out of which he must fight his way with only integrity, courage, and intelligence for his weapons. A different assortment was needed—those count only in a world of honor. But the world in which he used them was not a world of honor; it was a new-born, golden age of demagoguery, the age of rabble-rousers and fire-eaters, of Jeff Davis and Tillman and Bleese and Heflin, of proletarian representatives of the proletariat. (148)

Percy is categorically unwilling to consider the class perspective of the poor white, who, as C. Vann Woodward showed many years ago, had good reason to reject Bourbon political leadership. But for Percy, the poor white does not have a *claim;* he has a *nature:* it is *characteristic of him* to reject instinctively integrity, courage, intelligence, and legitimate leadership. Under such circumstances, defeat signifies virtue.

The poor white serves as an equally perfect antagonist in the Klan battle of 1922. There are, however, two important differences from the senatorial election. First, the scene is not Mississippi as a whole, but Greenville, Percy's own community. As Hobson notes, this change of scene follows Marcus Aurelius in its emphasis on individual action in a restricted arena, an emphasis made explicit in a letter of LeRoy Percy's included in *Lanterns on the Levee.*[13] Writing to a supporter after his defeat, LeRoy Percy affirmed that "[i]f I can keep this small corner of the United States in which I reside, comparatively clean and decent in politics and fit for a man to live in, and in such condition that he may not be ashamed to pass it on to his children, I will have accomplished all that I hope to do" (152). The community thus forms the final contested domain of *Lanterns on the Levee,* with the important consequence that the antagonist assumes the form not of the faceless poor white mob and its demagogic manipulators, but the townsfolk among whom Percy had been raised. "White folks and colored folks," Percy writes of Greenville prior to the Klan episode, "that's what we were—and some of us were nice and some weren't" (231). Percy describes Greenville as a community more willing than most to live and let live; a "certain laxity in church matters" leads the town to regard "drunkenness and lechery, Sab-

---

13. Hobson, *Tell about the South,* 280.

bath-breaking and gambling" as little more than "poor judgment or poor taste" (231). Ethical transgression is thus largely ignored within the private network of communal relationships, which presumes at least a tacit acceptance of collective norms. Yet within this pastoral scene, there are signs of trouble: "My townsfolk had got along pretty well together—we knew each other so well and had suffered so much together. But we hadn't suffered a common disaster, one that was local and our very own, like a flood or a yellow-fever epidemic, since the flood of 1913, and that had failed as a binder because it didn't flood the town" (230). More ominous is the arrival of an "alien breed of Anglo-Saxon" who "had drifted in since the war—from the hills, from the North, from all sorts of odd places where they hadn't been wanted" (230). This relatively disembodied threat to the community arrives in the physical form of one "Colonel" Camp, a Klan organizer who comes to speak at the local courthouse. Through sheer rhetorical force, LeRoy Percy drives the man from the podium with his own speech denouncing the Klan. Herein lies the second difference between this episode and the 1911 election: in both this scene and the later climactic election of an anti-Klan sheriff, the forces of ethical degradation are defeated.

Despite these differences, Percy's ethical reading remains consistent. In both episodes Percy configures historical action as ethical action, and in both cases the ethical norms through which those actions are interpreted are not seriously questioned. This is precisely the sense in which we can say the poor white is a perfect antagonist: he exerts little pressure against the stability of Percy's mythical community and the legitimacy of the social relationships presumed to exist therein. Thus, while history may come in the form of an impersonal assault upon tradition, it is an assault easily explained through recourse to ethical criteria: History is alien because it does not recognize ethics; the poor white is a threat because he is unethical. Nevertheless, the poor white represents a different kind of threat within the community than he does outside the communal boundary. In that external domain class relationships are intrinsically antagonistic, and as a consequence, no bulwark avails against the onslaught of history. Socialized space is nonexistent; rational discourse is impossible. Conversely, the community appears as a socialized space in which rational discourse is possible, a contrast made apparent in the public speaking scenes represented in the two episodes. During what Percy calls the "worst day" of the election campaign, LeRoy Percy gives a speech at Lauderdale Springs: "When Father rose to speak he was greeted with a roar of boos, catcalls, hisses, and cries of 'Vardaman! Vardaman!' It was impossible to hear a word he might say. The din was insane and intolerable, and it showed no sign of diminishing. Obviously the crowd was determined to make it impossible for him to speak at all" (150). Finally, LeRoy Percy "cowed them by sheer will-power and lashed them into silence by leaping invective" (150). In contrast, Colonel Camp's speech "was listened to with courtesy," although "any trained mind" could recognize its "lies" (233); thus, manners and rational judgment replace the "obscene pandemonium" of the Lauderdale Springs mob (150). As the chosen representative of "[o]ur best citizens, those who thought for the public good" (232), LeRoy Percy is able to defeat the outmatched Klan organizer, who, ironically, is escorted in defeat to his hotel by a Catholic deputy (233). If conflict is the primary operator in the public domain of history, we can see that while the Klan organizers and the alien breed of Anglo-Saxons bring history to the borders of the community, LeRoy Percy is able to defend those borders from the encroachment of history. The community thus survives because of the ideal relationship between it and its heroes.

Or so Percy would have it. In fact, two questionable premises underlie Percy's representation of the Klan episode. First, Percy's displacement of culpability onto the alien breed of Anglo-Saxons drifting in from the hills is contradicted by his emphasis on the communal suspicion engendered by the episode. "The most poisonous thing the Klan did to our town," he writes, "was to rob its citizens of their faith and trust in one another. Everyone was under suspicion: from Klansmen you can expect neither frankness nor truth nor honor, and you couldn't tell who was a Klansman" (237). Indeed, Percy relates that the Klan "had its genesis, as far as our community was involved, in the Masonic Temple" (234), hardly a gathering ground for poor whites. Percy's displacement of culpability is significant because it allows him to locate blame external to the community; to admit otherwise would be to admit the impossibility of resolving "the Delta problem." More importantly, the very concept of role—which we have said is grounded in a collective narrative or "plot"—would be internally subverted; already rejected by the outside world, LeRoy Percy and the role he epitomizes would have no communal ground upon which to support itself. This is precisely why "the whole town" (244) must gather to celebrate after the anti-Klan candidate for sheriff is narrowly elected. Only by strategically attenuating the community in this manner—by redrawing the communal boundary, if you will—is Percy able to configure aristocratic action as collective action. The second questionable premise involves the motivation behind LeRoy Percy's battle with the Klan. One would never know from reading *Lanterns on the Levee* that LeRoy Percy and his peers had a very material reason for wanting to keep the Klan out of Greenville. As Bertram Wyatt-Brown has shown, what he feared, and what formed the basis of his speech answering Captain Camp, was that Klan activity would cause the dispersal of the local black population, which provided the primary source of labor for the planter class. Pointing to an already serious "lack of labor," LeRoy Percy predicted that should the Klan gain a foothold, grass would soon be "growing in the streets of Greenville."[14]

In contrast to both episodes that center around the poor white, the 1927 flood episode does not permit Percy either to attenuate his community strategically or to ignore the instrumental motives of the aristocrat. Consequently, the flood episode represents a narrative crisis—especially so given that LeRoy Percy, the epitome of noblesse oblige, fails to conform to the aristocratic ethical ideal.[15] Immediately following the deluge, Will Percy was named chairman of the Flood Relief Committee, and after consulting the other committee members, decided to evacuate the Negroes who were at that time being sheltered on the levee. A group of planters, however, fearing that they would emigrate to the North, argued that they should remain where they were:

I was bursting with fury when Father overtook me on the levee. I explained the situation and he agreed I should not, of course, be intimidated by what the planters said, but he suggested that if we depopulated the Delta of its labor, we should be doing it a grave disservice. I insisted that I would not be bullied by a few blockhead planters into doing something I knew to be wrong—they were thinking of their pocketbooks; I of the Negro's welfare. (257)

14. LeRoy Percy qtd. in Wyatt-Brown, *House of Percy,* 230.

15. For interpretations of the flood episode that center around the latent antagonism between father and son, see King, *Southern Renaissance,* 94–95; and Kreyling, *Figures of the Hero,* 162–64.

Consulting the committee for a final time, Percy was astonished to learn that despite their previous support, to a man they now agreed that the Negroes should remain where they were. After his father's death, Percy learned that he had visited each of the committee members individually and convinced them that the Negroes should not be moved: LeRoy Percy "had accomplished his end in the one way possible and had sworn the committee to secrecy" (258). Despite Percy's attempt to downplay it, this incident forms the central *aporia* in the narrative because Percy weakly attempts to revoke a meaning he has already provided. When his father first attempts to change his mind, Percy explicitly deciphers the myth of Negro labor, the preservation of which is not, as his father has it, for the "good of the Delta," but for the good of the planters' pocketbooks. Yet, a page later, Percy attempts to restore his father's meanings: "He knew that the dispersal of our labor was a longer evil to the Delta than a flood. He was a natural gambler: he bet on warm weather and tents" (258). Two striking equivocations are apparent in this passage: First, "the Negro's welfare" has vanished utterly as a consideration, and second, when one bets in earnest, one stands to lose something.

Faced with a flat ethical contradiction, Percy shifts his narrative focus, as he typically does in the absence of black consent, to the Negro's reversion to type. The Negro community, inflamed by anti-Percy editorials in the *Chicago Defender* (which "climaxed an eloquent editorial by observing that until the South rid itself of William Alexander Percys it would be no fit place for a Negro to live" [263–64]), refused to unload the Red Cross boats that carried their food supplies. When, as a last resort, Percy consented to allow the police to round up a work crew, a Negro man refused to come and was shot. To quell an incipient uprising, Percy confronted the Negro community, "the surliest, most hostile group I ever faced" (266), from a church pulpit. Having learned a lesson from his father's election, Percy recognizes that consensual, socialized space is unavailable: "I knew there was no chance here to appeal to reason. Retreat was out of the question. Attack was imperative" (267). Although Percy's powerful rhetoric forces his audience to their knees in prayer, he gets only four volunteers to help unload the supplies. This scene is instructive because racial resentment is directed not at LeRoy Percy, but at his son, who has little difficulty in defending his own motives. Yet, because of his father's actions, the Negroes' resentment is, according to

Percy's own logic, at least partially *legitimate*. In his speech to the Negro community, for example, Percy hotly asserts that "[Every white man] served you with our money and our brains and our strength and, for all that we did, no one of us received one penny" (267), conveniently repressing the fact that, whatever his own motives, the material considerations of the planter class, his father among them, largely determined the white community's actions. While Percy was willing to denounce privately those landowners who "were guilty of acts which profoundly and justly made the negroes fear them," publicly he must *stand* for his father—ethically as well as physically—substituting his own intentions for his father's instrumental machinations.[16]

More than any other, the flood episode threatens to reveal the extent to which community constitutes an instrumental field, a means toward achieving the ends of the aristocrat. This is especially troubling because LeRoy Percy, the epitome of noblesse oblige, subverts his son's conception of aristocratic role, which need not require collective consent so long as it is collectively motivated. In placing the good of his pocketbook above the Negroes' welfare—and to reiterate, these are the meanings assigned by Will Percy himself—LeRoy Percy violated this absolute rule, thus calling into question three premises that fundamentally inform *Lanterns on the Levee*: that "the Delta" is based on culture rather than capital; that the role epitomized by LeRoy Percy is an unconscious manifestation of noblesse oblige rather than an alibi for instrumental, self-serving action; and that the community is consensual and collective rather than coercive and class-centered.

That the respective failures of the levee and of LeRoy Percy coincide is no mere coincidence, since Percy tacitly associates levee and aristocrat throughout his narrative. He begins "Hell and High Water," the chapter that immediately precedes the flood episode, by reprinting an 1893 Greenville *Democrat* notice equating a man's willingness to guard the levee with "those characteristics which would prove your patriotism in a time when your country is threatened" (242). He goes on to describe the levee guards of an older generation, men whom he idolized and whose personal achievements never interfered with their willingness to defend the community, a

16. Percy qtd. in Wyatt-Brown, *House of Percy*, 243.

duty that here is demonstrably collective in purpose. In short, the levee provides the ideal scene for the aristocrat to act out his role. "If you won't volunteer for that duty, " Percy writes, "you should return to the hills from
which obviously you came" (247). Carolyn Holdsworth has usefully suggested that the levee is equated metaphorically with a tradition that controls
"not just general nature but human nature" (38). As part of what George
Lakoff and Mark Johnson call an experiential gestalt whose rough form can
be stated as "the levee is an aristocrat," the levee marks a boundary between
the community and the alien threat to community, whether it be "nature" or
"human nature"; moreover, it constitutes a bulwark against that threat. The
complex of meanings associated with the levee thus includes both a prescriptive and a descriptive component: the levee *defends* against what is outside—that is, against what it *defines* as the alien antagonist. In turn, each
component roughly corresponds to a specific feature of Percy's representation of the aristocrat: the descriptive component corresponds to the ethics
that separate the aristocrat from the "alien breed of Anglo-Saxon," while the
prescriptive component corresponds to the aristocrat's duty or role to defend the community against that alien threat.[17]

That the ethical "boundary" associated with the levee collapses in the
flood episode is only too clear. But perhaps more importantly, Percy must
contend with the Negro's resistance to the category of "enemy." Although
his rhetorical attack on the Negro community from the church pulpit briefly
casts the Negro in this role, this is a strictly provisional stance that Percy
does not sustain. Unlike the poor white, whose illegitimate resentment allows Percy to exile him from the community as a hostile force, the Negro is
intimately bound within the community's network of social relationships.
As such, he is a figure against whom heroism cannot be brought to bear. The
ethical anxiety that accrues around the relationship between aristocrat and
Negro does not, however, necessitate that Percy overtly reject what his father represents; on the contrary, LeRoy Percy becomes an even more mythical figure as the narrative progresses. Percy's ethical anxiety is largely

17. Carolyn Holdsworth, "The Gorgon's Head and the Mirror: Fact versus Metaphor in
Lanterns on the Levee," Southern Literary Journal 14, no. 1 (1981): 38; George Lakoff and Mark
Johnson, *Metaphors We Live By* (Chicago: University of Chicago Press, 1980), 77–82. For an-
other view of the levee's metaphorical connotations, see Rocks, "Art," 821.

betrayed by the form of his work. In contrast to the narratively configured chapters leading up to and containing the flood episode, the chapters that follow appear more as essays than stories, and are marked by a near absence of narrative occurring in historical time. Although this shift allows a tenuous private recuperation of race relations, which have, as we have seen, broken down on a public or collective level, this recovery comes at a price: as Percy's voice becomes more purely subjective, it threatens to lose contact with the outside world. Percy's loss of what I call a narrative relationship with the community, evidenced by his radical division of public and private selves, indicates the difficulty of subjectively sustaining the concept of aristocratic role and the cultural narrative that emplots it. I am arguing, then, that Percy's failure of inheritance—his inability to imitate his father's ideal synthesis of virtue and activity—is driven not so much by personal weakness as an inability to naturalize the contradictions of racial paternalism and the aristocratic plot. For Percy this plot cannot be lived in, because to do so would be to assume its ethical contradictions and forfeit the aesthetic perspective necessary to maintain its formal coherence. In aesthetically objectifying the pattern embodied in his father, Percy no less than his contemporaries Lillian Smith and Katharine Du Pre Lumpkin suggests the difficulty of sustaining social contradictions at the level of selfhood.[18]

At the conclusion of Robert Penn Warren's *All the King's Men*—another work that deals with the crisis of inheriting aristocratic role—Jack Burden says that he "shall go out of the house and go into the convulsion of the world, out of history into history and the awful responsibility of Time."[19]

18. Both Smith in *Killers of the Dream* (New York: Anchor Books, 1963) and Lumpkin in *The Making of a Southerner* (New York: Alfred A. Knopf, 1947) represent the moral autonomy of selfhood as being antithetical to public racist ideology. Both works share the form of the conversion narrative, which can be mapped as a three-stage process: (1) the passive inheritance of racist ideology (2) the cognitive dissonance resulting from moral contradictions and contact with African Americans who fail to act "according to form," and (3) conversion, which involves the public renunciation of racial taboos. But where Smith and Lumpkin *convert*, Percy sublimates; see especially his discussion of miscegenation, a topic he defines as being unavailable to conceptual scrutiny (307–308).

19. Robert Penn Warren, *All the King's Men* (1946; reprint, New York: Harcourt Brace, 1984), 438.

Will Percy moves in the opposite direction: out of the untenable space of history into the timeless space of the garden. To understand the complexity of the garden metaphor, we must first consider Percy's essentially dualistic portrayal of community as an entity comprised of both a synchronic and a diachronic dimension, a "culture" and a "history." Early in his work Percy compares the South's "dreadful" Confederate monuments, which he fears a future anthropologist would "tragically and comically" take as "relics of and clues to the vanished civilization we call ours," to southern cookery, a "memorial," he asserts, that "would be more informative" (12). Implicit here is a hierarchy in which Percy privileges the rich symbolic texture of the lifeworld over his culture's grand historical narrative as the true measure of the South. Although the lifeworld largely supersedes history as the scene of the latter part of *Lanterns on the Levee,* the relationship between the two is far from oppositional, since the grand narrative permits the survival of the lifeworld, which in turn justifies (as the enabling term) the heroic action undertaken in its name. The hero, then, enables the historical articulation of the lifeworld. To take but one example of this ideal synthesis, Percy frames his apotheosis of the aristocratic hero in "A Small Boy's Heroes" with a tribute to the mint julep, a symbol that metonymically invokes a wide range of values, feelings, and relationships broadly associated with a way of life. Similarly, in Percy's homage to southern cooking, batter bread is not just batter bread: it is the concrete form of a lifeworld that might otherwise be irreducible to observation.

For Percy, the texture of community extends to social relationships, especially the bond between the aristocrat and the Negro, of which, he continually frets, the outside world receives a distorted view. In a letter to the *New Republic* reproduced in the Klan episode, Percy affirms that only the South's "unadvertised leaders of thought" can establish racial harmony (228). Not a matter for northern "criticism, suggested panaceas, [or] scorn," the race problem is an issue to be privately settled among southerners with "common kindness" as a guiding principle (229). In short, the race problem is a community issue whose solution is already grounded, if not yet brought to fruition, in the concrete social intercourse that occurs every day between white and black southerners. As Richard Weaver shows in *The Southern Tradition at Bay* and as Percy himself attests, this attitude represents the essence of southern conservatism.[20] But as Percy attempts to deploy this rationale in his discussion of race relations, the fissures in interracial consensus and social manners that first appear in the flood episode refuse to be mended.

Percy opens "Planters, Sharecroppers, and Such," the chapter that immediately follows the flood episode, by recounting the death of his parents, after which, he asserts, "my life seemed superfluous" (270). Nor does LeRoy Percy's death affect only his son. Acting as that central figure in southern racial discourse, the faithful retainer, an ex-slave named Holt guides Will Percy to his father's chair where, Holt affirms, "you b'long" (270). Distraught, Holt cries out, "the roof is gone from over my head and floor from under my feet. I am out in the dark and the cold alone. I want to go where he is" (270). Although Holt's grief mythically invokes the Negro's devotion, the aristocrat's seat he offers the younger Percy represents but another possession of the father that the son cannot inherit: an interracial relationship in which the Negro's labor mythically resolves itself into an organic bond between himself and the aristocrat. As King has suggested, Percy's subtitle—"Recollections of a Planter's Son"—represents not so much a fact as a narrative choice, since, literally speaking, Percy was every bit the planter his father was.[21] Yet Percy locates in the past a utopian view of race relations that does not exist, as we shall see, on his plantation. Whereas LeRoy Percy's Negroes are loyal and faithful retainers, his son confronts a world in which Negroes who "used to be servants, now . . . were problems" (312).

The tenuous nature of the paternalistic bond manifests itself most clearly in relation to Negro labor, the preservation of which, we recall, had driven LeRoy Percy's actions during the Great Flood. Attempting to preserve an ideal configuration of race relations and the economic form they assume,

20. For Weaver on the South's cultural preference for "a tested *modus vivendi*" over "the most attractive experiment," see *The Southern Tradition at Bay: A History of Postbellum Thought*, ed. George Core and M. E. Bradford (New Rochelle, N.Y.: Arlington House, 1968), 42. Compare Percy: "In the South our anxiety is not to find new ideas, but to bring to realization old ones which have been tested and proved by years of anguish—a far more difficult undertaking. We Southerners aren't as bright as we are right. But when we do hit on a new idea, it's not only wrong, it's inconceivable" (229).

21. King, *Southern Renaissance*, 94.

Percy recasts labor as an essentially social relationship. In his discussion of sharecropping, Percy represents the genesis of the institution as a family story involving his grandfather Fafar, whose life work was the restoration of white supremacy during Reconstruction. Although Fafar's participation in the southern grand narrative necessitated an initially antagonistic relationship with the Negro, after the "first fine frenzy of emancipation," he and the Negro come to a tacit understanding: "On ex-slave and ex-master alike it dawned gradually that they were in great need of one another—and not only economically, but, curiously enough, emotionally" (275). From this mutual need results the sharecropping system or "partnership contract" (as Percy prefers), a contract he presents as a verbal offer Fafar extends to the freedmen: "I have land which you need, and you have muscle which I need; let's put what we've got in the same pot and call it ours" (275). Although he admits that this fully socialized form of labor can survive only when land owners conceive of property as a trust rather than an opportunity for profit—a conception which entails strict adherence to the code of noblesse oblige—Percy sees this "one drawback" as a failure not of the system, but of a failure to "liv[e] up to the contractual obligations of the system" (283, 82). Although Richard King has faulted Percy for "opinions [on sharecropping] which jar our more enlightened sensibilities,"[22] the real scandal of this chapter occurs as Percy widens his focus to consider the entire history of his culture. In one of the few passages in which Percy implies continuity between himself and his forebears, he lists the obstacles that "had to be overcome before ever this poor beautiful unfinished present was turned over to us by the anonymous dead" (284). Beginning with the concrete fact of malaria, this list concludes with Percy lamenting "the pathos of a stronger race carrying on its shoulders a weaker race and from the burden losing its own strength!" (284). Moving beyond a legitimation of Negro labor, Percy implies that the authentic labor is expended by the aristocrat, whose "burden" causes the cumulative loss of cultural energy that constitutes, as we have said, one of the primary narrative problems to be solved.

For Percy, the Negro is a burden primarily because his refusal to accept

22. Ibid., 88. Percy admits that the Negro's redress for exploitative practices is "merely theoretical," a concession that evades sheer contradiction only if "contractual obligations" are considered to be social and thus extralegal.

paternalistic benevolence threatens Percy's perception of a cohesive, organic community. Percy configures race relations so that the Negro resists not merely his place in the social hierarchy, but the philanthropic intentions of the aristocrat. Percy's attempt to emplot the Negro within a communal narrative fails outright, primarily because he and the Negro interpret their mutual relationship in radically different ways, as evidenced by two important scenes in which Negroes actively voice their resentment. In the first, Percy relates how Ford, his "general factotum," informs him that a friend had claimed that Percy "went to Africa to 'range to have the niggers sent back into slavery," a sentiment Ford buttresses by claiming to have heard it "lots of times" (289). Stunned and hurt by the accusation, Percy demands the identity of another accuser. When Ford returns the next morning with the name of Percy's cook, "the mainstay and intimate of the household for fifteen years" (290), Percy enters the kitchen to confront her, only to find her pacing under a nail she had stepped on and hung under a door lintel. This ritual, she explains, will draw the soreness from her foot. Percy wryly concludes, "I didn't mention slavery then or later" (290). Instead of adjudicating what he perceives to be a case of miscommunication, Percy aestheticizes it; what originally had "hurt" now provides aesthetic—in this case, comic— pleasure. As in the flood episode, Percy responds to the absence of black consent by shifting his focus from racial *resentment* to racial *characteristics,* and in so doing uses the grounds of division as an alibi for the absence of unity. Complaints from people *of this kind,* he implies, need not be taken seriously.

In a second and more telling scene, Percy describes visiting his plantation and overhearing a Negro say of his car, "Dat's *us* car" (291). Musing on the "thought of how sweet it was to have the relation between landlord and tenant so close and affectionate that to them my car was their car," Percy is disabused of this notion by Ford, who informs him that the speaker "meant that's the car *you* has bought with *us* money" (291). This stark assertion of resentment, based as it is on the Negro's perception of his instrumental value to the landowner, does much to subvert the social "partnership" Percy affirms in his chapter on sharecropping. Yet if Percy does not confront this contradiction directly, he at least registers it, and after having Ford's interpretation confirmed by the plantation's managers, he registers his hurt. Indeed, this scene represents the climax of private racial tension just as fully as public racial tension culminates in the flood episode. Unlike that episode, however, and unlike all episodes involving the poor white, resentment does not generate more resentment; Percy's reaction to Ford's "bitter tutelage" is pain. Insofar as social division is marked, as Jameson suggests, by the "unavoidably autoreferential" nature of resentment that begets further resentment,[23] Percy's inability to classify the Negro as an enemy—that is, to exile him from the community as he does with the poor white—makes this conflict particularly troubling. Whereas the external domain of history requires conflict as a precondition for aristocratic heroism, conflict within the life-world disrupts the reciprocal exchanges through which the social order is verified and stabilized. In voicing his resentment, the Negro threatens to obliterate the objective social world in which Percy's identity finds meaningful form.

Percy's solution to the problem of community is not the evocation of a shared ethos, but of a social style through which ethical difference is mitigated. "[W]hile good morals are all important between the Lord and His creatures," he writes, "what counts between one creature and another is good manners" (286). Manners thus verify the coherence of community in spite of difference, which Percy, as a rule, defines when necessary, and defers when possible. Yet to maintain hierarchy—that is, the simultaneity of unity and division—Percy must mediate between an aesthetic stance that allows the perception of pastoral unity, and an ethical one that emphasizes social difference. As stated earlier, the Negro's aesthetic charm mitigates his ethical shortcomings, and as a consequence Percy is able to assert that his "beautiful manners," imitated by whites, make it possible for "two such dissimilar races [to] live side by side with so little friction, in such comparative peace and amity" (286). Yet at the same time, he is quick to invoke ethical failures of one sort or another—an aptitude for violent crime, a propensity for theft, a rejection of the white man's morality—as the primary obstacles blocking the Negro's social evolution. "How is it possible," he asks, "for the white man to communicate with people of this sort?" (299). Percy goes so far as to say that despite both races' belief that "they have an innate and miraculous un-

23. Jameson, *Political Unconscious*, 202.

derstanding of one another. . . . the sober fact is we understand one another not at all" (299). Although this assertion undermines the concrete evocation of the paternalistic bond—how, for example, could "people of this sort" rationally enter into the "partnership contract" of sharecropping?—it also blunts the concrete fact of racial resentment, since Percy can now represent his philanthropic intentions as being *misunderstood:* "I want with all my heart to help him. But . . . " (306). Percy is thus forced into a conceptual double bind: If the racial other is utterly alien, then the relationship and the manners through which it is maintained reveal themselves to be pleasant fictions; if this relationship is real, then the speech of either party must be taken seriously. Percy's refusal of the strong form of paternalistic rhetoric—captured memorably in Richard Wright's assertion that "The white South said that it knew 'niggers' "[24]—represents not a solution to, but a deferral of the Negro's resentment lest it flatly contradict the cohesive social order of which he is ostensibly a part.

Percy's inability to adjudicate conceptually the dilemma of race relations helps explain why one of his proposed titles for his narrative was *A Stranger Here Myself,* a title that suggests the attenuation of selfhood and alienation from community that occurs as the resistant social world drives the self inward. In an important essay on race and southern autobiography, William L. Andrews suggests that Percy leaves open-ended the issue of whether he "confronted his selfhood through the agency of the [racial] other." I contend that the form of *Lanterns on the Levee* allows us to answer this question in the negative—that the "bitter tutelage" offered by Ford is an education Percy cannot afford to receive. In *Theory of the Novel* Georg Lukács argues that the "autonomous life of interiority is possible and necessary only when the distinctions between men have made an unbridgeable chasm," the corollary of which is that "the world of deeds separates itself from men and, because of this independence, becomes hollow and incapable of absorbing the true meaning of deed in itself, incapable of becoming a symbol through deeds and dissolving them in turn into symbols." Lukács's description of

24. Richard Wright, *Black Boy: A Record of Childhood and Youth* (1945; reprint, Cleveland: World Publishing, 1947), 227.

"estrangement from the outside world" captures precisely Percy's representation of his selfhood even as it dictates the solution he adopts: the valorization of pure intention, of virtue as "an end in itself" (313).[25]

Although at several points Percy implies that virtue and action are mutually exclusive—he claims, for example, that virtues "are good even if they kill you" (313), with the clear implication that they probably will—he nevertheless conceptually coins a term through which this antinomy is putatively resolved: the "survival virtues" such as "hardihood and discipline," which "are not ornaments but weapons" (312). The need for "survival virtues" in Percy's narrative will no doubt be clear: they are the virtues that categorically subsume the pseudo-ethics of his father and the grand narrative sanctioning them, and that create the cultural space in which, as Kreyling says, contingency never undermines the purity of action. We have said that this space remains forever unavailable to Percy as a subjective ground or field; nevertheless, it constitutes an essential object within that field because it allows the perception of the ideal relationship between the role-playing aristocrat and the community.

This pattern of identity, however, must be objectified *qua* pattern; forever lost, it cannot be "acted out" from within. The question of why this "line of fortification" remains unavailable brings us to the heart of Percy's narrative project. According to Lukács the subject can only avoid succumbing to "moods"—defined as the despair resulting from the conceptualization of hostile and immutable laws "beyond the reach of man"—if the "arena of its actions, the normative object of its actions, is made of the stuff of pure ethics: if right and custom are identical with morality: if no more of the soul has to be put into the man-made structures to make them serve as man's proper sphere of action than can be released, by action, from those structures." According to Lukács, then, the organic community is lost when its social forms absorb more subjective energy than they reciprocate. This condition not being met, the scene is set for the despair and reification of hostile external forces that characterize Percy's stoic meditations. Yet Percy's

25. William L. Andrews, "In Search of a Common Identity: The Self and the South in Four Mississippi Autobiographies," *Southern Review* 24 (1988): 51, 54; Lukács, *Theory*, 66.

attempt to attenuate strategically the community so that all "enemies" lie outside its boundaries—a strategy we have associated with the levee—does not attend to the problem of race. If, as he has observed earlier, the greatest amount of subjective energy is lost in the arena of race relations, where philanthropic or paternal intention is repeatedly thwarted by the Negro's ethical immaturity, the reification of external forces (the "enemy") appears as a displacement, since the Negro, who resists categorization as an enemy, represents the primary obstacle resisting subjective intention. Moreover, the flood episode demonstrates that race relations provide the arena in which the ethical ground of the aristocrat is most tangibly eroded and in which the organic community most threatens to reveal itself as an instrumental field driven by economic necessity. If Tobin Siebers is correct in asserting that "aesthetic pleasure serves to put ethical dissatisfaction into a form that can be swallowed," we can conclude that the contradictions inherent in race relations drive the massive code switch from ethics to aesthetics that occurs in the last three chapters of *Lanterns on the Levee*. This switch allows us to reinterpret Percy's rhetoric of failure as, more properly, a rhetoric of exhaustion—exhaustion resulting not from fighting the good fight so much as needing to withdraw from the conflict so that its ethical contours can be preserved. By displacing ethical degradation beyond the communal boundary and aestheticizing the ideal relationship between the aristocrat and his community, Percy need not inherit the ethical contradictions that manifest themselves within the lifeworld.[26]

In the last three chapters of *Lanterns on the Levee*, Percy's narrative style itself seems to succumb to exhaustion. Percy's inability to internalize and naturalize the contradictions inherent in the concept of "survival values" parallels the breakdown of narrative structure, which we might define in this context as a way of emplotting the self within the lifeworld. Unable to live for the community as its hero, Percy finds it increasingly difficult to live in his community as a citizen. This breakdown is evidenced most clearly in "A Bit of a Diary." Although the diary entries that form the bulk of the chap-

---

26. Lukács, *Theory*, 65; Tobin Siebers, "Ethics ad Nauseam," *American Literary History* 6 (1994): 762.

ter show Percy as the social man *par excellence*—hosting visitors, attending committee meetings, offering advice to friends and strangers, collecting for charities, advising the press and the police force, even attending a Rotary luncheon—he nevertheless dismisses the exercise as "inconsequential and daft" (322). In closing the chapter, Percy indicates the symbolic vacuity of his actions in writing that "the more [facts] you set down, the less progress you seem to make toward a likeness" (331). "This bit of a diary," he continues, "if continued indefinitely, would not help my guardian angel to recognize me if he met me coming down the middle of a big road" (331). Percy's estrangement from the community could hardly be clearer. In reducing social intercourse to the status of facts, he implies that because it no longer contains subjective energy, the community no longer provides a meaningful field of action; the authentic self, finally, is extrasocial. To catch the likeness of this "queer creature" (as he calls himself), Percy will have to "ease up on him unbeknownst—say when he is sitting in the garden idly" (331). The diary form underscores the absence of a narrative relationship with the community: The disjointed "facts" of his existence come as mere sequence; they form no part of a larger story.

The loss of the concrete social world as a domain that *contains* identity nevertheless dictates its own solution: the perception of the lifeworld as an aestheticized object rather than a field for ethical action. In the context of Percy's final logic, aesthetic experience itself allows the perception of community. "It is given man to behold beauty and to worship nobility," he writes, "[o]nly when he is in their presence does the air taste native and the place seem home" (320). Although this aesthetic imperative might appear as a transcendent withdrawal from society, it nevertheless has clear social content. In "Jackdaw in the Garden," Percy perceives character types as natural facts: acid-loving azaleas explain to him a woman who "needed tragedy and couldn't thrive without it"; hybrid strains that cannot resist disease warn him of the dangers of "crossing" human beings and "fusing" bloods; plants dislocated from their proper environment remind him that "the heart too has its climate"; hardy roses that are "not too beautiful" teach him that "[a]fter all, strength is one of the primary colors" (333). "But the major moral afforded by a garden," Percy writes, "comes from watching the fight for sunlight waged by those unhappy things rooted against their will in shade. None of them will flower, but by desperate devices, tragic substitutes, some of them will live" (334). Although Carolyn Holdsworth criticizes these "hackneyed comparisons,"[27] they represent a tenuous solution to the chaos that threatens Percy's community. Through this symbolic reduction, community becomes, not the context, but the content—not the container of identity, but the thing contained within subjective perception. In short, Percy's garden metaphor involves the subjective imposition of a stable order on experience otherwise irreducible to that order. The garden thus reveals itself as a narrowed version of the plantation—that is, as a scene congenial to pure contemplation of a sort impossible in the concrete, resistant world of social intercourse.

By objectifying character types and reducing them to a collection of innate characteristics, Percy is able to restore aesthetically the reified fragments of his community, just as broken bits of glass might be combined in a mosaic. Indeed, this is a particularly apt metaphor for "Jackdaw in the Garden," a chapter whose stated purpose is for Percy to display "the jackdaw pickings of my curious and secret heart . . . bits of color and scraps of go-in-man . . . of no worth save to the miserly fanatic heart" (336). Just as the garden itself is "a substitute for things preferred but denied," these "tinsel hoardings"—memories of transitory, sublime moments in which self briefly locates pure analogs in the outside world—are presented as effete substitutes for the greater treasures tarnished by history. Indeed, "the only treasure," Percy writes, "that's exempt from tarnish is what the jackdaw gathers" (343). In shoring these fragments against his ruin and in divorcing the affective objects of consciousness from effective social action—which is largely what the juxtaposition of "A Bit of Diary" and "Jackdaw in the Garden" structurally accomplishes—Percy registers his deep sense of alienation.

If Percy's garden constitutes a narrowed, aestheticized version of the plantation, *Lanterns on the Levee* concludes in a third kind of garden. "Home," the final chapter of Percy's narrative, is set in the Greenville cemetery, "one of the pleasantest places near the home town" (344). "Here," Percy relates, "I come . . . not infrequently because it is restful and comforting. I am with my own people" (345). In this final scene the aesthetic perception

27. Holdsworth, "Gorgon's Head," 39.

of community involves a radical suspension of ethics: "While people are still alive we judge them as good or bad, condemn them as failures or praise them as successes, love them or despise them. Only when they are dead do we see them, not with charity, but with understanding. Alive they seem remote, even hostile; dead they join our circle and you see the family likeness" (347). Although such sentiments may seem strangely out of place in a narrative that reflects a rigid ethical code, Percy is merely applying the code that has come to dominate his text, a code that valorizes intention over action. As Percy says as he contemplates the graves of the erstwhile "enemies of me and mine and all that we held dear," "I know their stories, but not their hearts" (347). In considering that their world too offered resistance to the public articulation of self, Percy indicates how completely any stable medium of ethical norms has vanished. In the end, maintaining the conceptual integrity of community requires the renunciation of a narrative relationship with the world. Failing to inherit from his father the mythical substance in which virtue and action are conjoined, Percy ends his narrative asserting himself to his true father, Death.

Will Percy's thanatos syndrome identifies him as that peculiarly southern version of Narcissus.[28] If there is a literary analog of Will Percy wandering among the graves of the Greenville dead confronting his most troubling doubt—"I have loved no one so much as myself" (348)—it must surely be Allen Tate's speaker wandering among the Confederate dead, forever alienated from "the immoderate past," from "the furious murmur of their chivalry," and succumbing at last to narcissistic self-annihilation. In "Narcissus as Narcissus," his exegesis of the "Ode," Tate wrote that poem was "about Narcissism, or any other *ism* that denotes the failure of the human personality to function objectively in nature and society." "Society," Tate continues, "appears to offer limited fields for the exercise of the whole man, who wastes his energy piecemeal over separate functions that ought to come

28. To use Walker Percy's terminology, Percy risks trading immanence for transcendence, an ominous exchange, since it creates the condition necessary for suicide—a not irrelevant consideration given the setting of and death-wish apparent in "Home." For discussion of the relationship between the work of the two Percys, see Kreyling, *Figures of the Hero*, 154–82; and Lewis Lawson, "Walker Percy's Southern Stoic," *Southern Literary Journal* 3, no. 1 (1970): 5–31.

under a unity of being."[29] Like Tate's speaker, Percy fails to locate a social order in which he can function objectively since, in the end, the community partakes of the same disorder that Percy attempts to displace outside of its boundaries. Percy dwells in a community that does not reflect his experience of interiority, a world in which the Negro fails to authorize the paternal role of the aristocrat. His valorization of pure intention and pure subjectivity allows him to configure aesthetically the community as his home, but in the final analysis, the story he tells is one of exile.

29. Allen Tate, *Collected Poems, 1919–1976* (New York: Farrar Straus Giroux, 1977), 21, 22; Tate, "Narcissus as Narcissus," in *The Man of Letters in the Modern World: Selected Essays, 1928–1955* (New York: Meridian Books, 1955), 334.

4

Narrating the Community Narrating

William Faulkner's *Light in August*

In *The Southern Heritage* James McBride Dabbs describes, with tongue firmly in cheek, the white southerner's attitude toward the Negro under segregation: "We like the Negro in his place. The liking is a bonus for his staying there."[1] As we have seen in both Page and Percy, the paternalistic bond depended upon Negro consent; to the extent that he resisted his place, the Negro was defined as a contaminant. Indeed, it was his unique ability to contaminate that made the Negro's place possible and even necessary under the bizarre logic of segregation. If one drop of black blood could taint an entire person, then the corruptive properties of blackness were powerful indeed. Despite their commitment to the paternalistic bond, neither Page nor Percy question the possibility of Negro contamination. Discussing miscegenation, Percy writes, "It is academic to argue the wisdom or justice of this taboo. Wise or unwise, just or unjust, it is the cornerstone of friendly relations, of interracial peace" (308). It is precisely this kind of reticence, this categorical inability to submit the basic premise of segregation to conceptual scrutiny that makes the institution appear so bizarre and irrational to the modern mind. Where slavery had an obvious economic motive, segregation buried its economic subtext in a mass of arcane forms. Where slavery

1. Dabbs, *Southern Heritage*, 177.

had tough-minded, intellectually rigorous apologists, segregation had none. Paradoxically, it is the bizarre nature of segregation that allows it to be viewed from the relatively safe distance of three decades as a marginal component of southern culture, a kind of freak accident that need not disrupt contemporary nostalgia for the communities of an earlier era. William Faulkner's *Light in August* (1932) tells another story. Relentlessly revealing the symbolic logic of segregation, the narrative structures of *Light in August* demonstrate the deep interdependence between social cohesion and the contamination associated with black blood.

In many respects *Light in August* differs qualitatively from the narratives we have considered to this point, each of which involves a community that is essentially heterogeneous—that is, composed of at least two distinct classes whose hierarchical arrangement does not prevent the perception of interdependence and mutual obligation. And with the exception of *Georgia Scenes,* a work in which slaves play a negligible role, each of these works strategically incorporates blacks within the community. To be sure, that integration is tenuous and impure, but from Kennedy to Percy, the community obtains a pluralistic, interracial cast. In contrast, the community of *Light in August* excludes blacks absolutely. Lacking even a vestige of paternalistic rhetoric, *Light in August* is unusual among Faulkner's novels, which often contain, as Ralph Ellison noted in a 1953 essay, the "benign stereotype" of the "good nigger" so prevalent in the paternalistic tradition. Likewise, the figure of the family, so central elsewhere to Faulkner's representation of race, is nearly invisible. Not only is the community of *Light in August* exclusively white, it approaches monolithic whiteness. As Myra Jehlen observes, the community consists almost exclusively of plain folk, and thus lacks the nuanced hierarchy of white social classes so essential to the Faulkner canon. Although, as we shall see, the novel occasionally introduces class distinctions within the white community, they prove to be of a decidedly provisional nature: in the end, the community is white in a homogeneous sense approaching what W. J. Cash called the "savage ideal . . . whereunder dissent and variety are completely suppressed and men become, in all their attitudes, professions, and actions, virtual replicas of one another." *Light in August* thus replicates a broader American trend to conceive, as Walter Benn

Michaels shows in *Our America,* of culture and nationhood in terms of race at the level of a relatively humble Mississippi community.[2]

Another difference between *Light in August* and the works we have considered to this point involves narrative voice. Despite their many differences, our previous narratives have all contained a coherent narrating subject that frames and attempts to stabilize the social contradictions with which it is confronted. *Light in August* appears to offer no such stability, as its narrative voice is the single most unstable feature of the novel's intricate design. In contrast to our previous narratives, where stability exists at the subjective level and is largely threatened by dissonant objects of consciousness, the opposite is true of *Light in August,* a narrative whose complex shifts in focalization and voice work to undermine whatever subjective stability it might seem to offer. Reading Faulkner's novel, we are rarely sure quite where we are. The paradox of *Light in August* is that despite its tremendous centrifugal energy—that is, its numerous *kinds* of shifts that threaten to fracture the novel into a multitude of narrative shards—an equally powerful centripetal force prevents such a dispersal. In his classic essay on the novel in *The Yoknapatawpha Country,* Cleanth Brooks associates this centripetal force with the community itself, "the circumambient atmosphere, the essential ether of Faulkner's fiction" that is "at once the field for man's action and the norm by which his action is judged and regulated."[3] In this chapter I want to revise Brooks's terminology and claim that the essential ether of Faulkner's narrative is narrative itself, the social and epistemological mode through which society regulates itself. Narrative is how community happens; community, in one sense, is a form of narrative. As a social transaction and as an ideological vehicle, narrative obtains coherence in response to a central symbol: black blood. By focusing attention upon narrative as a communal activity, I

2. Ralph Ellison, "Twentieth-Century Fiction and the Black Mask of Humanity," in *The Collected Essays of Ralph Ellison,* ed. John F. Callahan (New York: Modern Library, 1995), 97; Myra Jehlen, *Class and Character in Faulkner's South* (New York: Columbia University Press, 1976), 91; Cash, *Mind of the South,* 90–91; Michaels, *Our America,* 23–40.

3. Cleanth Brooks, *William Faulkner: The Yoknapatawpha Country* (New Haven: Yale University Press, 1963), 52, 69. The opposition between centrifugal and centripetal forces is borrowed from Ellen Goellner; see note 15 below.

hope to demonstrate the interdependence of community, narrative, and black blood, thereby elucidating how the community responds to racial symbols in such a way as to make a collective subjectivity not only possible, but darkly necessary.

A passage near the middle of *Light in August* describes Joe Christmas as he lies bleeding after having been savagely beaten: "He was not thinking at all, not suffering. Perhaps he was conscious of somewhere within him the two severed wireends of volition and sentience lying, not touching now, waiting to touch, to knit anew so that he could move."[4] The "severed wireends of volition and sentience" remove Christmas from narrative time and the plot that is his life; when they "knit and made connection," he "entered the street which was to run for fifteen years" (222, 223). Christmas's suspended moment is predicated on the dissociation of volition and sentience, a key dualism not only in the context of his own story—one infused with issues of determinism and knowledge—but also in the context of the novel's narrative style. The reader first encounters Christmas in chapter 2, the first section of which will serve as a likely point of entry into an examination of that style and its tortured relationship between sentience and volition. The chapter begins simply enough: "Byron Bunch knows this: It was one Friday morning three years ago" (31), an embedding locution whose stable syntax (subject—verb—object) implies a stable epistemological relationship. The narrating instance of this chapter thus contains two important pieces of information: first, that the narrator (and not Byron) will narrate what Byron Bunch knows—that is, Byron, as focal character, "sees" but the narrator "speaks," to use Gérard Genette's important distinction between perspective and voice—and second, that the narrative discourse occurs in the present ("knows"), but describes events in a story that occurred three years prior to the act of narration.[5]

4. William Faulkner, *Light in August,* Corrected Text edited by Noel Polk (New York: Vintage, 1990), 220. This work will hereinafter be cited parenthetically by page number in the text.
5. Here, I am using Jonathan Culler's standardization of the terms "story," consisting of "a sequence of actions or events, conceived as independent of their manifestation in discourse," and "discourse," consisting of "the discursive presentation or narration of events." For further

In an extended reading of the section, Arthur F. Kinney takes the apparent stability of the narrating instance to its logical conclusion, making in the process at least three assumptions that illustrate the difficulties posed by Faulkner's complex regulation of narrative information. Working from Kant's notion "that reality is individually constructed by shaping ideas and images," Kinney argues that "Byron here is not a receiver of images but a creator of awarenesses—he calls it knowledge, 'Byron Bunch knows this'— because he chooses and shapes what he sees and so absorbs it into what he thinks." First, Kinney fails to distinguish Byron from the narrator, as evidenced by his claim that Byron "*calls* it knowledge." Not only is there a clear distinction between the two (since Byron is not called "I"), there is, as we shall see, internal evidence clearly indicating that the section is not even what Genette calls pseudo-diegesis, in which the narrator appropriates and tells another's story *as if* it were his own. Second, Kinney views Byron as the exclusive focal character, whereas internal evidence suggests not only that Byron does not *speak,* but that he does not *see* everything either. Consider the following passage, which comes just after the workmen learn Christmas's name: "It seemed to [Byron] that none of them had *looked especially at the stranger until they heard his name*" (33; emphasis added). If this section is focalized solely through Byron's consciousness, then the following passages, which occur *prior* to the men learning Christmas's name, represent a clear theoretical problem:

the men in faded and worksoiled overalls *looked* at his back with a sort of baffled outrage. "We ought to run him though a planer," the foreman said, "Maybe that will take that look off his face." . . . The others had not stopped work, yet there was not a man in the shed who was not again *watching* the stranger. . . . The others *watched* him go down to the sawdust pile. (32–33; emphases added)

How has Byron managed to both register *and* miss that the men have done nothing *but* look at Christmas since he makes his appearance? Third, Kinney attributes to Byron a level of cognitive volition that is highly problematized by narrative stylistics, claiming of the passage below, for example, that

---

discussion, see Culler, *The Pursuit of Signs: Semiotics, Literature, Deconstruction* (Ithaca, N.Y.: Cornell University Press, 1981), 169–71.

"Byron *wishes* to analogize ('like a tramp') or classify ('the stranger') in order *to give* some meaning to the images he perceives."[6]

> Byron Bunch knows this: It was one Friday morning three years ago. And the group of men at work in the planer shed looked up, and saw the stranger standing there, watching them. They did not know how long he had been there. He looked like a tramp, and yet not like a tramp either. His shoes were dusty and his trousers were soiled too. But they were of decent serge, sharply creased, and his shirt was soiled but it was a white shirt, and he wore a tie and a stiffbrim straw hat that was quite new, cocked at an angle arrogant and baleful above his still face. He did not look like a professional hobo in his professional rags, but there was still something definitely rootless about him, as though no city was his, no street, no walls, no square of earth his home. (31)

Extending to its logical conclusion the chapter's narrating instance, Kinney locates sentience and volition exclusively within the character of Byron. But if it looks as though "Byron Bunch knows this," we should note that the narrating instance is completely destablized as the section unfolds.

The immediate nominal shift from "Byron Bunch" to the "group of men" calls into question what we might call the focal path—that is, the subjective intermediaries—through which the narrator apprehends Christmas. The possible focal paths can be schematized according to the following diagram:

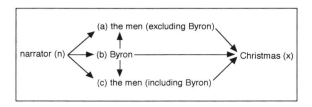

Even if we dismiss a straight n-b-x path, which fails to account for the presence of the men, there remain several alternative paths through which the passage can, at least provisionally, be read. In the n-a-x path the narrator

6. Arthur F. Kinney, *Faulkner's Narrative Poetics: Style as Vision* (Amherst: University of Massachusetts Press, 1978), 16–17, emphases added; Gérard Genette, *Narrative Discourse: An Essay in Method,* trans. Jane E. Lewin (Ithaca, N.Y.: Cornell University Press, 1980), 236.

shifts his focal location from Byron to the men. In the n-c-x path the focalizing locus shifts to the group of men including Byron, in which case the third person pronouns (them, they) can be transposed to the first person (us, we) with a minimal loss of meaning. In the n-b-a-c path the group of men (excluding Byron) provides the final locus of focalization, but their perceptions of Christmas are mediated through Byron's "framing" focalization: the narrator is conscious of Byron's consciousness of the men's consciousness of Christmas. Another path, which we might designate n-b-a/n-b-x, allows us to read Byron's focalization as being equally conscious of the men and Christmas. To further complicate matters, the absence of embedding locutions (he knew, they believed) in the latter part of the passage where the reader first "sees" Christmas makes it possible to read the passage as non-focalized narrative in which the narrator is conscious *of* Byron, the men, and Christmas as *equivalent* narrative units (with the signal difference that the narrator has access to the subjectivities of Byron and/or the men, but not that of Christmas) rather than becoming conscious of Christmas *through* one of the focal paths described above.

So who "owns" the knowledge of Joe Christmas? Who "decides"—if volition is even at issue—that "he looked like a tramp, yet not like a tramp either"? The syntactic structure of the sentence "He looked like a tramp"—the essential features of which are replicated throughout the passage—involves what Brian Macaskill calls middle voice utterance, a grammatical structure in which the agentive or instrumental phrase is called into question.[7] Although the reader might supply any number of ostensibly recoverable deletions ("He looked [to the narrator? the men? Byron?] like a tramp"), the actual syntactic structure assigns to Christmas the grammatical location typically afforded to the agent of the action. The accretion of middle voice utterance during the course of this passage causes an elision of agency: the qualities "attributed" to Christmas tend to "appear" as objective

---

Genette notes that the convention of the flashback in film, often introduced with a character's voice-over, is a common form of pseudo-diegetic discourse.

7. Brian Macaskill, "Charting J. M. Coetzee's Middle Voice," *Contemporary Literature* 35 (1994): 450–51.

qualities. At the same time, the range of Christmas's "appearance" makes it impossible to read the passage as a simple descriptive register. Interestingly, as the passage becomes more subjective, moving as it does from relatively objective qualities like Christmas's white shirt to analogic similes to (at the end) something like a proto-narrative ("as though no town nor city was his . . ."), it becomes less clear precisely which subjectivities are orienting the narrative. Yet even could we decide conclusively that, say, the focal path of the passage is n-c-x, and that the passage represents the men's active perception of Christmas ("the men thought that he looked like a tramp"), we must still consider the *mode* of representation—that is, the relationship between the language of this passage and the thoughts, feelings, and conceptualizations of the men. Did the men literally say to themselves, "He look[s] like a tramp," or is the narrator providing language and analogies that capture the vague feelings and impressions of the focal characters? By the end of the passage, it is difficult to ascribe the heightened diction to what Byron and his peers might conceivably say or even think. In short, what happens between "Byron Bunch knows this" and the conclusion of the passage? I propose that we cannot know. Faulkner's narrative style so radically and systematically dissembles any Cartesian model of epistemology than any decision regarding how knowledge happens is inherently precarious. Nor are these destabilizing techniques peculiar to this passage; the instabilities I have considered here are replicated throughout the novel.

The fuzzy edges of Faulkner's narrative style are, as it were, central to *Light in August,* a novel obsessed not only with maintaining boundaries, but with the problem of defining them. Although these boundaries are, of course, thematized at the cultural level of gender and especially race, they are immanently at work in the novel's narrative style, which, in its continual forays into private and public subjectivities, obscures both the locus and the status of the cognitive work being performed. Further, this style modulates between mimesis and diegesis without clearly marking either; we are never quite sure what we are being shown and what we are being told. As an index of this textual characteristic, critics of the novel are fairly evenly divided between referring to the narrator as a "narrative consciousness" (a mimetic metaphor) and "narrative voice" (a diegetic metaphor). Although Hugh

Ruppersburg and Stephen Ross have provided useful heuristic taxonomies for distinguishing between the various "voices" and "perspectives" of Faulkner's novel, neither accounts for the phenomenon noted by David M. Toomey, who observes that the narrator of *Light in August* "blends so easily into character's speech or thought that in many instances their certain differentiation is impossible. . . . *Light in August* seems not only to eschew such indicators; it seems actually to obscure the places narrative transitions would naturally occur."[8]

Consider, for example, the following passage from chapter 5, which takes place just after Christmas has beaten Brown and shortly before he kills Joanna Burden:

> He stood in the darkness above the prone body, with Brown's breath alternately hot and cold on his fingers, thinking quietly *Something is going to happen to me. I am going to do something* Without removing his left hand from Brown's face he could reach with his right across to his cot, to his pillow beneath which lay his razor with its five inch blade. But he did not do it. Perhaps thinking had already gone far enough and dark enough to tell him *This is not the right one* Anyway he did not reach for the razor. (104)

The passage begins with a nonfocalized representation of action (Christmas standing above Brown), before shifting to a location associated with Christmas's consciousness (*Something is going to happen to me. I am going to do something,* the chiasmus of which perfectly illustrates the problem of volition and agency). The italicized internal discourse of Faulkner's novel has generated substantial critical commentary: Ruppersburg claims that it represents "for all intents and purposes" a merger of narrator and character; Joseph Reed locates at least one instance of it "at a level just below speech, more or less formulated for speech"; while Ross claims that although Faulkner "never interferes with the mimetic illusion that a character is thinking in his or her

---

8. Hugh M. Ruppersburg, *Voice and Eye in Faulkner's Fiction* (Athens: University of Georgia Press, 1983), 30–56; Stephen M. Ross, *Fiction's Inexhaustible Voice: Speech and Writing in Faulkner* (Athens: University of Georgia Press, 1989), 51–58, 147–54; David M. Toomey, "The Human Heart in Conflict: *Light in August*'s Schizophrenic Narrator," *Studies in the Novel* 23 (1991): 456.

own idiom," such discourse, which Ross categorizes under the heading "psychic voice," "transcends the limits of any individual consciousness and comes to be a shared or at least a sharable discourse." Although I tend to read the majority of italicized "thinking" as what Ann Banfield calls nonreflective consciousness—that is, consciousness not yet articulated in language—the generic idiom in which it is articulated suggests at least some intervention on the part of the narrator. We should clarify, however, that nonreflective consciousness rarely involves a total shift in focalization; the narrator is equivalently conscious *of* Christmas's physical and mental activity. This passage is typical of Faulkner's representation of nonreflective consciousness in that it is not, to use Genette's phrase, emancipated from narrative patronage.[9]

The remainder of the passage, however, complicates this focal model. Immediately, the reader confronts a sentence that appears to be focalized *through* Christmas. The narrative here registers not merely distances, but intentions: insofar as Christmas is *thinking about* reaching for his razor, the passage is focalized through him. Two factors, however, suggest that the focalization is not absolute. First, there is an excess of information; even though he is apparently thinking about the razor and its proximity, Christmas would not be thinking about it having a five-inch blade. Second, the repetition of "his" rather than "the" ("his cot," "his pillow," "his razor") represents a subtle infiltration of the narrator's language; were the passage fully focalized, "his" would clearly be anomalous. Mieke Bal has labeled this technique "transposed focalization," which she defines as when the narrator "assumes the character's view but without thereby yielding the focalization to him."[10] Following the external shift in the next sentence ("But he did not do it")—which, focalized through Christmas, would be some version of "No"—the focal model becomes even more convoluted. The embedding locution "Perhaps thinking had already gone far enough and dark enough to

9. Ruppersburg, *Voice and Eye,* 37; Joseph W. Reed, Jr., *Faulkner's Narrative* (New Haven: Yale University Press, 1973), 121; Ross, *Fiction's Inexhaustible Voice,* 149, 150; Ann Banfield, "Reflective and Non-Reflective Consciousness in the Language of Fiction," *Poetics Today* 2 (1981): 63–67; Genette, *Narrative Discourse,* 174.

10. Mieke Bal, "The Narrating and the Focalizing: A Theory of the Agents in Narrative," *Style* 17 (1983): 252.

tell him" qualifies the "thought" (*"This is not the right one"*) as a narrative speculation, thereby overtly calling attention to the narrator's presence for the first time in what had existed, despite its shifts in focalization, as a minimally narrated *register* of physical and psychological events. As in the opening passage of chapter 2, the narrative becomes less stable, less authoritative, as it begins to concern itself with issues of causation and motivation—in short, as it becomes concerned with meanings.

As the novel moves inward, then, we find problems of focalization, mode of representation, and narrative authority similar to those we noted above as the novel moves among different characters. The stylistic techniques producing this phenomenon systematically obscure how norms, conceptualizations, and causal scenarios enter the discursive space of the novel. For Christmas to have "looked like a tramp, and yet not like a tramp either" or for Christmas's hypothetical thought to be "dark," someone—or rather, some subjectivity, since, as Ruppersburg says, the narrator is "[i]n no sense a character or even a person"[11]—must have decided so. Yet determining precisely where that subjectivity exists—or indeed, whether a subjectivity is even tangibly present, since many valuations and conceptions are presented as objective "facts"—is a difficult matter indeed. That the narrative discourse sometimes appears as a relatively passive medium in which the events of the story are merely registered, but at others assumes the texture of a story being actively told, adds complications upon complexities. Yet for all its complexities, the narrative style of *Light in August* is singularly fitted to capture the nuances of this particular social world, with its uncertain and unstable boundaries between private and public space, between subject and object, between individual and community. *Light in August* posits a grammar, or set of structural imperatives, that cannot be reduced to the level of the individual and that, to some extent, is shared between individuals. In thus establishing something like the community's continuous mind, Faulkner's narrative style refuses to recognize the discrete cognitive boundaries normally associated with individual persons. To put the matter another way, although the community is *different* from, it is not *separate* from the individuals who comprise it. While *Light in August* frequently reifies "the com-

---

11. Ruppersburg, *Voice and Eye,* 32.

munity" as an agent in and of itself—an entity greater than the sum of its citizens, so to speak—it also registers how the community is part of the minds of its citizens.

The continuous mind does not simply form conceptions and make judgments; it also tells stories. And if the community does not tell stories in precisely the same way as the primary narrator of the novel, the alignment of the two entities makes it impossible to differentiate between them with any precision. (Indeed, as I shall argue, the limited critique of community that emerges in the novel is in no sense dependent upon norms external to the community.) Before turning our attention to the significance of these narrative techniques in relation to communal ideologies of race, let us return to the opening section of chapter 2 and consider the second feature we identified as being communicated by the embedding locution "Byron Bunch knows this." Like the relationship between the narrator and Byron, the tense of the section—the temporal configuration it assumes—undergoes subtle and sometimes problematic shifts. Consider the following passage:

> And that was the first time Byron remembered that he had ever thought how a man's name, which is supposed to be just the sound for who he is, can be somehow an augur of what he will do, if other men can only read the meaning in time. It seemed to him that none of them had looked especially at the stranger until they heard his name. But as soon as they heard it, it was as though there was something in the sound of it that was trying to tell them what to expect; that he carried with him his own inescapable warning, like a flower its scent or a rattlesnake its rattle. Only none of them had sense enough to recognize it. They just thought that he was a foreigner. (33)

Although we have noted how the men have already been watching Christmas obsessively, and thus that Byron's exclusive focalization is rendered problematic, another important feature of this passage is the temporal paradox contained within it. If, as the passage indicates, Christmas's name is an "augur of what he will do," this insight, specifically attributed to Byron three years prior to the present tense of the section's telling, is predicated on what Byron does not yet know *even in the present tense:* namely, that Christmas has "black blood." "They"—which apparently refers to the men exclusive of Byron, since the augur hypothesis is specifically attributed to him—do not recognize the "inescapable warning" of Christmas's name precisely because, as the ensuing language explicitly indicates, they "just thought that he was a foreigner," a categorization which, in indicating only a slight (and hence insufficient) deviation from the norm "white," clearly points to "Negro" as the proper category. Not making this mistake thus stands in a causal relation to being able to recognize the warning. And yet nowhere do we have any evidence that Byron is inclined to view Christmas with *any* undue suspicion—Byron is, in fact, *less* suspicious than the other men, one of whom later says that Byron "stays out of meanness too much himself to keep up with other folks'" (43)—much less that he intuits Christmas's black blood. Unless the reader is here willing to grant Byron a prescience he sorely lacks elsewhere, the passage is possible only insofar as it posits a future tense providing the necessary perspective from which "Byron Bunch knows"—a tense perhaps suggested by the embedding locution "Byron remembered"—in which case the original attribution of the hypothesis to Byron three years ago represents a clear contradiction. We might label this the problem of embedded foreshadowing, since Byron himself is represented as possessing something like narrative license—the ability to select significant events within a chain of signification whose ultimate signified is not yet available. To put the matter another way, Byron is unable to "read the meaning in time," and yet still recognizes the warning, despite that these features theoretically cancel one another out.

A similar temporal shift occurs later in the section, just after a passage describing the few facts the men have of Christmas around six months after he had begun working at the mill:

This is not what Byron knows now. This is just what he knew then, what he heard and watched as it came to his knowledge. None of them knew then where Christmas lived and what he was actually doing behind the veil, the screen, of his negro's job at the mill. Possibly no one would have known it if it had not been for the other stranger, Brown. But as soon as Brown told, there were a dozen men who admitted having bought whiskey from Christmas for over two years, meeting him at night and alone in the woods behind an old colonial plantation house two miles from town, in which a middleaged spinster named Burden lived alone. But even the ones who bought the whiskey did not know that Christmas was actually living in a tumble down negro cabin on Miss Burden's place, and that he had been living in it for more than two years. (36)

Although the aegis of the first sentence, which directly contradicts the first sentence of the section, is not clearly delineated, the real enigma of this passage is what "Brown told" that caused a dozen men to admit that they had bought whiskey from Christmas. Clearly these men are not the mill workers, who later inform the innocent Byron that Christmas and Brown sell whiskey to *other* men, although the speaker carefully qualifies Christmas's involvement as hearsay (43). Nor are these men numbered among the "young men and even boys" who buy whiskey from Brown in town. Even at the end of the section, the town "still do[es] not know for certain if Christmas is connected with it, save that no one believes that Brown alone has sense enough to make a profit even from bootlegging, and some of them know that Christmas and Brown both live in a cabin on the Burden place" (46). So who are these dozen men—a group clearly distinct from Byron, the mill workers, and "the town," which has one piece of knowledge unavailable to the dozen men (that Christmas and Brown live in Joanna Burden's Negro cabin) but lacks another (that Christmas is definitely involved)—and what does Brown tell that causes them to admit their purchases? The first question is admittedly insignificant except insofar as it creates a discrete group, but the second is more intriguing. Because this discrete group exists and because the offhand narrative reference to Brown's telling points to a collectively known event, the most likely reference is to Brown's assertion to the sheriff in chapter 4 that Christmas has "nigger blood." If this is true, then the narrative consciousness extends not only beyond Byron for reasons that are altogether obvious, but beyond the present tense of the section's telling. The second section of chapter 2, narrated largely in the present tense, takes place on the afternoon after Christmas kills Joanna Burden; Brown, however, does not reach the sheriff until the evening of that day.

According to the normal rules of narrative, such prescience can logically be attributed only to the narrator. Indeed, the narrator demonstrates foreknowledge throughout the text, notably at the conclusion of chapter 17, where Hightower's relief at Byron and Lena's departure ("And this must be all") is followed by the ominous narratorial comment, "But it is not all. There is one thing more reserved for him" (414). Such passages embody, on a formal and not merely thematic level, what Joseph Reed describes as the novel's momentum from *was* to *must be*. Discussing this feature of *Light in August*, Brian Richardson contends that such metafictive elements "dra[w] attention to the paradoxical status of causality in fiction": "Any coincidence, determinism, or teleology within a fictional world is present because it has been placed there by the author. At some level, destiny is always a fabrication."[12] I would contend, however, that destiny is fabricated not merely at the level of authorial discourse, but at the levels of narratorial and communal discourse as well. As the community attempts to explain the meaning of Joe Christmas, its causal sequences are revealed to exist only after the fact.

We have now tentatively defined some of the features of *Light in August*'s narrative style, taking the first section of chapter 2 as a provisionally representative text. Essentially, these features organize themselves around issues of sentience and volition, or, to revise these terms slightly, of focalization and agency. We have further seen how narrative stylistics place both focalization and agency in a continual state of deferral. As "the town"—which we can take as a nominalization of the various focalizing subjectivities involved, and which explicitly provides the final (collective) focalization of the section—comes to "know" Christmas, the responsibility for or original ownership of this knowledge, although provisionally ascribed to Byron, is systematically obscured, as is, insofar as Byron's embedded foreshadowing and the reference to Brown's telling call into question the temporal perspective of the narrating instance, the *motivation* structuring the narrative through which Christmas becomes known. To put the matter this way is certainly to use circular logic, but such logic is extremely relevant to *Light in August*, a novel in which stories consistently present themselves as repetitions of the already-told or, alternatively, as tellings of the already-there. In considering how narrative functions within the community, both in terms of the "outside narratives" constructed by the community and "inside narratives" that the characters inhabit, I want to call attention to how, on the one

12. Reed, *Faulkner's Narrative,* 113; Brian Richardson, "Death by Fiction in *Light in August*," *Faulkner Journal* 3, no. 2 (1988): 28.

hand, the novel systematically traces how stories are built, thus providing an opportunity to examine how ideological pressures influence and distort the evolution of tales presenting themselves as objective registers of "things as they are," and how, on the other, stories consistently appear as objective forms existing prior to any individual or group appropriating and telling them. *Light in August* asks us to take seriously the idea of social role in its literal dramatic sense, as a playing out of already-scripted actions and words. Narrative is extremely malleable; it is also perfectly rigid. Paradoxically, the community's stories are always in the process of becoming what they already are.

Deferral occurs not only in relation to the focal shifts of *Light in August*'s normative diegesis, but also at the level of its embedded storytelling. From Byron Bunch's early revelations to the furniture dealer's tale that closes the novel, the reader receives a great deal of information via second-level narrators. This technique has several important consequences. First, as has been commonly recognized, the reader is placed within the world of the novel, receiving the information and its stylistic texturing along with the character(s) to whom it is directed. Second, Faulkner's embedding techniques often foreground the unstable nature of the narrative discourse by obscuring, on different occasions, both the teller and the tale. Third, the embedding techniques foreground the nature of storytelling as a social transaction, a shared attempt to understand and socialize phenomena through the framework of communal norms.

As an introduction to embedded narrative in *Light in August*, let us consider the two versions of Hightower's history told in chapter 3 by anonymous narrators. The first instance is an example of what Genette calls the pseudo-iterative[13]—an event presented as occurring repeatedly, but whose specificity ensures that the reader does not take this claim literally: "a stranger happening along the quiet and remote and unpaved and littleused street would pause and read the sign [in front of Hightower's house] and then look up at the small, brown, almost concealed house, and pass on; now and then the stranger would mention the sign to some acquaintance in

---

13. Genette, *Narrative Discourse*, 121.

the town. 'Oh yes,' the friend would say. 'Hightower. He lives there by him-self'" (59). The ensuing story, which occupies just under a page of text, re-counts the basic plot of Hightower's life in Jefferson—how his wife "went bad on him" because, as "[s]ome folks claimed," "he couldn't or wouldn't sat-isfy her himself"; how he "had to resign from the church but wouldn't leave Jefferson" after "she got killed, in a house or something in Memphis"; how he remains in town living alone and mostly forgotten (59). The unnamed narrator tells a tentative story, qualifying several of his facts as hearsay, re-fusing to speculate on why Hightower remains ("We don't know why he stays here"), and focalizing his tale through a communal perspective. In short, this brief history, set off from the normative diegesis as a recurrent tale, realistically depicts what a citizen of Jefferson might actually say if asked about Hightower.

In contrast, the immediate retelling and elaboration of Hightower's life in Jefferson (60–73) involves a greater degree of narrative license. Although the ostensible narrator is a collective "they" who had recounted the tale to Byron seven years previously, as the story progresses it becomes farther re-moved from its narrative instance and closer to the normal diegetic mode of the novel. The embedding locutions "they told him" or "they told Byron" ap-pear ten times, five times within the first three pages of text. Although the story is consistently focalized through the community—"the people" and the "the town" are cited repeatedly—what originally appears as transposed speech ("they" speaking *through* the narrator) gradually demonstrates more and more features of narratized speech (the narrator speaking *for* "them"), finally terminating in what appears very much like pseudo-diegesis.[14] The effect of this narrative transfer is to align the primary narrator and the em-bedded collective narrator, the latter of which seems to merge with the for-mer without a clear line of demarcation being drawn. The narrator thus (pseudo-diegetically) assumes the community's perspective not only at the level of focalization, but at the level of narration itself.

Yet as the reader consumes Hightower's story, he or she is also forced to apprehend the discursive practices producing that story. In a provocative

14. The terms are Genette's; see his discussion of the "narrative of words" in *Narrative Dis-course*, 169–85.

essay on *Light in August* Ellen Goellner argues that gossip acts simultaneously as a centripetal force (a dispersed public voice representing communal
judgment) and a centrifugal force (a "non-mainstream, alternative, subversive set of histories"). Although I find little evidence that gossip serves any
subversive role, Goellner's analysis of the novel's normative narrative mode
as "an amalgamated talking" not dissimilar from the gossip contained within
it represents an important insight into the narrative dynamics of *Light in
August*.[15] One important feature of gossip is how it defers the origin of the
narrating subject. Gossip in *Light in August* is virtually originless; in one
sense, it is not narrated at all, but merely repeated as a story that already exists. Byron, for example, is told about how Hightower's "wife was hardly
cold in the shameful grave before the whispering began. About how he had
made his wife go bad and commit suicide because he was not a natural husband, a natural man, and that the negro woman was the reason. And that's
all it took; all that was lacking. . . . that was all that it required: that idea,
that single idle word blown from mind to mind" (71). The "whispering" occurs as an event *within* the embedded narrative Byron receives; the collective narrator neither assumes nor assigns responsibility for it. And while it
has no concrete origin, the story, or rather the "single idle word" is immediately disseminated among the members of the community, which here, as
elsewhere, demonstrates an almost obsessive *desire* for stories, even those, as
Byron believes with respect to another lurid tale involving Hightower,
"which they did not believe themselves" (74). In another instance the town
circulates a rumor that Hightower had insured his wife's life and had her
murdered: "But everyone knew that this was not so, including the ones who
told and repeated it and the ones who listened when it was told" (71).

Not only, then, do these narratives lack a proper narrator, they also frequently lack a verifiable referent. What these stories do possess is an eager
audience for which they serve an essential social function. Such narratives
contain violence in both senses of the word: although that "single idle word"
terminates in Hightower's being savagely beaten by the Klan, after he is
beaten, "all of a sudden the whole thing seemed to blow away, like an evil

15. Ellen Goellner, "By Word of Mouth: Narrative Dynamics of Gossip in Faulkner's
Light in August," *Narrative* 1 (1993): 107.

wind. It was as though the town realised at last that he would be a part of its life until he died, and that they might as well become reconciled. As though, Byron thought, the entire affair had been a lot of people performing a play and that now and at last they had all played out the parts which had been allotted them and now they could live quietly with one another" (73). The image of the wind, which seems to "bring" stories and then to "blow them away," is a highly suggestive one, as is the metafictional equation of social action and "performing a play"—one whose predetermined plot permits no deviation. The one image suggests transience and instability, the other strict rigidity: the story originates from nowhere, yet seems to be intractably emplotted. Yet, after the story has reached its climax, Hightower, like Joanna Burden and for a certain time Joe Christmas, comes to inhabit what we might call (to borrow an idea from Brooks) a narrative cyst, by which I mean that he has been narrated in such a way as to render him nearly invisible to public view. I say nearly invisible because such cysts constantly threaten to rupture, as evidenced by the renewed threat of violence when Hightower delivers a stillborn child rumored to be his, an incident that "was just too close to that other business . . . even despite the fifteen years between them" (74).

In many respects, Hightower prefigures Christmas as an object in the town's narrative consciousness. Like Hightower, Christmas lives largely off-stage during the years between his arrival in Jefferson and his killing of Joanna Burden; in chapter 13, for example, he is described as "another stranger . . . about whom, despite the fact that he had lived in Jefferson for three years, even less was known than about Brown" (295). As with Hightower, the rupture he causes by killing Joanna engenders two separate tellings: Byron's embedded narrative told to Hightower in chapter 4 and the diegetic narrative told in chapter 13, between which lie the intervening chapters (6–12) recounting Christmas's childhood and life up to the actual killing. And in each case the narrative and social dynamics surrounding the two characters work according to a principle of deferral. Byron's account in chapter 4, interspersed within his account of meeting Lena at the mill and taking her to town, begins with a mimetic representation of Byron telling his story. As the episode proceeds, however, we find, as with the collective narration of the story about Hightower, the boundary between embedded storytelling and pseudo-diegesis becoming increasingly indistinct. The first major shift occurs as Byron begins to tell Hightower about his decision to take Lena, to whom he has revealed that Lucas Burch lives in Jefferson, to a boarding house in town: "Byron continues in that flat voice: about how at six oclock . . ." (82). Several factors clearly mark the ensuing narrative as pseudo-diegesis: Byron is referred to in the third person; the narrative is no longer set off with quotation marks; the style of the narrative represents a clear shift from Byron's dialect; and on one occasion the private thoughts of a character other than Byron are represented, thereby subverting even Byron's exclusive focalization. Byron's narrative thus fades into pseudo-diegesis:

And Byron talking quietly, thinking, remembering: It was like something gone through the air, the evening, making the familiar faces of men appear strange, and he, who had not yet heard, without having to know that something had happened which made of the former dilemma of his innocence [i.e., his dilemma over telling Lena about Burch/Brown] a matter for children, so that he knew before he knew what had happened, that Lena must not hear about it. . . . It seemed to him that fate, circumstance, had set a warning in the sky all day long in that pillar of smoke, and he too stupid to read it. And so he would not let them tell—the men whom they passed, the air that blew upon them full of it—lest she hear too. (83)

As Byron brings Lena into town, he is engulfed by a narrative he does not yet know, despite having been given a warning whose status as such, as with Christmas's name earlier, is recognizable only after the fact, when mere circumstance reveals itself to have been part of a fated pattern. The recurrent image of narrative "in the air" asks to be taken almost literally; once again, a story appears as a physical object within the community.

The narrative finally returns to Byron's embedded narration, which he concludes by relating to Hightower, in what purport to be his own words, the story he had not known in the passage above. Although the reader is never shown how this story is transmitted, Byron has apparently received it well. His tale, which embeds both the countryman's account of finding the fire and Brown's account of the killing is, indeed, *too* authoritative. In spite of the mimetic presentation of Byron's narrative, which is set off by quotation marks and which contains numerous locutions ("I reckon," "he said that," "he told how") maintaining the appearance that Byron literally tells it, the overabundance and authoritativeness of the information contained therein, combined with a shift to the present tense ("the sheriff says"), makes it difficult to interpret the story as either a literal tale of what happened or a literal register of what Byron might have told, and impossible to interpret it as both. How, for example, does Byron gain access to the interview between the sheriff and Brown, which he relates in detail to Hightower? His story makes clear that the interview is *heard* by no one else but the marshal: a parenthetical comment (Byron's? the narrator's? we are never quite sure) relates that "they had locked the door [to the cabin where the interview takes place], but the windows was lined with folks' faces against the glass" (97). Later, as the marshal brings Brown from the cabin, the spectators ask if Brown is "the one that done it" (100), information they would have if they had been able to hear Brown's account and the sheriff's reaction to it. Interestingly, Byron's embedded narrative concludes with the marshal's refusal to answer the men's questions, although this contact provides the most likely site for the transmission of Brown's account. Yet even if we allow Byron both indirect access to "the facts" and a liberal amount of narrative license, he would still be unable to tell his story *this way*, since Byron reproduces verbatim not only the speech between Brown and the authorities, but speech within that speech, at one point quoting Brown's quoting of conversation between himself and Christmas that had occurred some time prior to the killing. Even if Byron could piece together the events he relates, a realistic telling, such as the first embedded narrative in chapter 3, would surely not extend this far, since, as Genette observes, "the presence of a narrator . . . is in principle contrary to novelistic mimesis."[16]

Byron's story combines elements of embedded narrative and pseudo-diegesis; indeed, at the end of his story, very little distinguishes him from the primary narrator, especially in this important respect: neither the primary narrator nor Byron demonstrates how the narrative came to exist. At the normal diegetic level, the reader of *Light in August* (or for that matter, any narrative that lacks, as Faulkner's novel does, a sustained extradiegetic level) simply suspends disbelief and accepts the narrative on its own terms:

16. Genette, *Narrative Discourse*, 210.

diegetic narrative "just happens." At the level of embedded narrative, how-ever, the impossibility of Byron narrating *this* crucial moment in *this* way raises serious questions concerning the ontology of his story, which, like many in the novel, seems to appear from out of the blue. This is especially salient given that Byron "quotes" the revelation enabling all of the commu-nity's subsequent narratives about Christmas:

> "'You're so smart,' he [Brown] says. 'The folks in this town is so smart. Fooled for three years. Calling him a foreigner for three years, when soon as I watched him three days I knew he wasn't no more a foreigner than I am. I knew before he even told me himself. . . . He's got nigger blood in him.' . . .
>
> 'A nigger,' the marshal said. 'I always thought there was something funny about that fellow.' . . .
>
> 'Well,' the sheriff says, 'I believe you are telling the truth at last.'" (98–99)

Despite the problems we have noted concerning Byron's story—to which we can add the unreliability of Brown's assertion that he knew all along about Christmas's black blood, one of many obvious lies that the sheriff shrewdly exposes—the implied reader, let me suggest, tends to accept the reliability of Brown's revelation *as both an event and a fact;* it is almost as if the event being narrated temporarily overwhelms whatever scruples the reader might have concerning the authenticity of its transmission. Because the stories concerning Christmas have been focalized through the commu-nity, and because the reader has been provided with ample opportunity to observe along with the town that "there was something funny about that fellow," the resulting alignment between reader and community tends to create a sense of fulfilled expectation, of things having finally "fallen into place." Yet at the same time, the various instabilities surrounding Brown's revelation ensure that this moment of gestalt is in no sense final for either the community or the reader.

The sheer impossibility of Byron's story replicates on a formal level the problem of positive knowledge that plagues the community itself. Christ-mas's own uncertain knowledge of his black blood is subject to a regressive series of narratives terminating in the murky conversation between Doc Hines and the circus owner (374), and an even more complex progressive series of narratives (from Brown to the sheriff and marshal, through an anonymous intermediary or intermediaries, to Byron, and through Byron to Hightower), which finally reveals the presence of black blood to the reader of *Light in August*. Yet at each stage of transmission—even those not represented—"black blood" produces, as a kind of irresistible force, a narrative *at the next level:* black blood abolishes narrative ellipsis. Simultaneously, however, the narrating subjectivity in question is not permitted to repress fully its unstable genealogy, its reliance on previous, potentially unreliable narratives. Yet for the story of Joe Christmas to make sense—that is, for a causal series of otherwise random events to be established—black blood must be present, as Christmas himself recognizes when he tells Joanna Burden that if he is not black, "damned if I haven't wasted a lot of time" (254). Like the community itself, Christmas is deeply invested in the presence of black blood, since without it, his life obtains no narrative coherence and devolves instead into a series of unorganized, "wasted" episodes. As an object within a story—indeed, as the defining object in the stories that accumulate in and finally comprise *Light in August*—black blood *enables* the narrating subject: hence the possibility of Byron's impossible story. Christmas's black blood thus permits a tentative convergence of the various narrating subjects, against which is counterbalanced the deferral of these same subjects, none of which has the authority to state positively the presence of black blood. Although this deferral threatens, as in Byron's retelling of Brown's story, to undermine the very foundations of narrative representation, the potentially arbitrary nature of such representation is suspended or abolished at the moment black blood is present. The circular logic of *Light in August,* then, dictates that without black blood, there's no story, and since the story exists, then there must be black blood. Although lacking both a stable, authoritative subject and a verifiable object, the story of Christmas's black blood is one that continues to be told, that keeps on happening.

In an important sense, it is a story that has already happened. The following passage from chapter 13—prior to Brown's revelation in story time but subsequent to it in discursive time—describes the crowd that gathers to watch Joanna's house go up in flames:

Among them the casual Yankees and the poor whites and even the southerners who had lived for a while in the north, who believed aloud that it was an anonymous negro crime committed not by a negro but by Negro and who knew, believed, and hoped that she had been ravished too: at least once before her throat was cut and at least once afterwards. (288; emphasis added)

Hence the need for black blood. Yet of the many critics who discuss this passage, few foreground the italicized text, and for reasons that will be quite apparent: the displacement of guilt onto poor whites, Yankees, and quasi-southerners—that is, onto people *outside* of the community—appears to subvert the corporate rape narrative many critics are concerned to establish. Considered *as* a displacement, however, the story is simply *already there;* the community need not, as with the whispering that surrounds Hightower, take responsibility for it. The narrative of Negro rape, then, exists as an objective plot in search of its actors, one of whom is dead, while the other simply requires Brown's story in order to be revealed. Yet the absence of focalization *through* the community in this passage raises the issue of the narrator's complicity in this displacement, for the narrator clearly displaces the rape narrative onto *disreputable* social groups—that is, those other than "true southerners."

The relationship between the community and the narrator is indeed a complex one. As we have seen, two techniques in particular tend to align the two: the pseudo-diegetic shifts that modally align the primary narrator with embedded narrators, and the subtle focal shifts to either members of the community or the community itself reified as "the town" or a collective "they." We have also seen how the narrator complicates such alignments by reserving a space for himself after ostensibly deferring to another focalizer ("Byron Bunch knows this") or an embedded narrator, often asserting his presence in theoretically troublesome ways, as in, for example, his pseudo-diegetic appropriation of the town's and Byron's speech.

Nevertheless, these theoretical complications do not create a marked division between narrator and community. Ross, who notes that Faulkner wrote the early chapters as "quoted colloquial narration" (that is, "pure" embedded narrative), points out "how surprisingly few major stylistic distinctions exist between the authorial voice and a town narrator." Traces of this original form remain, lending the primary narrator's voice something of a corporate *texture:* traces such as colloquial expressions ("*Anyway* he did not do it"), aphorisms directly attributable to the narrator ("Man knows so little about his fellows" [47]), or temporal references ("one day *about six months ago* another stranger appeared at the mill") that fix the narrator in narrative time rather than the timeless present usually reserved, as Genette points out, for extradiegetic narrators.[17] As a voice, the narrator thus occasionally implies his "presence" in the diegetic world, as he does (as an eye) in passages like the following, where the combination of nonfocalization, deictics, and present-tense verbs seem to situate the narrator physically within the scene: "[Lena] stands there just inside the door, watching him intently but without alarm, with that untroubled, faintly baffled, faintly suspicious gaze. Her eyes are quite blue" (51).

Although the narrator's initial alignment with, and location within, the community might seem to explain the displacement of guilt onto poor whites and other marginalized groups in the passage quoted above, the ensuing narrative clearly demonstrates the spread of the rape narrative to the community at large. Because it is one of the very few passages in which the narrative overtly distances itself from the community's continuous mind, I will quote it at length:

They came too and were shown several different places where the sheet had lain, and some of them with pistols already in their pockets began to canvass about for someone to crucify.

But there wasn't anybody. She had lived such a quiet life, attended so to her own affairs, that she bequeathed to the town in which she had been born and lived and died a foreigner, an outlander, a kind of heritage of astonishment and outrage, for which, even though she had supplied them at last with an emotional barbecue, a Roman holiday almost, they would never forgive her and let her be dead in peace and quiet. Not that. . . . Because the other made nice believing. Better than the shelves and the counters filled with longfamiliar objects bought, not because the owner desired or admired them, could take any pleasure in the owning of them, but in order to cajole or trick other men into buying them at a profit; and who must now

---

17. Ross, *Fiction's Inexhaustible Voice*, 152; Genette, *Narrative Discourse*, 220. For further discussion of Faulkner's revision in these early chapters, see Regina K. Fadiman, *Faulkner's "Light in August": A Description and Interpretation of the Revisions* (Charlottesville: University Press of Virginia, 1975), 152–61.

and then contemplate both the objects which had not yet sold and the men could buy them but had not yet done so, with anger and maybe outrage and maybe despair too. Better than the musty offices where the lawyers waited lurking among ghosts of old lusts and lies, or where the doctors waited with sharp knives and sharp drugs, telling man, believing that he should believe, without resorting to printed admonishments, that they labored for that end whose ultimate attainment would leave them nothing whatever to do. And the women came too, the idle ones in bright and sometimes hurried garments, with secret and passionate and glittering looks and with secret frustrated breasts (who have ever loved death better than peace) to print with a myriad small hard heels to the constant murmur *Who did it? Who did it?* periods such as perhaps *Is he still free? Ah. Is he? Is he?* (289–90)

The crucial feature of this passage is that the "other, which made nice believing" does not merely contain the violence generated by Burden's death, but assumes, as a kind of surrogate narrative, violence that already exists and that is specifically attributed to the "anger and maybe outrage and maybe despair" generated by abortive transactions. This is a community entirely unlike anything the reader has previously encountered, a town whose normal systems of exchange have broken down and whose citizens are virtually at each other's throats. Yet out of this community seething with violence, the rape narrative produces not only a consensus, but a single body. The crowd gathers

with faces identical one with another. It was as if their individual five senses had become one organ of looking, like an apotheosis, the words that flew among them wind- or airengendered *Is that him? Is that the one that did it? Sheriff's got him. Sheriff has already caught him.* . . . Behind them in turn the dying fire roared, filling the air though not louder than the voices and much more unsourceless *By God, if that's him, what are we doing, standing around here? Murdering a white woman the black son of a* (291)

It is clear from internal evidence, especially the "sourceless," "wind- or airengendered" italicized text, that "the other" is closely related to the rape narrative originally and explicitly attributed to a group marginalized in relation to the normative group marked as "southerners." Yet "the other" is just as clearly attributed to this normative group, which here includes, besides an entire gender, three socially prominent professions. Just as we noted earlier how "black blood" engenders, through a kind of suspension of disbelief, a conflation of narrative subjectivities, it appears that a similar phenomenon is occurring in this passage: the rape narrative, initially displaced outside of the community, threatens to engulf the collective of the crowd gathered to watch the house burn.

Recognizing that this transfer of violence coincides with a radically new representation of the community, we are forced to ask why, if the narrator disapproves of this transfer—as he clearly does; Reed is perfectly correct in labeling this a "passage of condemnation, almost vituperation"—he is initially complicit in its displacement onto the extranormative group. This displacement, we should further note, was frequently replicated in public rhetoric contemporaneous to the novel. Discussing the aristocratic "convention that no white man of any self-respect would participate in a lynching or indulge in nigger-hazing of any sort," W. J. Cash concluded in *The Mind of the South* that while "common whites have usually done the actual execution," "they have kept on doing it, in the last analysis, only because their betters either consented quietly or, more often, definitely approved." In a 1957 interview at the University of Virginia, Faulkner himself asserted that "not all Mississippians wear the sheet and burn the sticks. That they scorn and hate and look with contempt on the people that do, but the same spirit, the same impulse is in them too."[18] It is precisely this invocation, and then suspension, of white hierarchy that Faulkner's narrative so brilliantly registers as a mechanism of displacement. As the rape narrative spreads from the "poor whites" to the community at large, it is as if the narrator, formally complicit in the narrative exchanges constituting the community's cohesive bonds, must divorce himself from a story that arbitrarily articulates the object of violence upon which those bonds are revealed to be dependent.

This violence might be said to produce, on a formal level, a bifurcation of the ensuing narrative into two distinct—although interrelated—modes, which I will label the detective story and the narrative of desire. By the former I mean not only the literal attempt to apprehend Joe Christmas, but the

18. Reed, *Faulkner's Narrative*, 136; Cash, *Mind of the South*, 308, 311; William Faulkner, *Faulkner in the University: Class Conferences at the University of Virginia, 1957–1958*, ed. Frederick L. Gwynn and Joseph L. Blotner (1959; reprint, New York: Vintage, 1965), 94.

more complex effort on the part of the community to comprehend him—to incorporate and subsume him within its ideologies, norms, codes, and laws. Hayden White has suggested that "narrativity, whether of fictional or the factual sort, presupposes the existence of a legal system against or on behalf of which the typical agents of a narrative account militate." This raises, White continues, "the suspicion that narrative in general . . . has to do with the topics of law, legality, legitimacy, or, more generally, authority."[19] Whatever its merits as a general theory, White's assertion of the interdependence of the law and narrative has important implications for *Light in August,* a novel in which law and storytelling function similarly as forms of authority, punitive mechanisms that regulate and contain threatening social phenomena. Christmas, of course, generates the majority of embedded narratives in the novel, most of which involve a community spokesman—a law-abiding citizen, so to speak—who attempts to incorporate him within communal norms. We do not hear from the citizens consumed by a lynch mentality, and when we see them, it is through a narrative perspective not dissimilar to that a law-abiding citizen might inhabit. Although what I am calling the detective mode entails a dispersal of subjectivities such as we have previously encountered, its main actors are the sheriff (who enforces the code) and the lawyer Gavin Stevens (who applies it at the final level of collective interpretation). Although the detective mode entails violence—from the sheriff's literally beating a story out of a Negro to Stevens's figuratively violent division and reification of black and white blood—it also structures and contains violence. The sheriff in particular receives a peculiar brand of narrative sanction due to his ability to control the crowd canvassing about for someone to crucify and his later (unsuccessful) attempt to control Percy Grimm. He is, the narrator tells us, a "good officer" (330).

By narratives of desire, I am designating a more amorphous group of stories whose common feature is that they threaten to spiral out of control. Indeed, the community's level of control may be the primary distinction between the two modes I am describing. Like the magazine Christmas reads "of that type whose covers bear either pictures of young women in underclothes or pictures of men in the act of shooting one another with pistols"

---

19. White, *Content of the Form,* 13.

(110), the narrative of desire typically centers around an amalgamation of sex and violence, producing desire in excess of the ability of societal codes to contain it.[20] These narratives tend to appear out of nowhere, and generally follow a sexual paradigm of rising action, climax, and denouement. Where the effect of what I am calling the detective mode is primarily to structure and maintain an equilibrium, the narrative of desire works in the opposite direction, elaborating and exacerbating the tensions latent in the community. Its dominant actors are Doc Hines and Percy Grimm, the latter of whom, significantly, is initially committed to the imposition of order. Where the one mode is enabled by the law, the other is essentially anarchic, producing an excess of violent energy. Where the one acts as a mode of social transaction, the other is antisocial in any normative sense, although, as in the case of Hightower's beating, the violent climax of such narratives is often followed by the reestablishment of the social equilibrium. Both narrative modes produce a consensus, although again a distinction can be drawn between the community produced by the one and the mob produced by the other. In this context we can usefully juxtapose the rape narrative and the rage it feeds upon, which, as we have seen, is attributed to failed economic transactions, with the "detective" narration of Armstid and Winterbottom concerning the arrival of Lena Grove. Although the two men's bargaining does not produce an exchange of goods, and thus represents a potential site of frustration implied by the sarcastic rhetoric Winterbottom employs, as John N. Duvall notes, "in a semiotic sense there has been a successful contract executed through their dialogue concerning Lena's origin."[21]

Heuristically dividing the narrative into these two modes allows us to make discriminations concerning the problematic relationship between narrative ideology and communal ideology. Although Brooks's conservative reading of the novel has been subjected to countless hostile critiques for its

20. Goellner's assertion that gossip disrupts the Freudian model of desire that "achieves discharge in a moment of epiphanic of heuristic climax" ("By Word of Mouth," 106) seems particularly surprising in this context precisely because gossip does generate the need for such climax. Indeed, the narrative of desire in *Light in August* follows closely the sexual paradigm several theorists have associated with narrative generally.

21. John N. Duvall, *Faulkner's Marginal Couple: Invisible, Outlaw, and Unspeakable Communities* (Austin: University of Texas Press, 1990), 26.

valorization of communal norms, many of Brooks's critics have had difficulty in locating a critique of the community within the text. Such critics have generally argued one of two positions: (1) that narrative ideology differs from that of the community, or (2) that the narrator is "transparently" complicit in this ideology—that is, complicit in such a way as to be textually "obvious," usually through some version of an implied author. Arguing the latter strategy, James A. Snead locates numerous racist assumptions permeating the novel's diegetic level: for example, "the text's repeated notion that blacks smell different than whites do" or narrative assertions such as, "only a negro can tell when a mule is asleep or awake" (10). "To find these [racist] rhetorics in well-socialized speakers is one thing," Snead writes, "but it is quite another to find them in the voice of the narrator." Labeling these assertions "outrageous," "duplicitous," and "transparent," Snead concludes that Faulkner exposes "omniscience as unreliability," adding that "[t]he unreliability is an active deception. There is no deficiency, of either intelligence or perspicacity: the narrator is actively creating error." Although he has difficulty showing how the text *exposes* this creation of error, Snead is correct in asserting a certain ideological consonance between narrator and town, which merge, as we have seen, at the level of perception and narration. This consonance extends beyond racial ideologies to more general norms: the imperative to extend charity, for example, to Lena and even to the disgraced minister in the form of food, which acts as a basic unit of exchange within the community. Snead's paradigm, however, cannot account for the central passage enabling the argument of Joseph Reed, who finds the narrator to be overtly hostile to the town. Claiming that the mob scene in Chapter 13 "rules all of this book's prior references to community," he asserts unequivocally that the "narrative . . . does not attempt to form an alliance between us and the community."[22]

Both groups of critics, I believe, are searching in vain for a stable relationship between the narrator and the community he represents. In fact, such a relationship is nowhere to be found: the narrative neither sanctions nor censures the community in absolute terms. It is my contention that a dissonance between the narrator and the community manifests itself only in

22. James A. Snead, "*Light in August* and the Rhetorics of Racial Division," in *Faulkner and Race,* ed. Doreen Fowler and Ann J. Abadie (Jackson: University Press of Mississippi, 1987), 157, 157, 160; Reed, *Faulkner's Narrative,* 139.

the presence of the narrative of desire, and extends only so far as the community submits to such narratives. This submission is, in turn, often subject to a peculiar kind of after-the-fact censorship by the community itself. Consider the various stories that circulate about Hightower, all of which elaborate a basic plot of transgressive desire involving miscegenation, homosexuality, or both. After Hightower is beaten because of his supposed liaison with the male cook, "the town knew that that was wrong" and offers to prosecute the perpetrators, in effect taking legal recourse against the punitive act generated by the collective story (72). Conversely, the tale of how Hightower fathered the stillborn Negro child fails to engender violence because, as Byron speculates, it results more from habit than passion or actual belief; it is, in short, an incipient narrative of desire that fails to suspend disbelief powerfully enough to overcome communal censorship. Yet even when it is fully realized, the frenzy associated with this kind of story is only temporary, leaving in the collective mind a feeling akin to guilt. After the passing of the "wind- or airengendered" rape narrative in chapter 13, "[i]t was as if the very initial outrage of the murder carried in its wake and made of all subsequent actions something monstrous and paradoxical and wrong, in themselves against both reason and nature" (296). The dissonance felt here by the community registers only after the fact the incommensurability between the "initial outrage" and its ostensible cause that the narrator more explicitly articulates and critiques while the frenzy rages at full force.

The narrator is thus critical of the community in a way that it is critical of itself. The community's "everyday racism"—by which I mean to refer to the racial norms acceptable in the community's public discourse—likewise finds expression in the narrator. In one instance the narrative refers, without embedding or focalization of any kind, to the "vacuous idiocy" of a Negro nursemaid's "idle and illiterate kind" (59), clearly employing the kind of racial category that a white citizen would likely use. On other occasions, such racial categories originate between the narrator and a character, as in the following passage: "Hightower knew that the man would walk all the way to town and then spend probably thirty minutes more getting in touch with a doctor, in his fumbling and timeless negro fashion, instead of asking some white woman to telephone for him" (74). Although the category "fumbling and timeless negro fashion" is attributed to Hightower's "knowledge," its status remains unclear. Because of the verb "knew" and the transposed focalization, it is possible to read the passage as either the narrator's representation of what Hightower is thinking or, alternatively, an assertion that Hightower is aware of an objective fact ("Hightower knew X, and X is true"). In either case, the category of "negro fashion"—which, according to the rules of the detective mode, reduces ambiguity and explains behavior— enters the diegesis with the narrator's sanction, which is to say that the embedded narrative does not enter the text dialogically, as a contested site between the narrator and the character responsible for either focalization or embedded narration.

I contend that insofar as embedding is concerned, there are very few dialogic elements in *Light in August.* Standing at what we might think of as the top of the continuous mind, the narrator sanctions the detective mode and the racial norms it entails up to and including Gavin Stevens's infamous blood theory. I am claiming, then, that the narrator is complicit in the community's attempt to assimilate Joe Christmas within its already-existing structures of meaning, which is simply to say that the narrator, like the town, attempts to *narrate* him, to tell his story. *Light in August* is a novel nearly without irony, except for the greatest irony of all: Christmas's story proves imminently resistant to the detective mode and the norms it presumes. He is captured, but never arrested.

The detective mode is doomed to failure on two counts. First, it involves bad detective work. As Stephen Meats has argued, the sheriff accepts Brown's assertion that Christmas has black blood "in spite of the strong circumstantial evidence against Brown, and in the face of the near certainty that everything Brown has told them is a lie" (272). The detective mode is predicated, from the beginning of the manhunt to Gavin Stevens's theorizing, on Christmas's "black blood," the presence of which the narrative never establishes, but which has the unique ability, as we have said, to produce a story at the next level. This ability to overcome narrative ellipsis is reflected in the missing "murder" scene, to which neither the community nor the narrator has access, but which both, with Brown's introduction of black blood, specifically label as murder. Duvall, who has called attention to this misidentification (legally, the killing is either manslaughter or self-defense), suggests that the word "murder" enters the diegetic level of the novel largely through a character's speech or through indirect discourse: for example, in the passage quoted above ("the murder carried in its wake . . ."), where, according to Duvall, the narrator "speaks for" the men arriving on the train.[23] There is, however, little evidence for indirect discourse in this passage—the narrator might "see with" the men, but he clearly does not "speak for" them—and in any case the point is mooted when the narrator clearly uses the word in a later passage when Brown and the deputy "drove out to the scene of the fire and murder" (428). At the very least, the narrative is complicit in the community's identification of the killing as murder just as it is generally aligned with the community's racial norms.

The second problem with the detective mode is more serious: under certain conditions, it produces more violence rather than assimilating and containing it. The detective mode is contractual in nature: the transgressing party must consent to the community's punitive sanctions after they have been applied through narrative. Lena Grove in particular meets this criterion; it is precisely because she subjects herself to communal norms that she is able to invoke the community's charity. Conversely, Hightower's history demonstrates the consequences of this condition not being met, and in doing so defines the conjunction between the detective mode and the narrative of desire. The town's story begins as a corporate effort to make sense of its disgraced minister: "the town said that if Hightower had just been a more dependable kind of man, the kind of man a minister should be instead of being born about thirty years after the only day he seemed to have ever lived in—that day when his grandfather was shot from the galloping horse—she would have been all right too" (62). The town is not only shrewd, but right, as Hightower himself later comes to realize; their request that he resign his pulpit is, by the contractual standards of the community, a perfectly legitimate one. As Brooks puts it (correctly, I think), "*Naturally,* he was asked to resign" (emphasis added). Yet Hightower refuses the contract; his refusal to conform to the community's codes and resign—his inability, in short, to see himself as having *been* disgraced—produces that "single idle word" that categorizes him as something other than a "natural man." It is as

23. Stephen E. Meats, "Who Killed Joanna Burden?" *Mississippi Quarterly* 24 (1971): 272; Duvall, *Faulkner's Marginal Couple,* 21.

if there is an imperative for the community to produce a more grotesque, more arbitrary transgression to verify its norms and to justify its punitive measures. (Curiously, while the community overproduces deviance in order to verify its sense of normalcy, that overproduction is itself perceived to be deviant and thus subject to censorship.) At this moment of nullified reciprocity, the detective mode becomes transformed into a narrative vehicle that assumes the community's latent, free-floating violence, although, as with the displacement of the rape narrative onto "poor whites" in chapter 13, a marginal group—here, the Klan—actually articulates the violence. In its broad contours this shift from the detective mode to the narrative of desire replicates the generic shift Tzetvan Todorov locates in the 1930s from the whodunit to the thriller, the latter of which replaces the bloodless investigation of the former with "violence—in all its forms, and especially the most shameful—beatings, killings. . . . love—preferably vile—violent passion, implacable hatred" (48).[24] My distinction between the detective mode and the narrative of desire, then, must be qualified in light of the former's ability to merge almost seamlessly with the latter in the absence of consent.

Although Richard Godden has interestingly suggested that "*Light in August* can be read as a thriller whose villain is the word 'nigger,'"[25] the thriller aspects of the novel really appear only after the community's interpretive resources have been exhausted. After Christmas gives himself up in Mottstown, the talk that "went here and there about the town" is concerned not with vigilante retribution but with classifying Christmas and understanding his actions:

He don't look any more like a nigger than I do. But it must have been the nigger blood in him. . . . He never acted like either a nigger or a white man. That was it. That was what made the folks so mad. For him to be a murderer and all dressed up and walking the town like he dared them to touch him, when he ought to have been skulking and hiding in the woods, muddy and dirty and running. It was like he never even knew he was a murderer, let alone a nigger too. (349–50)

24. Cleanth Brooks, *On the Prejudices, Predilections, and Firm Beliefs of William Faulkner* (Baton Rouge: Louisiana State University Press, 1987), 37; Tzetvan Todorov, *The Poetics of Prose,* trans. Richard Howard (Ithaca, N.Y.: Cornell University Press, 1977), 48.

25. Richard Godden, "Call Me Nigger! Race and Speech in Faulkner's *Light in August,*" *Journal of American Studies* 14 (1980): 240.

The embedded story, set off with quotation marks, that contains this passage is another example of quasi-iterative diegesis; although the specificity of information and the singular "I" who speaks clearly indicate a single narrative event, the embedding locution ("*they* told it *again*") indicates a collective story narrated multiple times. Implying the (theoretically impossible) dispersal of a single story, this technique asks us to take seriously the existence of a collective narrator. At this crucial point the collective mind is disturbed not only by Christmas's resistance to racial categories, but also by his refusal to play his role as murderer, a role that dictates that one should skulk and hide in the woods waiting to be apprehended by the law. Although the community's attempt to establish a causal relationship between Christmas's black blood and his actions is contravened by his refusal to consent to the role of "nigger murderer," the narrative of desire has not manifested itself in the collective mind, which at this point is dominated by the law. When Doc Hines begins his ranting, "folks were beginning to think that maybe the place for him was in the jail with the nigger," and when the Mottstown sheriff informs the crowd that "it was his sworn word given to them on the day they elected him that he was trying to keep" (354), the crowd offers only halfheartedly the sentiment that he should be lynched (355). Even as Percy Grimm walks to the sheriff's house to ask his permission to keep the peace, he crosses "a quiet square empty of people peacefully at suppertables about that peaceful town and that peaceful country" (454).

Mottstown, like Jefferson as Gavin Stevens describes it, is willing to keep the peace by permitting the law to assimilate Christmas—to allow him to "die 'decent,'" as Stevens puts it, and be "[d]ecently hung by a Force, a principle; not burned or hacked or dragged dead by a Thing" (445). Even in Jefferson, when Doc Hines escapes from his wife and begins "preaching lynching . . . his audience was more interested than moved" (447). Significantly, it is Stevens who here calls attention to Jefferson's willingness to submit to the law, for he articulates the causal principles that stabilize the meaning of black blood and thereby allow Christmas's death to make sense. Although recent critics have almost unanimously argued that Stevens's blood theory is intended to be read as ironic, irony proves elusive in this context. However ludicrous it may appear, Stevens's embedded narrative is fully sanctioned by the narrator, who clearly offers it as a corrective to the three alternative explanations as to why Christmas had fled to Hightower's house. Moreover, the narrative *approves* of Stevens: that he is well-educated, that "[h]is family is old in Jefferson," that he "has an easy, quiet way with country people, with the voters and the juries" (444). In addition, Stevens's account contains several insights and intuitions that are supported elsewhere in the text. For example, his assertion that Mrs. Hines wants Christmas to "die decent" echoes her own assertion to Byron and Hightower that "[i]f he done it, I would not be the one come between him and what he must suffer" (388). Stevens, of course, has had, by the time he tells his story, individual contact with the Hineses. Yet, even if we attribute to this contact much of the information he relates, he still demonstrates an almost uncanny insight, suggesting, for example, that Christmas fled to Hightower's house because his grandmother "somehow" communicated to him that it "was a sanctuary which would be inviolable not only to officers and mobs, but the very irrevocable past" (448).[26] Hightower himself believes, as he remarks on several occasions, that he has "bought his immunity." That he has, in fact, done so forms the basis for Byron's plan that he provide an alibi: "And it wont be like you haven't done it before, haven't already paid a bill like it once before," he tells Hightower, "It oughtn't be so bad now as it was then" (390).

In a more substantial instance of narrative overlap, Stevens relates that Christmas flees "[n]ot pursuers: but himself: years, acts, deeds omitted and committed" (448), while Christmas himself has already thought, "I have never broken out of the ring of what I have already done and cannot ever undo" (339). The similarity between these two passages is particularly striking in that both are immediately followed by the physical presence of blackness in Christmas's body: the black blood that "would not be quiet" (449) and "the black tide creeping up his legs, moving from his feet upward as death moves" (339), respectively. Elaine Scarry has suggested that "when there is within a society a crisis of belief—that is, when some central idea or ideology or cultural construct has ceased to elicit a population's belief either because it is manifestly fictitious or because it has for some reason been di-

---

26. For a discussion of this detail of Stevens's narrative as "demonstrably incorrect," see Jay Watson, *Forensic Fictions: The Lawyer Figure in Faulkner* (Athens: University of Georgia Press, 1993), 96.

vested of ordinary forms of substantiation—the sheer material factualness of the human body will be borrowed to lend that cultural construct the aura of 'realness' and 'certainty.'"[27] While Stevens's blood theory precisely illustrates what Scarry calls analogical verification, the narrator performs an identical symbolic act in producing the image of the black tide. Just as the black tide predicts, as something like a physiological fact, the social role Christmas has apparently chosen to play, so it is a physiological fact that permits Stevens to explain Christmas's performance of that role—his passive suicide. To reiterate, although recent critics have been skeptical of Stevens's causal link between black blood and Christmas's actions, it is fully consonant with the narrative's repeated reification of blood not only as a meaningful social metaphor, but as an *agent* as well.[28] This is true not only of the community's attempts to make sense of Christmas ("it must have been the nigger blood in him"), but from the perspective of other characters—Nathaniel Burden's French blood does not permit him, Joanna explains, to take revenge on Colonel Sartoris (254–55); Christmas himself attempts "to expel from himself the white blood and the white thinking and being" (226)—and the narrator as well: "[Christmas's] blood began again, talking and talking" (116).

Black blood, then, gains legitimacy as an agent that not only defines social caste, but that also causes and explains behavior. Like the stock scene in detective fiction where the investigator accounts for everything, Stevens's account provides a closure to the story of Joe Christmas. Yet, while I would assert unequivocally that Stevens's theory is not ironic, neither does it fully contain the meaning of black blood; the closure his story provides is, as it were, immediately reopened. As in the case of Hightower, meanings that are putatively stabilized through storytelling retain a latent power to generate additional, more violent narratives. Such is the case with Stevens's parable of black blood, which limits itself to black blood as it acts upon an objectified Joe Christmas. By containing black blood within the black body, Stevens

27. Elaine Scarry, *The Body in Pain: The Making and Unmaking of the World* (New York: Oxford University Press, 1985), 14.

28. That Faulkner later termed Stevens's theory a "rationalization" (*Faulkner in the University*, 72) does nothing to undermine my assertion, since I am claiming only that the narrator is complicit in this rationalization.

need not similarly objectify the community, and so his story ends with the death of an armed and presumably dangerous felon, which from the community's perspective is not only legal, but perfectly defensible. But that is not the whole story. By narrowing the field of his narrative, Stevens censors the role played by Percy Grimm.

But Percy Grimm exists, and despite the narrative's hostility toward his all-American racial fanaticism, black blood in its most arbitrary form drives him to commit a horrific deed. Hightower has already predicted so: "Is it certain," he asks Byron, "that he has negro blood? Think, Byron; what it will mean when the people——if they catch .... Poor man. Poor mankind" (100). Having no faith in the law, Hightower is a pariah in the special sense of being exiled from the community's interpretive norms. Alone among the characters of *Light in August,* he is able to inspect those norms, a condition not unrelated to his separation from—or immunity to—the community.

He paces on, thinking quietly, peacefully, sadly: 'Poor man. Poor fellow. No man is, can be, justified in taking human life; least of all, a warranted officer, a sworn servant of his fellowman. When it is sanctioned publicly in the person of an elected officer who knows that he has not himself suffered at the hands of his victim, call that victim by what name you will, how can we expect an individual to refrain when he believes that he has suffered at the hands of *his* victim?' (414)

Echoing the Mottstown sheriff, who defends his office in terms of his legal contract with the community, Hightower critiques that office, refusing, on the grounds that revenge is at least authentic, the very distinction Stevens makes between being hung by a principle and being hacked by a thing. In *Violence and the Sacred* René Girard concurs, claiming that "the principle of [legal] justice is in no real conflict with the concept of revenge," to which he adds, however, the crucial qualification that "on the social level, the difference is enormous." According to Girard, because the law removes vengeance from the hands of the public and places it in the hands of "a sovereign authority specializing in this particular function," it deflects the cycle of violence that threatens any community, a role, significantly, also played by scapegoating or sacrificial rituals, which arbitrarily fix communal violence on a surrogate victim whose death allows the cycle of violence to be broken and a collective equilibrium to be reestablished.[29] Here we can recall how the incipient sacrifice of the "Negro rapist" in chapter 13 creates a mob out of individual community members previously at one another's throats—a mob, moreover, which, "beginning to canvas about for someone to crucify," almost arbitrarily selects its potential victim: *"Is that him? Is that the one who did it? . . . By God if that's him, what are we doing standing around here? Murdering a white woman the black son of a."*

Girard's equation of legal justice and sacrificial rituals echoes throughout the Percy Grimm section, which immediately follows Stevens's embedded narrative and is narrated by the primary narrator. Byron Bunch has noticed the ominous air around the men lurking outside of the grand jury, men "who had a generally identical authoritative air, like policemen in disguise and not especially caring if the disguise hid the policemen or not" (415–16). The words "Grand Jury" evoke something "secret and irrevocable and something of a hidden and unsleeping and omnipotent eye watching the doings of men" (456). The incipient executioner is himself fanatically committed to the law. "We got to preserve order," Grimm says, "We must let the law take its course. The law, the nation. It is the right of no civilian to sentence a man to death" (451–52). Like Grimm, the community has a tremendous investment in the distinction between hanging and hacking: indeed, it is Grimm's commitment to this distinction that leads the town "to accept him with respect and perhaps a little awe and a deal of actual faith and confidence, as though somehow his vision and patriotism and pride in the town, the occasion, had been quicker and truer than theirs" (456–57). At the same time we should note that this distinction is the product of an elaborate symbolic apparatus, which, in producing a principle (justice) that establishes the literal guilt of the hung, censors the brute literality of hacking, which establishes merely the symbolic value of the hacked. (Here again we can recall the potential hackers in chapter 13 who conceive of Joanna's "murder" as a "crime committed not by a negro but by Negro.") Justice, we might say, *objectifies* the victim of ritual punishment, and thus conceals the potentially arbitrary

29. René Girard, *Violence and the Sacred*, trans. Patrick Gregory (Baltimore: Johns Hopkins University Press, 1977), 16, 15.

nature of a victim whose selection might conceivably result from subjective imperatives.

If the community accepts Grimm as its representative in terms of his commitment to the law, the relationship between the two is more complicated in relation to Grimm's castration of Christmas. Clearly Grimm articulates the latent communal desires very nearly articulated outside of Joanna's burning house, but that also—and recent critics have been reluctant to see this point—have been largely censored through the community's legal structures that remove vengeance from private hands. The question, then, becomes the extent to which the community is implicated in Grimm's actions. Brooks, for whom the issue is crucial in recuperating the organic community, argues that Grimm demonstrably fails to represent the community in this decisive instance.[30] But at the same time, Grimm is clearly not a free agent. As he tracks Christmas down with "the implacable undeviation of Juggernaut or Fate," Grimm moves with "that lean, swift, blind obedience to whatever Player moved him on the board" (460, 62). Even after the Player "who moved him for a pawn" leads him, automatic blazing, into the kitchen with "unfailing certitude," "the Player was not done yet": "Then Grimm too sprang back, flinging behind him the bloody butcher knife. 'Now you'll let white women alone, even in hell,' he said" (462, 64). The Player punishes Christmas not for murder, but for the rape of a white woman, and in so doing reveals himself to be a bad detective, for this is one offense that Christmas has not committed. Indeed, the Player appears to seize arbitrarily on transgressive or aberrant forms of sexuality: upon hearing Hightower's alibi for Christmas, Grimm asks, in a voice "like that of a young priest," "Has every preacher and old maid in Jefferson taken their pants down to the yellowbellied son of a bitch?" (464). Through these stories, the Player has Grimm—and not only Grimm, but his accomplices as well—physically in his grasp: "It was upon them, of them: its shameless savageness" (463).

Whence the Player? Reed claims, correctly, that he "has always been there. . . . He is the logical conclusion, the personified agent of all the habits to which the book's strategy has been accustoming us."[31] This is especially

---

30. Brooks, *Yoknapatawpha Country*, 52, 60–62.
31. Reed, *Faulkner's Narrative*, 117.

true of the several scenes of pursuit terminating in a violent confrontation in which, further, the pursuer is represented as being moved by some supernatural (whether deific or demonic) force. In addition to Grimm's pursuit, McEachern finds Christmas dancing with Bobbie Allen in a building that "he had neither reason nor manner of knowing" would be having a dance, and "if he were thinking at all, he believed that he had been guided and were now being propelled by some militant Michael Himself as he entered the room" (204). Doc Hines hunts down his daughter and her "Mexican" lover by choosing out of a half-dozen roads the right one: "And yet it wasn't any possible way that he could have known which road they had taken. But he did" (375). Even the normally passive Byron Bunch, chasing down Lucas Burch to fight what he knows will be a losing battle, is moved by a "desire . . . more than desire: it is conviction quiet and assured; before he is aware that his brain has telegraphed his hand he has turned the mule from the road and is galloping along the ridge" (425). Insofar as each of these scenes implies the presence of a Player, we might designate that agent as one simultaneously requiring and enabling violent retribution, often cloaked in sacred rhetoric, against transgressions associated with sexuality. That these transgressions are frequently of dubious authenticity matters little, since retribution at times appears to necessitate the crime and not vice versa.

Within the world of *Light in August*, where violence usually accumulates around sexuality, the relationship between the two is an integral one: both represent latent threats to the social order and must, as a consequence, come under some kind of regulation or discipline. Significantly, both violence and sexuality are reified as contaminants in the form of blood: black blood and menstrual blood, respectively. Both forms of blood have the ability to contaminate, to infect, just as the stories they engender threaten to contaminate the community. To the mob gathered at the burning house, Joanna's "blood . . . cried out for vengeance"; the "sourceless" rape narrative that arises spontaneously selects black blood as the culprit and likely sacrificial victim. Menstrual "filth" resonates mainly in relation to Christmas, who, upon having the physiological process described to him as a boy, buys his "immunity" from it through the grisly sacrifice of a sheep (185–86). When, later, Bobbie Allen explains that she is menstruating, and therefore cannot have sexual intercourse with him, he encounters on his way home "suavely shaped urns . . . cracked and from each crack there issued something liquid, deathcolored, and foul" (189). Overcome by the contagion of sexual violence, Joe vomits—precisely the reaction of the men who come upon Grimm as he is castrating Christmas. Although the symbolic weight of menstrual blood does not systematically register in the collective mind, its effect on Christmas's conception of his own black blood is, as Joseph Urgo observes, profound: through it, he analogically internalizes black blood as the "secret, irremovable 'filth' of his own existence." As a result, Christmas needs to present himself as filth as when, for example, he informs white prostitutes that he has "nigger blood" or when, as Godden says, he takes delight in despoiling the cooking of Mrs. McEachern and Joanna Burden.[32] For Christmas, identity is contingent upon his ability to contaminate.

As Mary Douglas shows in *Purity and Danger*, the presence of filth indicates the presence of a system. "[I]f uncleanness," Douglas says, "is matter out of place, we must approach it through order. Uncleanness or dirt is that which must not be included if a pattern is to be maintained. To recognize this is the first step toward insight into pollution."[33] The symbolic field of Jefferson, with its elaborate protections against the filth and violence it associates with blood, is, in a darkly ironic way, the ideal setting for Christmas's negative assertion of self. Yet the community fails Christmas in a crucial way: it allows the law to take its course. Until Christmas escapes, all indications are that the community will allow him to plead guilty to murder and take a life sentence. Insofar as we can posit a reason for his escape—his "plans to passively commit suicide," as the town aptly puts it (443)—it must surely have to do with the difference between the crime for which he *is* being punished and the crime for which he *needs* to be punished in order to verify, in effect, his existence. Although Christmas would receive a life sentence for murder, he is killed by the Player for raping a white woman.

Christmas's rationale must, however, remain a somewhat speculative matter, since the novel shifts exclusively to the community's perspective

32. Joseph Urgo, "Menstrual Blood and 'Nigger' Blood: Joe Christmas and the Ideology of Sex and Race," *Mississippi Quarterly* 41 (1988): 395; Godden, "Call Me Nigger!" 241.

33. Mary Douglas, *Purity and Danger: An Analysis of Concepts of Pollution and Taboo* (New York: Frederick A. Praeger, 1966), 40; for a fuller application of Douglas's theory to *Light in August*, see Godden, "Call Me Nigger!" 239–42.

after chapter 14. What is clear is that Christmas invokes the contest between the two narrative modes through which he and black blood obtain social meaning, clarifying in the process the alternative systems—the law, which segregates and exiles black blood, and the lynching ritual, which purges the community through sacrificial bloodletting—through which the community isolates or eliminates "filth" so that its contagion cannot spread. That "filth" is, from the community's perspective, nothing more than a reification of violence is made abundantly clear throughout the novel, nowhere more so than in Stevens's narrative, which brings to closure the detective story inaugurated by Brown's revelation. For Stevens, black blood contains and absorbs violence and death: "It was the black blood," he says, "which swept him by his own desire beyond the aid of any man, swept him up into that ecstasy out of a black jungle where life has already ceased before the heart stops and death is desire and fulfillment" (449). Consciously or not, Stevens legitimates the act of segregation that has produced Freedman Town, which can be considered a legal separation by means of which the community maintains its symbolic cleanliness—that is to say, its separation from violence. The symbolic logic of segregation thus repeats the primitive practice of segregating women during menstruation, an analogy further reinforced when the narrative associates Freedman Town, "the original quarry, the abyss itself" (116), with "the lightless hot wet primogenitive Female" (115).

Although Stevens segregates black blood even within the confines of Christmas's body, it reappears in a different form in Hightower's kitchen: "Then his face, body, all, seemed to collapse, to fall in upon itself, and from out the slashed garments about his hips and loins the pent black blood seemed to rush like a released breath. It seemed to rush out of his pale body like the rush of sparks from a rising rocket; upon that black blast the man seemed to rise soaring into their memories forever and ever" (465). The crucial feature of this passage is the *diffusion* of violence produced by the "black blast" of Christmas's "pent black blood." At this critical moment the narrative, previously complicit in the association between black blood and violence, reifies black blood as an image "of itself alone serene, of itself alone triumphant" (465). The narrative's complicity, then, seems to have moved in a different direction, as does its relationship to the story of Negro rape: although unequivocally hostile to its presence earlier, here the narrative appears to mitigate—or even invert, insofar as violence produces serenity—its bloody consequences. Snead is thus partially correct in finding the narrator culpable for "offer[ing] a 'serene' and 'triumphant' recollection of a vigilante murder." But it is not a "vigilante murder," and not only because Grimm's *killing* of Christmas is perfectly justified from a legal perspective. It is what happens after the killing that matters, for when Grimm castrates Christmas, his actions are translated from the realm of law to the realm of sacrifice. According to Girard, sacrifice "purifies" violence by metaphorically transforming blood from an agent of contamination to an agent of purification. "The same substance," he writes, "can stain or cleanse, contaminate or purify, drive men to fury and murder or appease their anger and restore them to life."[34] The sacrifice of Joe Christmas works according to an identical logic; having arbitrarily designated black blood to absorb violence—violence intimately linked to sexuality—the community is able to protect itself through the purifying sacrifice of black blood: hence the diffusion of violence produced by Christmas's "black blast," which appears here as a dark parody of orgasm. And despite the narrative's previous hostility toward lynching and toward Percy Grimm, its complicity in this diffusion involves a complete alignment with the community and its sacrificial rite.

In the end, the story of Joe Christmas makes nothing happen; the center holds, and mere anarchy is exiled from this particular narrative world. Besides the serene and triumphant apotheosis that provides closure to his story, the clearest indication that his sacrifice enables the community's regeneration is the novel's conclusion, which, despite countless critical treatments attempting to make it more complicated than it is, represents nothing more than the happy ending many early commentators perceived and criticized as being extraneous to the novel's main action. Both the embedding context (the furniture dealer in bed with his wife) and the embedded story (Lena and Byron riding off, more or less, into the sunset) portray in the one case and predict in the other a sexual drive that has assumed its properly socialized form—that is, a form in which the cycle of violence that surrounds sexuality throughout the novel has broken. Although sexually transgressive

---

34. Snead, "Rhetorics of Racial Division," 168; Girard, *Violence and the Sacred,* 36–37. For a discussion of Christmas's death as an ineffective sacrifice, see Eric Sundquist, *Faulkner: The House Divided* (Baltimore: Johns Hopkins University Press, 1983), 93.

herself, Lena has, of course, been protected by the community all along, a point Brooks emphasizes in his portrayal of the organic community. Yet in labeling the novel "a bloody and violent pastoral,"[35] Brooks largely ignores the extent to which the pastoral mode is *predicated* upon blood—black blood—since the community expends upon Christmas aggressive impulses that, without mechanisms of surrogate victimization, might well have prevented charity in other scenarios. This is not, of course, to imply that Lena would have come to a bad end had Christmas not been available in the specific way that he is, but to assert the deep connection between the symbolic function served by black blood and the symbolic exchanges that constitute communal virtue, which we may take as the positive form of the community's suppression of violence. Insofar as the tragedy of Joe Christmas enables the comedy of Lena Grove, Lena may be more perspicacious than she realizes in confusedly perceiving Christmas to be the father of her child (409).

But *Light in August* is not simply a story about a sacrifice and its consequences; it is also a story about narrative. Black blood serves the function that it does only because of the stories told about it. And for those stories to displace violence onto black blood, the community must elide any ruptures between discourse and story. The central instance enabling the community's collective gestalt is, as we have seen, Brown's revelation of Christmas's black blood, an event that leads the entire community to say, along with the unnamed proprietor of the general store, "I said all the time that he wasn't right. Wasn't a white man. That there was something funny about him" (309). Brown's revelation, like the clue that breaks the case, enables the community's detective mode, revealing the structure that "was there all along" and thereby permitting collective racial norms to emanate from Christmas's story. In this respect, the community's collective narrative—that is, the sum total of the various embeddings and focal shifts through which the continuous mind is established—reflects the basic structure of literary narrative, which, as White says, typically "contains a plot [i.e., discourse] which imposes a meaning on the events that comprise its story level by revealing at

35. Brooks, *Yoknapatawpha Country*, 54.
36. White, *Content of the Form*, 19.

the end a structure that was immanent in events all along."[36] The community, however, has a great deal invested in repressing the fictional status of its stories in this specific sense. What the community requires is a hard-boiled detective story that gets to the bottom of things through the revelation of evidence—that is, the revelation of events that form parts of an *already-existing narrative.*

By assigning priority to story over discourse, then, the community need not *impose* meaning. And yet this is not only precisely what it does, but precisely what the story of Joe Christmas threatens to reveal. As Jonathan Culler remarks, the hierarchy of story over discourse easily reverses itself when events are presented "not as givens but as products of discursive forces or requirements." When "meaning is not the effect of a prior event but its cause," the whole logic of causation is disrupted.[37] Reading Brown's revelation as an *effect* of an existing discursive requirement—specifically, the desire for a black culprit—threatens to destabilize the socially essential meaning of black blood as a magical substance that contains violence. The community has, of course, long associated Christmas himself with violence, from his first appearance at the sawmill to his shadowy career as a moonshiner, one violent detail of which leads a man to comment, "Would it surprise you to hear that that fellow Christmas hadn't done no worse than that in his life?" (87). But the community's case against Joe Christmas is not a strong one—as Byron points out, "all the evidence they got against him is Brown's word, which is next to none" (390)—and their case, ultimately, is not against him at all. Divested of evidence against black blood by Christmas's physical appearance and by his refusal, as the Mottstown citizen puts, "to act like a nigger," the community must suspend disbelief and dispense with justice as a mechanism of objectification in order to maintain the sacrificial efficacy of Christmas's black blast. In the end, Gavin Stevens's detective narrative, which "discovers" that black blood causes violence, gives way to the sacrificial imperative of the Player's narrative of desire, the tacit logic of which dictates that violence, since it exists, must be attributable to black blood—a kind of *post facto* causality, if you will. And if Stevens shows how the meaning of Joe Christmas will be stabilized in a socially acceptable form, the

37. Culler, *Pursuit of Signs,* 172.

castration of Christmas in Hightower's kitchen threatens to expose the arbitrary, purely discursive nature of that meaning. It is not merely that the community brings its racial norms to bear on its stories, but that the stories themselves generate those norms. Hence the intolerable circularity of *Light in August* and the necessity of the *black* blast emanating from Christmas's loins: without it, the elaborate fiction, the collective design degenerates into chaos, and the violence is random violence.

That the narrative finally participates in Grimm's sacrificial rite suggests deep interdependence of the community's everyday racism and its hysterical racism, for both ultimately respond to the same symbol. Writing four years before *Light in August* was published, Ulrich Bonnell Phillips wrote that white supremacy, "whether expressed with the frenzy of a demagogue or maintained with a patrician's quietude, is the cardinal test of a Southerner and the central theme of Southern history."[38] *Light in August,* I think, corroborates, if not that precise thesis, at least the centrality of racial scapegoating to the southern community. Whether it appears in Gavin Stevens's patrician theorizing, Doc Hines's frenzied ranting, or on Percy Grimm's bloody knife, black blood serves as a kind of vanishing point at which all white perspectives converge. In the end, black blood provides the central symbol whose segregation or sacrifice permits the maintenance of the collective mind. That mind and the stories it tells reveal a society in crisis, a culture in the process of becoming reflexively aware of its racial ideology, deferring only at the last moment knowledge that would profoundly alter southern communities everywhere.

38. Ulrich Bonnell Phillips, "The Central Theme of Southern History," *American Historical Review* 34 (1928): 31.

Epilogue: Whence the Community?

Some Thoughts on Contemporary Southern Narrative

In *A Homemade World,* his idiosyncratic study of American modernism, Hugh Kenner calls William Faulkner the "last novelist." After Faulkner, Kenner writes, "[w]hatever goes in, satire is what comes out." Writing in the context of southern literature, Michael Kreyling argues a similar point. Kreyling is eager to valorize post-Faulknerian parody for its exposure and suspension of "the South" conceived as a mimetic given unmediated by representation rather than a "way of making and maintaining meaning" that, by the 1970s, "had ceased functioning, as it were, on involuntary muscles and had become a kind of willed habit." Kreyling's central insight seems inescapable: Faulkner's style defines a key moment in southern literature, a moment after which "the South" ceases to function "on involuntary muscles"—or, to use Polanyi's terminology, as a tacit dimension. Indeed, Kreyling largely sees, from the perspective afforded by several decades and an entirely different ideological view, what Allen Tate predicted in a 1945 essay: that "without regionalism, without locality in the sense of local continuity in tradition and belief," a generation of novelists would appear who "see *with,* not *through* the eye."[1]

1. Hugh Kenner, *A Homemade World: The American Modernist Writers* (Baltimore: Johns Hopkins University Press, 1975), 220; Michael Kreyling, "Fee, Fie, Faux Faulkner: Parody and Postmodernism in Southern Literature," *Southern Review* 29 (1993): 1; Allen Tate, "The New

We should first clarify that the "finality" of "Faulkner" is in no sense chronological: many writers since have forgotten what the author of his books knew. Yet insofar as it embodies a collective way of knowing, Faulkner's style threatens to become reflexively conscious of itself, a point at which its positivist tendencies, its displacement into things, devolves into mere textuality and ceases to function involuntarily. The question of the relationship between Faulkner and the end of southern literature is, of course, a massive one, only one facet of which will I examine here. That facet has to do with how Faulkner defines the limits of the southern community as a possibility for fiction. As we have seen, the community has never been a truly autochthonous ground; as a constant site of deferral, the community requires a constant investment of energy lest its self-evident organization begin to appear as something entirely different. Yet Faulkner's community remains self-evident in the limited sense that social roles based on race and class remain operative. Faulkner once commented that the tragedy of Joe Christmas was that "he didn't know what he was, and so was nothing. He deliberately evicted himself from the human race because he didn't know which he was."[2] Note the shift in pronouns. It apparently never occurred to Faulkner, nor does it register in his fiction, that "which he was" might bear no essential relation to "what he was." And if *Light in August* has only two basic classes of characters, the history of Yoknapatawpha County shows clearly that "aristocrat," "poor white," "plain white," and "Negro" all retain a collective tacit meaning. Such categories might verge on the arbitrary, but they are never meaningless.

A novel including such types today would, almost by default, devolve into a novel "about" the aristocrat, the poor white, the plain white, or the Negro—that is, these types would likely devolve into stereotypes. As Kreyling suggests, after Faulkner's massive encoding of these types, mere repetition is impossible. To put the matter another way, Faulkner is able to exploit the collective meaning of these social types in a way that is unavailable to the

Provincialism: With an Epilogue on the Southern Novel," in *Man of Letters in the Modern World, 1928–1955* (New York: Meridian Books, 1955), 322.

2. *Faulkner in the University*, 72.

contemporary novelist, whose knowledge of type is, almost by definition, focal rather than tacit. As Jack Butler says, "There's still a lot of sheriffs out there with cowboy hats, big fat bellies, and mirror shades, but try getting away with using one as a character."[3] Another way of stating the problem is to say that after Yoknapatawpha County, Hazzard County is all that's left. In turning his narrative eye upon the tacit dimension, Faulkner defined the reflexive limit at which collective meaning becomes collective fiction and at which, moreover, "collective" itself becomes a fiction. In so doing, he defined the limits of community—at least, one kind of community.

At about the same time as Faulkner, the Agrarians were confronting the problem of reflexivity as well. As Richard Weaver says in "Agrarianism in Exile," "as soon the agrarian anywhere adds, or allows to be added, the *ism*, he is preparing the way for his own exile. We are simply confronted with different planes of human consciousness. Every *ism* is an intellectual manufacture; it has, in all sobriety, little relation to the people who till the soil for a living." No one felt this dilemma more than Allen Tate, who observes in "Remarks on the Southern Religion" that "the act of loyalty, or the fact of loyalty, must be spontaneous to count at all; tradition must, in other words, be automatically operative before it can be called tradition." Choice precludes tradition, and even to frame the issue this way is to conceive of tradition in a manner antithetical to its nature. When Tate advises the southerner to take hold of his tradition "by violence," he is advising the choice of an option, and his sense of inevitable exile is tangible enough.[4] As Tate well realized in his prose and his poetry, the traditional community cannot be entered by an act of will.

Even as they attempted to recuperate the traditional community, the Agrarians registered a kind of reflexive dissonance that would manifest itself more tangibly as the century progressed. While an uneasy ambivalence toward traditional modes of social order would dominate midcentury fiction—one thinks of Jack Burden's attitude toward Burden's Landing in *All*

---

3. Jack Butler, "Still Southern after All These Years," in *The Future of Southern Letters*, ed. Jefferson Humphries and John Lowe (New York: Oxford University Press, 1996), 38.

4. Richard M. Weaver, "Agrarianism in Exile," in *Southern Essays of Richard M. Weaver*, 40; Tate, "Southern Religion," 162, 174.

the King's Men, for example, or any number of works by Eudora Welty—it would remain for Walker Percy to confront reflexivity as a given. In broad terms, where Quentin Compson and Jack Burden find that they can no longer sustain the tacit dimension of a traditional culture, Binx Bolling appears on the first page of *The Moviegoer* without having that dimension available, even as an option. And yet, paradoxically, Binx is confronted with a plenitude of options, not the least of which is his choice of community. If he is not the first character in southern literature to choose where he lives, he is probably the first to live there without first renouncing where he comes from. Another first (or near first) in *The Moviegoer* is the appearance of a suburban landscape full of "shopping centers and blocks of duplexes and bungalows and raised cottages." To call Gentilly a community is to abuse the term. What remains, vestigially, of the traditional community is associated with the Garden District, where Binx's Aunt Emily resides. "[B]ut whenever I try to live there," Binx relates, "I find myself first in a rage during which I develop strong opinions on a variety of subjects and write letters to editors, then in a depression during which I lie rigid as a stick for hours staring straight up at the plaster medallion in the ceiling of my bedroom." Although Binx would have some literary company in this regard, it is nearly impossible to imagine him raging about anything. He is in exile as the novel opens; even the imperative to resist traditional roles has dissipated. Identity conferred by class, family, and community is already a null category. Reflecting on his attachment to bureaucratic documents that would have chilled Agrarian blood, Binx opines, "It is a pleasure to carry out the duties of a citizen and to receive in return a receipt or a neat styrene card with one's name on it certifying, so to speak, one's right to exist."[5]

The traditional South makes an appearance in the character of Binx's Aunt Emily, whose likeness to Will Percy, to whom *The Moviegoer* is dedicated, has not gone unnoticed. Like "Uncle Will" and his "Fode," Aunt Emily has a faithful retainer named Mercer. At least she thinks so: "My aunt truly loves him and sees him as a faithful retainer, a living connection with a bygone age." Binx is not so sure; he fully understands the performative, dramatic nature of Mercer's role, and he constantly frets that Mercer will forget

---

5. Walker Percy, *The Moviegoer* (1961; reprint, New York: Noonday Press, 1967), 9, 6, 7.

his lines. "My main emotion around Mercer," he says, "is unease in that threading his way between servility and presumption, his foot might slip." As its title suggests, *The Moviegoer* is a novel about performance and its reception; indeed, Binx's defining character trait is his tendency toward an endless regress of spectatorship. He not only observes, but he observes spectators (at the Mardi Gras parade, for example), and he observes his own act of spectatorship. He is reflexively aware of the performative demands placed upon him and upon everyone else. He remembers his aunt informing him that his brother was dead and asking him "to act like a soldier": "I could easily act like a soldier."[6] But if acting is at one remove from reality, so spectatorship is at two removes, and so on in a potentially infinite regressive series. Yet paradoxically, what is least real to Binx is a direct confrontation with reality; it is the hyperreality conferred by movies and other spectacles that suspends the tyranny of the "everyday."

Although it is not my purpose to untangle the complex metaphysics behind Binx's (and Percy's) conception of reality, I will observe that this conception makes it impossible for him to dwell in the common ground that enables normal social relationships. If Binx is not precisely beyond ideology, certainly he is beyond the ideology of his Aunt Emily, who states her objections to his behavior, in terms of tacit knowing. "I have been assuming," she says, "that between us words mean roughly the same thing, that among certain people, gentlefolk I don't mind calling them, there exists a certain set of meanings held in common." Besides learning that she and Binx do not share this "certain set of meanings," Aunt Emily learns that Binx cannot explain why; when pressed, he replies, "My objections, though they are not exactly objections, cannot be expressed in the usual way. To tell the truth, I can't express them at all."[7] This is a curious silence on the part of a character who is perfectly at home in his reflexive consciousness, and it is a deafening silence, a silence that marks the terminal limits of community in any traditionalist sense. For Binx meaning has deserted the social world and can be conceived only in otherworldly—specifically, religious—terms. Connection requires not a set of givens, but a leap of faith.

Where Binx is silent, many novelists of the 1950s and 1960s were vocal,

6. Ibid., 23, 22, 4.
7. Ibid., 222, 225.

vehemently and explicitly objecting to the racial sins of the fathers. "Race novels," many examples of which have justifiably faded into the woodwork of southern literary history, did not reflexively define the limits of community so much as attempt to abolish it outright. The community in Douglas Kiker's *The Southerner* (1957), which I will consider (somewhat arbitrarily) as a kind of epitome of this form, exerts an unequivocally insidious pressure against Kiker's hero. The plot of the novel is simple enough. Jess Witherow, a newspaper reporter, observes an African American friend, Will Taylor, attempt to enroll his son in a white school; when the principal of the school falsely accuses Will of assault, Jess is called upon to testify in Will's behalf. Kiker halfheartedly attempts to introduce some ambiguity into Jess's politics, an effort that consists primarily of having Jess know "that there was an element of truth in Southerners' claims about Negroes." These racial faults include the following: Negroes turn houses into slums, they rarely bathe, they buy "flashy automobiles when their houses are leaking," and they "go into massive sex demonstrations right on the dance floor." Although Jess protests that "being identified as some fanatical champion of the race revolted me," there is, in fact, little evidence for this claim; the best reason Kiker can muster for having Jess refuse to testify is that he must give up, for reasons that are never quite explained, an aristocratic beauty named Dugan Phillips.[8] What Jess thinks of as a dilemma is anything but, and because his duty is so unambiguously clear, *The Southerner,* like many novels of a similar stripe, rarely rises above the level of a morality play.

In his polemical 1968 Lamar Lectures, *The Death of Art,* Floyd C. Watkins argued this point heatedly, suggesting that the post-1954 southern novel had been contaminated by depicting African American characters "as too good to be true."[9] *The Death of Art* includes as case studies several novels that hardly substantiate Watkins's thesis, and it tacitly but clearly communicates a reactionary political stance on the Civil Rights movement. There is, nonetheless, some truth in Watkins's charge. With Kiker's Negro, we are virtually back where we were with Page, and perhaps even a little further back, since even Page's black characters are complex in ways that elude authorial intention. Conversely, Kiker's Negro does precisely what he wants.

8. Douglas Kiker, *The Southerner* (New York: Rinehart, 1957), 189.
9. Floyd C. Watkins, *The Death of Art: Black and White in the Recent Southern Novel* (Athens: University of Georgia Press, 1970), 12.

Will is eminently respectable, a perfect spokesman for the cause—he is also, it should be noted, neatly separated from the unwashed, dialect speaking Negro, who is mentioned in passing but rarely shown. Compared with the Renascence novel it most resembles—Faulkner's *Intruder in the Dust* (1948), itself often criticized for being too rhetorical in driving home its moral— *The Southerner* is in every respect an impoverished novel; its characters unambiguously fail Lukács's criterion for the type: that "all the humanly and socially essential determinants are present." Where Lucas Beauchamp is both man and "Negro," Will Taylor is "just plain Will," a man to whom Jess can speak like any other. Where Chick Mallison's duty to Lucas is intricate and convoluted due to his community's racial norms, Jess's duty to Will is perfectly clear: it is the duty of one man to another.

In *The Southerner* "Negro" has ceased to have any meaning—or to put the matter another way, those for whom it retains meaning are exposed as vicious bigots. Perhaps not so curiously, the same is true of "southerner." Despite the novel's title, Jess effortlessly renounces his "heritage of hatred"— and that is precisely what his heritage consists of. Yet near the end of the novel, as Jess is preparing to leave the South, he catalogues the crimes of the southern "forces of violence and hatred" before qualifying his denunciation: "The irreconcilable part of it was that, in repudiating the evil in the South, you also had to repudiate the good, the good people—and the great majority of Southerners were good people—and the good things about the place—the loyalty of friendship, the charity, the honor. But you could not reject a part without rejecting the whole because, God help us, we were all bound together in this thing."[10] Although it is too weighty a theme for a weak writer, it is interesting to note how, despite that the "good people" and "good things" Jess mentions are nowhere in evidence in a novel whose South consists mainly of hypocritical aristocrats and depraved poor whites (one of whom keeps a Negro toe as a souvenir of a lynching), he is essentially stating a point that the White Citizens Councils were making at about the same time: that with the disappearance of its racial hierarchies, the southern tradition would disappear as well. This is probably a half-truth, but the half that is true is not insignificant. Insofar as southern hegemony depended

10. Kiker, *The Southerner*, 294.

upon racial hierarchies, then *The Southerner* might be said to mark, as a somewhat arbitrary but still representative point of reference, the point at which hegemony is marked as morally irredeemable.

Whether this marks the termination of the southern community as a possibility for narrative is a somewhat more complicated issue. While the community figures less prominently in postwar fiction, this shift can to some extent be ascribed to the massive social and economic changes that spawned strip malls and suburbs, and eroded communities conceived in a traditional sense. If community is not merely a kind of place, but a mythology of place, it may well be that a certain kind of place must be there to mythologize. Significantly, *The Southerner* is set not in Jess's hometown of Cleo, a small mill community, but in Antioch, a large city seething with commerce; among the novel's many artifactual virtues is its depiction of how industrialism, boosterism, and the demands of the market combine to create an imperative that the South renounce its "backward" ways. The connection between industrialism and the breakdown of social hierarchies has long been a staple of both conservative and liberal rhetoric; what the one has lamented, the other has celebrated. But while the relationship between demographics and ideology is far too complex to examine here, I will hazard the general observation that as segregation ended, southern narrative tended to become more segregated. I do not take this as a necessarily pernicious development, especially given the kind of quasi-integration we have traced in writers like Kennedy, Page, and (more fitfully) Percy, for whom the black southerner acts as a keeper of the white conscience. (Here we can think of Alice Walker commending Flannery O'Connor for leaving her black characters undeveloped, for not presuming to know.) On the other hand, it often seems as if that coercive relationship, instead of evolving on a more authentically consensual ground, has simply disappeared, which, in a curious way, is what the conservative tradition had been warning all along. It is eerie to hear George Fitzhugh's irony a century and a half later: "The old relation has become unsuitable, obsolete, perhaps unjust; and the remedy is, abolish it; let there henceforth be no relation at all."[11]

11. Alice Walker, "Beyond the Peacock: The Reconstruction of Flannery O'Connor," in *In Search of Our Mothers' Gardens* (San Diego: Harcourt Brace, 1983), 52–54; Fitzhugh, *Cannibals All!* 11.

* * *

Community survives in southern literature, but in an ideologically diluted form. Community is rarely equated with hegemony; personal relationships are rarely mediated by social categories; the very concept of a social order is all but anachronistic. To what extent, then, does community survive? First, it survives vestigially in the sense of place that has long been designated (and often exaggerated) as a distinctive and defining trait of southern literature. Even if there is nothing distinctively southern about place, it is equally clear that place has served a distinctive function in southern literature, where historically it has tended to absorb and negate, as a concrete icon, many anxieties associated with the hegemonic order. Place is, on some level, a name for and a form of ideology; it is never "just place." While place continues to exert a weak pressure in contemporary narrative, it seems apparent that place serves more as a mere setting and less as a determinant than it did in the fiction of a half century ago; place means less because less meaning is displaced to it. As James Justus bluntly puts it, "The old piety of place so common to the agrarian generation is no longer operable." Julius Rowan Raper sees this as a positive development. Finding modernist representations of place to be consonant with the "control of reality" exerted by "the advertisers and ideologues of the age," Raper contends that "in modern Southern literature the sense of place takes on a role better played by a sense of self." Borrowing a page from Alain Robbe-Grillet, Raper suggests that postmodernist subversions of verisimilitude may allow southern writers, at last free of collective guilt and shame, and possessed of a "solid" sense of self, to "dispense with the grandiose loyalties grounded in the piety of place."[12] Raper's conception of place as a defense mechanism, a pathological surrogate for selfhood, parallels his trust, derived from Jungian psychoanalysis, in the utopian possibilities of individualism.

What piety remains tends to accumulate around alternative or marginalized places. Many communities in contemporary southern fiction involve an implicit act of segregation. Communities of women abound in the work of

12. James H. Justus, Foreword to *Southern Writers at Century's End*, ed. Jeffrey J. Folks and James A. Perkins (Lexington: University Press of Kentucky, 1997), xiii; Julius Rowan Raper, "Inventing Modern Southern Fiction: A Postmodern View," *Southern Literary Journal* 22 (1990): 10, 3, 13.

Alice Walker, Lee Smith, Anne Tyler, Gail Godwin, Jill McCorkle, Sherley Anne Williams, and Kaye Gibbons. Discussing several of these writers in a 1990 essay, Linda Wagner-Martin writes that *The Color Purple* is typical of contemporary fiction written by women in that it produces "ego identities" that have "strangely permeable boundaries." According to Wagner-Martin, "What formerly constituted 'self' as some rigidly defined unit becomes 'self' as a part of some sharing whole."[13] This whole, however, can never be comprehensive, since community in this sense can appear only as an enclave opposed to, excluded from, or otherwise outside the hegemonic order. Although Wagner-Martin and Raper may disagree as to the desirability of discrete ego identities, they are describing two distinct—and not necessarily mutually exclusive—reactions to community conceived in a traditionalist sense: a valorization of enclaves in the one case, and a subversion of the "pieties of place" associated with hegemony in the other. Both reflect trends within contemporary fiction that are part of a larger shift away from the conception of social reality in comprehensive terms.

Insofar as the traditional community remains a possibility for realistic narrative, it does so in an increasingly tenuous way. The possibility exists that "the South" has become available exclusively to discourse and not to narrative, in Benveniste's sense of these terms; the contemporary (not to mention postmodern) southern writer finds it difficult (if not undesirable) to dwell in the tacit dimension upon which an objective, "mimetic" South (to use Kreyling's label) is contingent. It would be an overstatement to say that the South no longer produces collective fictions because it is one, but there is a perceptible shift in this direction. It is difficult to write about the South without being conscious of the act. As Fred Hobson observes in *The Southern Writer in the Postmodern World,* the contemporary southern writer is "in danger of writing a sort of twentieth-century local color" resulting from the self-reflexive violation of the autochthonous ideal. This is not a problem exclusive to writers, since one way southernness survives is as a kind of nonreferential performance. It is possible—even profitable—to "act southern" today in a way that would have been inconceivable a century ago.

---

13. Linda Wagner-Martin, " 'Just the Doing of It': Southern Women Writers and the Idea of Community," *Southern Literary Journal* 22 (1990): 21.

Eating grits, for example, can mean something entirely different today from what it did then to the Mississippi sharecropper who ate them because that's what he had. Eating grits today can be manipulated as a sign of southernness: to eat grits is, in one sense, to identify oneself a southerner. And curiously, one can make a living from eating grits, as the career of Jeff Foxworthy adequately demonstrates. Hobson sees several contemporary writers as succumbing to a similar temptation.

Among the most symptomatic works in this regard is Clyde Edgerton's *Raney* (1985), a work that commits, in its representation of a small North Carolina community, what Davidson might call the ethnographic heresy. Edgerton's attempt to represent an "authentic" voice from this culture results in egregious ventriloquism; the title character is so radically overdetermined as a repressed hick that it is impossible to take her seriously. As Jack Butler observes, the erosion of cultural givens has necessitated that the contemporary writer "accumulate real-world details," an effort that, without "the entire culture backing them up . . . may seem antiquated or worse, clichéd" (38). Edgerton too often seems clichéd. Raney thinks vegetarians are born that way; Raney thinks Jesus turned water into grape juice; Raney thinks "segregation" means "integration"; Raney thinks that "a person shouldn't say 'nigger' *to* a nigger—unless maybe the nigger acts like one";[14] the list goes on. Although I do not doubt that every detail has an actual referent somewhere in the contemporary South, the cumulative effect is one of overkill; in the end, *Raney* crosses the limit at which the mimetic representation of "the South" devolves into performative self-indulgence.

If *Raney* produces the traditional community as mimetic object, it does so in a manner that is ultimately unconvincing. In this respect it might be said to represent the first of three modes by which the traditional southern community survives in contemporary narrative: (1) as a tenuously authentic, autochthonous community available to realist narration, (2) as an oppressive social order necessitating alternative communities or enclaves, and (3) as an object of postmodern deconstruction or parody. It is the third that I would like to consider in more detail, particularly in light of Kreyling's discussion

14. Fred Hobson, *The Southern Writer in the Postmodern World* (Athens: University of Georgia Press, 1991), 80–81; Butler, "Still Southern," 38; Clyde Edgerton, *Raney* (New York: Ballantine Books, 1985), 126.

of the "collision of the southern 'immovable object' and the postmodern 'irresistible force.'" Rejecting the hopes of Hobson and Lewis Simpson that "southern literary history will continue on its classic, renaissance foundations," Kreyling contends that there is "no escape from a world mediated through representations, no recourse to the totalizing and totally authoritative referent: capitalism, patriarchy, the novel, the South." Although Kreyling's literary examples of postsouthern parody from Reynolds Price to Barry Hannah tend to move in an exclusively deconstructive direction, his "cautionary" step provocatively opens a way in which "the South" might survive postmodern interrogation: "To put quotation marks around the real is not to efface the real; rather, it is to put it into a condition of multiple codes rather than the traditional realistic mimetic system. History still exists; we now acknowledge that we know it through a system of representations rather than in an unmediated, direct way. . . . Postmodernism does not deconstruct the past and meaning, except by interrogating the systems by which those entities have been known as such."[15] The "except" in the last sentence is a massive one, since to interrogate the systems by which knowledge is produced is, in a fundamental sense, a deconstructive act. In many respects the narratives we have considered here are primarily concerned with deferring such interrogation, for to know a system *qua* system is to produce a radically different kind of knowledge. Insofar as post-Faulknerian parody participates in what might be called (borrowing a page from cubism) analytic postmodernism, so much for the good: the traditional South was based on social hierarchies whose arbitrary and pernicious character necessitated this kind of analysis. But at the same time, the analysis and deconstruction of meaning can be extended indefinitely: anything that means, can potentially mean something else. To function as social beings, we need, at some level, to defer the textuality of things so that belief can exist—a kind of synthetic or pragmatic postmodernism, if you will. As the postmodern condition is an agnostic one, this belief will probably be less like that of the old, autochthonous dispensation and more like Wallace Stevens's "supreme fiction": a fiction we know as such and can still live with.

15. Michael Kreyling, *Inventing Southern Literature* (Jackson: University Press of Mississippi, 1998), 155, 153, 155.

It is not, I think, theoretically impossible to put "the South" in quotation marks and then remove them under a pragmatic aegis. In short, my hope is that after interrogating the meaning-producing systems—that is, the ideology—of the South, it might be possible to identify certain foundation assumptions by means of which a legitimate community could be sustained. As Sacvan Bercovitch reminds us, ideology is not simply what the rich do to the poor, it is "the ground and texture of consensus." Nor, as Bercovitch says, is ideology "simply repressive": "the very terms of cultural restriction [can become] a source of creative release: they serve to incite the imagination, to unleash the energies of reform, to encourage diversity and accommodate change—all this, while directing the rights of diversity into a rite of cultural assent."[16] To be sure, Bercovitch is speaking of American ideology; his comments, historically at least, are less applicable to the ideology of "Uncle Sam's other province," where the rites of assent have too often been the product of sheer coercion. Consequently, any attempt to recuperate a southern ideology must begin in a spirit of tough-minded critique, lest it degenerate into a facile attempt to extract a sanitized tradition in much the same manner as postbellum writers like Page recuperated an iconic "Old South" while evading the concrete evils of slavery. Yet analytic postmodernism, for which ideology is always false consciousness, would preclude community altogether.

Even in a postsouthern age circumstances are not altogether unfavorable for negotiating community on new terms. For one thing, the transition between a traditional agrarian economy and multinational capitalism has been especially abrupt in the South, resulting in a rich matrix of juxtapositions between traditional and contemporary forms of culture. An hour's drive from Atlanta or Charlotte can still open one's eyes. In one context, this interaction has produced *Southern Living,* Southern Comfort whiskey, *The Dukes of Hazzard,* and other commodifications of southernness. More hopefully, however, the residual culture of an earlier age may situate southern writers in a position to mediate meaningfully between postmodernity and tradition. A second favorable circumstance involves a durable belief in

16. Sacvan Bercovitch, "The Problem of Ideology in American Literary History," *Critical Inquiry* 12 (1986): 635.

southern distinctiveness. Although Hugh Ruppersburg is correct in asserting that contemporary writing often lacks the sense—so prevalent in the Renascence era—of the "South as an alternative to what many regard as depersonalizing and hostile in the rest of the world,"[17] many southerners continue, incontrovertibly, to think of the South in precisely these terms. Even if the South is less distinctive than it used to be, the redemptive mythology that continues to accrue around southern distinctiveness is, perhaps, something to go on.

In *Intruder in the Dust* Gavin Stevens predicted that the South's sheer experience in interracial relationships promised an eventual redemption. He was, to be sure, a windbag, but a provocative one nonetheless. Yet, if we are indeed "all bound together in this thing," many of our contemporary writers have failed to show us exactly how. Contemporary narrative written by whites has tended to efface social categories that still function powerfully: although race continues to hold immense and manifold meanings in the South and in the nation as a whole, one searches almost in vain for a major novel after *The Confessions of Nat Turner* that thematizes race at a metacultural level. The types are still out there, but their encoding occurs far more powerfully—and, I would contend, more perniciously—in mass culture than in narrative. This is one reason, I think, why commentators like Hobson find "the *big* novel" to be conspicuously absent in contemporary fiction.[18] The loss, rather than the evolution, of the interracial community in southern narrative reflects, I think, a lost opportunity. Like Raney, we still do not know the meaning of "integration."

With a word so encrusted with taboo and political rhetoric, it will take a special style—an acidic one, perhaps—to uncover what an integrated community might really look like. The stylists are among us, and not all of them have averted their eyes from the issue. Barry Hannah, one of the great sentence-level writers to appear in the past three decades, dares to be offensive in his treatment of race in a way that allows the meaning of race to emerges powerfully and disturbingly. Lewis Nordan's *Wolf Whistle*, a novel

17. Hugh Ruppersburg, "James Wilcox: The Normality of Madness," in *Southern Writers at Century's End*, 34.

18. Fred Hobson, "Of Canons and Culture Wars: Southern Literature and Literary Scholarship after Midcentury," in *Future of Southern Letters*, 85.

based on the 1955 murder of Emmett Till, is one of a handful of truly significant novels to appear in this decade. The collision of racial rage and parody that dominates his novel is one way of formalizing the rage that is still there. Like Hannah, Nordan employs types that are so overdetermined, so over-the-top, that they avoid cliché. In an entirely different key, Josephine Humphreys employs a distinctively southern brand of synthetic postmodernism that brilliantly interrogates words like "family" and "romance," but her style and the vision it encompasses extend to race relations in a compelling way. Well into *The Fireman's Fair*, an African American character informs a white friend of a shocking fact: he has been treated as a "nigger friend" whose sole job is to listen and offer sage advice. It is a disorienting moment for the white character and the reader. In *Dreams of Sleep*, Humphreys's protagonist wonders:

> What will happen to all these black people, now the movement is dead, their heroes tucked away in public offices? Was the whole civil rights movement nothing but a minor disturbance in the succession of years? White people have started telling jokes again. Blacks and whites live farther apart than ever, like the double curve of a hyperbolic function, two worlds of identical misery and passion but occupying opposite quadrants, nonintersecting. In a way, equal but separate. One day something will blow up, but Alice doesn't know whether it will be the world or the South or the Reese family.[19]

As one of our leading contemporary novelists of manners, Humphreys is asking important questions about the structure of race relations in a post-southern world. Southern writers would do well to ask these questions more frequently, for as Alice Reese recognizes, the promise of an interracial community emerging from the Civil Rights movement has conspicuously failed to materialize in many ways. It is too soon to say whether "something will blow up" in our own time, but the possibility is there. The need for a collective ideology—a ground of consensus—has never been greater.

In a postmodern world of dissensus, information overload, and truculent differences, community itself begins to look like a conceptual dinosaur, and it

19. Josephine Humphreys, *The Fireman's Fair* (New York: Viking, 1991), 226; Humphreys, *Dreams of Sleep* (New York: Penguin, 1984), 134.

may well be that community is too far gone to serve as the kind of public space or ground for ideological negotiation that I have in mind. But I do not think so. Jameson says that all narratives point toward utopia, and with that in mind, let me end mine with a community that I would like to read about. In 1994 a young woman in Union, South Carolina, killed her two children by drowning them in a car she pushed into a lake. She was eventually arrested, convicted, and sentenced to life in prison. The story would probably not have garnered national attention had the woman not concocted a story about an African American assailant who had kidnaped her children. A half-century earlier that story would surely have produced a lynching, as several black leaders in Union attested. Yet the woman's story did not work as she envisioned. The battle lines did not appear in the expected way, and a dialogue emerged across racial lines that would be inconceivable in New York or even Atlanta. To be sure, there is more to this horrific episode than the happy ending that I perhaps have appended, and which a television producer somewhere perhaps constructed. Yet to all appearances, a southern community in crisis extended the old ideals of responsibility, connectedness, and manners across racial lines. If the southern community is to remain a vital ground for fiction and a resource for interracial dialogue, it will take a writer who is willing to look behind appearances, to interrogate both "southern" and "community," and see if there is anything left to recuperate. If I'm not mistaken, there's a story there.

Bibliography

Andrews, William L. "In Search of a Common Identity: The Self and the South in Four Mississippi Autobiographies." *Southern Review* 24 (1988): 47–64.

————. "Inter(racial)textuality in Nineteenth-Century Southern Narrative." In *Influence and Intertextuality in Literary History*, edited by Jay Clayton and Eric Rothstein, 298–317. Madison: University of Wisconsin Press, 1991.

Bakhtin, M. M. *The Dialogic Imagination.* Edited and translated by Michael Holquist and Caryl Emerson. Austin: University of Texas Press, 1981.

————. *Problems of Dostoevsky's Poetics.* Edited and translated by Caryl Emerson. Minneapolis: University of Minnesota Press, 1984.

Bakker, Jan. *Pastoral in Antebellum Southern Romance.* Baton Rouge: Louisiana State University Press, 1989.

Bal, Mieke. "The Narrating and the Focalizing: A Theory of the Agents in Narrative." *Style* 17 (1983): 234–69.

————. "Notes on Narrative Embedding." *Poetics Today* 2, no. 2 (1981): 41–59.

Banfield, Ann. "Reflective and Non-Reflective Consciousness in the Language of Fiction." *Poetics Today* 2, no. 2 (1981): 61–76.

Barthes, Roland. *Mythologies.* Translated by Annette Lavers. New York: Hill and Wang, 1972.

Benveniste, Emile. *Problems in General Linguistics.* Translated by Mary Elizabeth Meek. Coral Gables, Fla.: University of Miami Press, 1971.

Bercovitch, Sacvan. *The Office of the Scarlet Letter.* Baltimore: Johns Hopkins University Press, 1991.

————. "The Problem of Ideology in American Literary History." *Critical Inquiry* 12 (1986): 631–53.

Bleicher, Joseph. *Contemporary Hermeneutics: Hermeneutics as Method, Philosophy, and Critique.* London: Routledge, 1980.

Booth, Wayne C. *The Rhetoric of Fiction.* Chicago: University of Chicago Press, 1961.

———. *A Rhetoric of Irony.* Chicago: University of Chicago Press, 1974.

Bourdieu, Pierre. *Outline of a Theory of Practice.* Translated by Richard Nice. Cambridge, U.K.: Cambridge University Press, 1977.

Bradford, M. E. "Where We Were Born and Raised." In *The Reactionary Imperative: Essays Literary and Political.* Peru, Ill.: Sherwood Sugden, 1990.

Brooks, Cleanth. *On the Prejudices, Predilections, and Firm Beliefs of William Faulkner.* Baton Rouge: Louisiana State University Press, 1987.

———. "William Faulkner." In *The History of Southern Literature,* edited by Louis D. Rubin, Jr. et al., 333–42. Baton Rouge: Louisiana State University Press, 1985.

———. *William Faulkner: The Yoknapatawpha Country.* New Haven: Yale University Press, 1963.

Brown, Carolyn S. *The Tall Tale in American Folklore and Literature.* Knoxville: University of Tennessee Press, 1987.

Burke, Kenneth. *The Philosophy of Literary Form: Studies in Symbolic Action.* Berkeley and Los Angeles: University of California Press, 1973.

Butler, Jack. "Still Southern after All These Years." In *The Future of Southern Letters,* edited by Jefferson Humphries and John Lowe, 33–40. New York: Oxford University Press, 1996.

Cash, W. J. *The Mind of the South.* New York: Alfred A. Knopf, 1941.

Chafe, William H. *Civilities and Civil Rights: Greensboro, North Carolina, and the Black Struggle for Freedom.* Oxford, U.K.: Oxford University Press, 1981.

Cohen, Hennig, and William B. Dillingham, eds. *Humor of the Old Southwest.* 3rd ed. Athens: University of Georgia Press, 1994.

Cox, James M. "Humor of the Old Southwest." In *The Comic Imagination in American Literature,* edited by Louis D. Rubin Jr., 105–106. Washington, D.C.: Voice of America Forum Series, 1974.

Culler, Jonathan. *The Pursuit of Signs: Semiotics, Literature, Deconstruction.* Ithaca, N.Y.: Cornell University Press, 1981.

Dabbs, James McBride. *The Southern Heritage.* New York: Alfred A. Knopf, 1958.

———. *Haunted by God.* Richmond: John Knox Press, 1972.

———. *Who Speaks for the South?* New York: Funk and Wagnalls, 1964.

Davidson, Donald. "The Artist as Southerner." *Saturday Review,* 15 May 1926, 781–83.

————. "The Southern Poet and His Tradition." *Poetry* 40 (1932): 94–105.

Davis, Lennard J. *Resisting Novels: Ideology and Fiction.* New York: Methuen, 1987.

Dixon, Thomas. "The Southern Question." In *Living Problems in Religion and Social Science.* New York: Charles T. Dillingham, 1889.

Douglas, Mary. *Purity and Danger: An Analysis of Concepts of Pollution and Taboo.* New York: Frederick A. Praeger, 1966.

Dupuy, Edward J. "The Dispossessed Garden of William Alexander Percy." *Southern Quarterly* 29, no. 2 (1991): 31–41.

Durkheim, Emile. *The Division of Labor in Society.* Translated by W. D. Halls. New York: Free Press, 1997.

Duvall, John N. *Faulkner's Marginal Couple: Invisible, Outlaw, and Unspeakable Communities.* Austin: University of Texas Press, 1990.

Eakin, Paul John. *Touching the World: Reference in Autobiography.* Princeton: Princeton University Press, 1992.

Edgerton, Clyde. *Raney.* New York: Ballantine Books, 1985.

Elkins, Stanley M. *Slavery: A Problem in American Institutional and Intellectual Life.* 1959. Reprint. New York: Grosset and Dunlap, 1963.

Ellison, Ralph. "Twentieth-Century Fiction and the Black Mask of Humanity." In *The Collected Essays of Ralph Ellison,* edited by John F. Callahan, 81–99. New York: Modern Library, 1995.

Fadiman, Regina K. *Faulkner's "Light in August": A Description and Interpretation of the Revisions.* Charlottesville: University Press of Virginia, 1975.

Faulkner, William. *Faulkner in the University: Class Conferences at the University of Virginia, 1957–1958.* Edited by Frederick L. Gwynn and Joseph L. Blotner. 1959. Reprint. New York: Vintage, 1965.

————. *Intruder in the Dust.* New York: Random House, 1948.

————. *Light in August.* 1932. Corrected Text edited by Noel Polk. New York: Vintage, 1990.

Fitzgerald, O. P. *Judge Longstreet: A Life Sketch.* Nashville: Publishing House of the Methodist Episcopal Church, 1891.

Fitzhugh, George. *Cannibals All! or, Slaves without Masters.* Edited by C. Vann Woodward. Cambridge, Mass.: Belknap Press, 1960.

Gates, Henry Louis. *The Signifying Monkey: A Theory of African-American Literary Criticism.* New York: Oxford University Press, 1988.

Genette, Gérard. *Narrative Discourse: An Essay in Method.* Translated by Jane E. Lewin. Ithaca, N.Y.: Cornell University Press, 1980.

Genovese, Eugene D. *Roll, Jordan, Roll: The World the Slaves Made.* New York: Pantheon Books, 1972.

———. "The South in the History of the Transatlantic World." In *What Made the South Different?* edited by Kees Gispen. Jackson: University Press of Mississippi, 1990.

———. *The Southern Tradition: The Achievement and Limitations of an American Conservatism.* Cambridge, Mass.: Harvard University Press, 1994.

Girard, René. *Violence and the Sacred.* Translated by Patrick Gregory. Baltimore: Johns Hopkins University Press, 1977.

Godden, Richard. "Call Me Nigger! Race and Speech in Faulkner's *Light in August.*" *Journal of American Studies* 14 (1980): 235–48.

Goellner, Ellen. "By Word of Mouth: Narrative Dynamics of Gossip in Faulkner's *Light in August.*" *Narrative* 1 (1993): 105–23.

Gramsci, Antonio. *Selections from the Prison Notebooks of Antonio Gramsci.* Edited and translated by Quintin Hoare and Geoffrey Nowell-Smith. New York: International Publishers, 1971.

Gray, Richard. *Writing the South: Ideas of an American Region.* Cambridge, U.K.: Cambridge University Press, 1986.

Habermas, Jürgen. *Communication and the Evolution of Society.* Translated by Thomas McCarthy. Boston: Beacon Press, 1979.

———. *The Theory of Communicative Action.* Vol. 2, *Lifeworld and System: A Critique of Functionalist Reason.* Translated by Thomas McCarthy. Boston: Beacon Press, 1987.

Hahn, Steven. "The Yeomanry of the Nonplantation South: Upper Piedmont Georgia, 1850–1860." In *Class, Conflict, and Consensus: Antebellum Southern Community Studies,* edited by Orville Vernon Burton and Robert C. McGrath Jr. Westport, Conn.: Greenwood Press, 1982.

Hobson, Fred. "Of Canons and Culture Wars: Southern Literature and Literary Scholarship after Midcentury." In *The Future of Southern Letters,* edited by Jefferson Humphries and John Lowe, 72–86. New York: Oxford University Press, 1996.

———. *The Southern Writer in the Postmodern World.* Athens: University of Georgia Press, 1991.

———. *Tell about the South: The Southern Rage to Explain.* Baton Rouge: Louisiana State University Press, 1983.

Holdsworth, Carolyn. "The Gorgon's Head and the Mirror: Fact versus Metaphor in *Lanterns on the Levee.*" *Southern Literary Journal* 14, no. 1 (1981): 36–45.

Holman, C. Hugh. *The Roots of Southern Writing.* Athens: University of Georgia Press, 1972.

Holmes, William F. "William Alexander Percy and the Bourbon Era in the Yazoo-Mississippi Delta." *Mississippi Quarterly* 26 (1972–73): 71–88.

Hubbell, Jay B. *The South in American Literature, 1607–1900.* Durham, N.C.: Duke University Press, 1954.

Humphreys, Josephine. *Dreams of Sleep.* New York: Penguin, 1984.

———. *The Fireman's Fair.* New York: Viking, 1991.

Jakobson, Roman. "Two Aspects of Language and Two Types of Aphasic Disturbances." In *Selected Writings.* 2 vols. The Hague: Mouton, 1971. 2:239–2:259.

Jameson, Fredric. *The Political Unconscious: Narrative as a Socially Symbolic Act.* Ithaca, N.Y.: Cornell University Press, 1981.

Jehlen, Myra. *Class and Character in Faulkner's South.* New York: Columbia University Press, 1976.

Justus, James H. Foreword to *Southern Writers at Century's End,* edited by Jeffrey J. Folks and James A. Perkins. Lexington: University Press of Kentucky, 1997. xi–xiii.

Kennedy, John Pendleton. *Swallow Barn; or, A Sojourn in the Old Dominion.* Rev. ed. New York: G. P. Putnam, 1851.

Kenner, Hugh. *A Homemade World: The American Modernist Writers.* Baltimore: Johns Hopkins University Press, 1975.

Kibler, James E., Jr. Introduction to *Georgia Scenes,* by Augustus Baldwin Longstreet. Nashville: J. S. Sanders, 1992.

Kiker, Douglas. *The Southerner.* New York: Rinehart, 1957.

King, Kimball. *Augustus Baldwin Longstreet.* Boston: Twayne, 1984.

———. Introduction to *In Ole Virginia; or, Marse Chan and Other Stories,* by Thomas Nelson Page. Chapel Hill: University of North Carolina Press, 1969.

King, Richard. *A Southern Renaissance: The Cultural Awakening of the American South, 1930–1955.* New York: Oxford University Press, 1980.

Kinney, Arthur F. *Faulkner's Narrative Poetics: Style as Vision.* Amherst: University of Massachusetts Press, 1978.

Kreisworth, Martin. "Plots and Counterplots: The Structure of *Light in August.*" In *New Essays on "Light in August,"* edited by Michael Millgate. Cambridge, U.K.: Cambridge University Press, 1987. 55–79.

Kreyling, Michael. "Fee, Fie, Faux Faulkner: Parody and Postmodernism in Southern Literature." *Southern Review* 29 (1993): 1–15.

————. *Figures of the Hero in Southern Narrative.* Baton Rouge: Louisiana State University Press, 1987.

————. *Inventing Southern Literature.* Jackson: University Press of Mississippi, 1998.

Lakoff, George, and Mark Johnson. *Metaphors We Live By.* Chicago: University of Chicago Press, 1980.

Lawson, Lewis. "Walker Percy's Southern Stoic." *Southern Literary Journal* 3, no. 1 (1970): 5–31.

Leinwand, Theodore B. "Negotiation and the New Historicism." *PMLA* 105 (1990): 477–89.

Lenz, William B. "Augustus Baldwin Longstreet." In *Fifty Southern Writers before 1900,* edited by Robert Bain and Joseph M. Flora. Westport, Conn.: Greenwood Press, 1987. 312–22.

[Longstreet, Augustus Baldwin]. "The Causes of the Frequency of Murders, Suicides, and Insanity in the United States." *State Rights' Sentinel,* 17 April 1834, 1.

Longstreet, Augustus Baldwin. "Darby, The Politician." In *Stories with a Moral,* edited by Fitz R. Longstreet. Philadelphia: John C. Winston, 1912. 50–87.

————. *Georgia Scenes: Characters, Incidents, &c. in the First Half Century of the Republic.* 1835. Savannah: Beehive Press, 1975.

————. *A Voice from the South.* Baltimore: Samuel E. Smith, 1848.

Lukács, Georg. *Studies in European Realism.* New York: Grosset and Dunlap, 1964.

————. *The Theory of the Novel.* Translated by Anna Bostock. Cambridge, Mass.: MIT Press, 1990.

Lumpkin, Katharine Du Pre. *The Making of a Southerner.* New York: Alfred A. Knopf, 1947.

Lynn, Kenneth. *Mark Twain and Southwestern Humor.* 1959. Reprint. Westport, Conn.: Greenwood Press, 1972.

Macaskill, Brian. "Charting J. M. Coetzee's Middle Voice." *Contemporary Literature* 35 (1994): 441–75.

MacKethan, Lucinda H. *The Dream of Arcady: Place and Time in Southern Literature.* Baton Rouge: Louisiana State University Press, 1980.

————. Introduction to *Swallow Barn; or, A Sojourn in the Old Dominion,* by John Pendleton Kennedy. 1853. Reprint. Baton Rouge: Louisiana State University Press, 1986.

Meats, Stephen E. "Who Killed Joanna Burden?" *Mississippi Quarterly* 24 (1971): 271–77.

Meriwether, James B. "Augustus Baldwin Longstreet: Realist and Artist." *Mississippi Quarterly* 35 (1982): 351–64.

Michaels, Walter Benn. *Our America: Nativism, Modernism, and Pluralism.* Durham, N.C.: Duke University Press, 1995.

Newlin, Keith. "Georgia Scenes: The Satiric Artistry of Augustus Baldwin Longstreet." *Mississippi Quarterly* 41 (1987–88): 21–37.

Nordan, Lewis. *Wolf Whistle.* Chapel Hill, N.C.: Algonquin Press, 1993.

Oriard, Michael. "Shifty in a New Country: Games in Southwestern Humor." *Southern Literary Journal* 12, no. 1 (1980): 3–28.

Osborne, William S. Introduction to *Swallow Barn; or, A Sojourn in the Old Dominion,* by John Pendleton Kennedy. 1853. Reprint. New York: Hafner Publishing, 1962.

Page, Thomas Nelson. *The Negro: The Southerner's Problem.* New York: Scribner's, 1904.

———. *In Ole Virginia; or, Marse Chan and Other Stories.* 1887. Reprint. Chapel Hill: University of North Carolina Press, 1969.

———. *The Old South: Essays Social and Political.* New York: Scribner's, 1906.

Percy, Walker. *The Moviegoer.* 1961. Reprint. New York: Noonday Press, 1967.

Percy, William Alexander. *Lanterns on the Levee: Recollections of a Planter's Son.* New York: Alfred A. Knopf, 1941.

Phillips, Robert L., Jr. "The Novel and the Romance in Middle Georgia Humor and Local Color." Ph.D. diss., University of North Carolina at Chapel Hill, 1971.

———. "Multiculturalism and the Scholarly Journal." Paper delivered at SAMLA Annual Convention, Knoxville, Tenn., November 1992.

Phillips, Ulrich Bonnell. "The Central Theme of Southern History." *American Historical Review* 34 (1928): 30–43.

[Poe, Edgar Allan]. "Georgia Scenes." *Southern Literary Messenger* 2 (1836): 287–92.

Polanyi, Michael. *The Tacit Dimension.* Garden City, N.Y.: Doubleday, 1966.

Raper, Julius Rowan. "Inventing Modern Southern Fiction: A Postmodern View." *Southern Literary Journal* 22, no. 2 (1990): 3–18.

Reed, Joseph W., Jr. *Faulkner's Narrative.* New Haven: Yale University Press, 1973.

Richardson, Brian. "Death by Fiction in *Light in August.*" *Faulkner Journal* 3, no. 2 (1988): 24–33.

Ridgely, J. V. *John Pendleton Kennedy.* New York: Twayne, 1966.

Rocks, James E. "The Art of *Lanterns on the Levee.*" *Southern Review* 12 (1976): 814–23.

Romine, Scott. "Framing Southern Rhetoric: Lillian Smith's Narrative Persona in *Killers of the Dream.*" *South Atlantic Review* 59 (1994): 95–111.

Ross, Stephen M. *Fiction's Inexhaustible Voice: Speech and Writing in Faulkner.* Athens: University of Georgia Press, 1989.

Rubin, Louis D., Jr. *The Edge of the Swamp: A Study in the Literature and Society of the Old South.* Baton Rouge: Louisiana State University Press, 1989.

———. "The Other Side of Slavery: Thomas Nelson Page's 'No Haid Pawn.'" *Studies in the Literary Imagination* 7 (1974): 95–99.

Ruppersburg, Hugh M. "James Wilcox: The Normality of Madness." In *Southern Writers at Century's End,* edited by Jeffrey J. Folks and James A. Perkins. Lexington: University Press of Kentucky, 1997. 32–43.

———. *Voice and Eye in Faulkner's Fiction.* Athens: University of Georgia Press, 1983.

Scarry, Elaine. *The Body in Pain: The Making and Unmaking of the World.* New York: Oxford University Press, 1985.

Siebers, Tobin. "Ethics ad Nauseam." *American Literary History* 6 (1994): 756–78.

[William Gilmore Simms]. "Miss Martineau on Slavery," by A South Carolinian. *Southern Literary Messenger* 3 (November 1837): 641–57.

———. *Woodcraft; or, Hawks about the Dovecote.* 1854. Reprint. New York: Norton, 1961.

Simpson, Lewis Press. *The Brazen Face of History: Studies in the Literary Consciousness of America.* Baton Rouge: Louisiana State University Press, 1980.

———. *The Dispossessed Garden: Pastoral and History in Southern Literature.* Athens: University of Georgia Press, 1975.

Smith, Lillian. *Killers of the Dream.* Rev. ed. New York: Anchor Books, 1963.

Snead, James A. "*Light in August* and the Rhetorics of Racial Division." In *Faulkner and Race,* edited by Doreen Fowler and Ann J. Abadie, 152–69. Jackson: University Press of Mississippi, 1987.

Styron, William. *The Confessions of Nat Turner.* New York: Random House, 1967.

Sundquist, Eric. *Faulkner: The House Divided.* Baltimore: Johns Hopkins University Press, 1983.

Tate, Allen. *Collected Poems, 1919–1976.* New York: Farrar Straus Giroux, 1977.

———. *The Man of Letters in the Modern World: Selected Essays, 1928–1955.* New York: Meridian Books, 1955.

———. *Memoirs and Opinions, 1926–1974.* Chicago: Swallow Press, 1975.

———. "Remarks on the Southern Religion." In *I'll Take My Stand: The South and the Agrarian Tradition,* by Twelve Southerners. 1930. Reprint. Baton Rouge: Louisiana State University Press, 1977. 155–75.

Taylor, William R. *Cavalier and Yankee: The Old South and American National Character.* 1961. Reprint. New York: Oxford University Press, 1993.

Todorov, Tzetvan. *The Fantastic: A Structural Approach to a Literary Genre.* Translated by Richard Howard. Cleveland: Press of Case Western Reserve University, 1973.

———. *The Poetics of Prose.* Translated by Richard Howard. Ithaca, N.Y.: Cornell University Press, 1977.

Toomey, David M. "The Human Heart in Conflict: *Light in August*'s Schizophrenic Narrator." *Studies in the Novel* 23 (1991): 452–69.

Tucker, George. *The Valley of Shenandoah; or, Memoirs of the Graysons.* 1824. Reprint. Chapel Hill: University of North Carolina Press, 1970.

Tuttleton, James W. *The Novel of Manners in America.* Chapel Hill: University of North Carolina Press, 1972.

Twelve Southerners. *I'll Take My Stand: The South and the Agrarian Tradition.* 1930. Reprint. Baton Rouge: Louisiana State University Press, 1977.

Urgo, Joseph. "Menstrual Blood and 'Nigger' Blood: Joe Christmas and the Ideology of Sex and Race." *Mississippi Quarterly* 41 (1988): 391–401.

Wade, John Donald. *Augustus Baldwin Longstreet: A Study in the Development of Culture in the South.* New York: Macmillan, 1924.

Walker, Alice. "Beyond the Peacock: The Reconstruction of Flannery O'Connor." In *In Search of Our Mothers' Gardens.* San Diego: Harcourt Brace, 1983.

Wagner-Martin, Linda. " 'Just the Doing of It': Southern Women Writers and the Idea of Community." *Southern Literary Journal* 22, no. 2 (1990): 19–32.

Warren, Robert Penn. *All the King's Men.* 1946. Reprint. New York: Harcourt Brace, 1984.

———. "The Briar Patch." In *I'll Take My Stand: The South and the Agrarian Tradition,* by Twelve Southerners, 246–64. 1930. Reprint. Baton Rouge: Louisiana State University Press, 1977.

Watkins, Floyd C. *The Death of Art: Black and White in the Recent Southern Novel.* Athens: University of Georgia Press, 1970.

Watson, Jay. *Forensic Fictions: The Lawyer Figure in Faulkner.* Athens: University of Georgia Press, 1993.

Watson, Richie Devon. *Yeoman versus Cavalier: The Old Southwest's Fictional Road to Rebellion.* Baton Rouge: Louisiana State University Press, 1993.

Weaver, Richard M. *Language Is Sermonic: Richard M. Weaver on the Nature of Rhetoric.* Edited by Richard L. Johannesen et al. Baton Rouge: Louisiana State University Press, 1970.

————. *The Southern Essays of Richard M. Weaver.* Edited by George M. Custis III and James J. Thompson Jr. Indianapolis: Liberty Press, 1987.

————. *The Southern Tradition at Bay: A History of Postbellum Thought.* Edited by George Core and M. E. Bradford. New Rochelle, N.Y.: Arlington House, 1968.

Welsh, Alexander. "On the Difference between Prevailing and Enduring." In *New Essays on "Light in August,"* edited by Michael Millgate, 123–47. Cambridge, U.K.: Cambridge University Press, 1987.

White, Hayden. *The Content of the Form: Narrative Discourse and Historical Representation.* Baltimore: Johns Hopkins University Press, 1987.

Williamson, Joel. *After Slavery: The Negro in South Carolina during Reconstruction, 1861–1877.* Chapel Hill: University of North Carolina Press, 1965.

Wilson, Clyde N. Introduction to *In Ole Virginia; or, Marse Chan and Other Stories,* by Thomas Nelson Page. Nashville: J. S. Sanders, 1991.

Winthrop, John. "A Modell of Christian Charity." In *The English Literatures of America, 1500–1800,* edited by Myra Jehlen and Michael Warner, 151–59. London: Routledge, 1997.

Woodward, C. Vann. *The Strange Career of Jim Crow.* New York: Oxford University Press, 1957.

Wright, Richard. *Black Boy: A Record of Childhood and Youth.* 1945. Reprint. Cleveland: World Publishing, 1947.

Wyatt-Brown, Bertram. *The House of Percy: Honor, Melancholy, and Imagination in a Southern Family.* New York: Oxford University Press, 1994.

Index